HOLT MATHEMATICS

Holt, Rinehart and Winston, Publishers
New York · Toronto · London · Sydney

Eugene D. Nichols
Distinguished Professor of Mathematics
Education and Lecturer
Mathematics Department
Florida State University
Tallahassee, Florida

Paul A. Anderson
Elementary School Teacher
Clark County School District
Las Vegas, Nevada

Leslie A. Dwight
Former Head of the Department
and Professor of Mathematics
Southeastern Oklahoma State University
Durant, Oklahoma

Frances Flournoy
Professor of Elementary Education
University of Texas
Austin, Texas

Joella Hardeman-Gipson
Professor and Program Director
College of Education
Wayne State University
Detroit, Michigan

Sylvia A. Hoffman
Resource Consultant in Mathematics
Illinois Office of Education
State of Illinois

Robert Kalin
Professor, Mathematics Education Program
Florida State University
Tallahassee, Florida

John Schluep
Professor of Mathematics
State University College
Oswego, New York

Leonard Simon
Former Assistant Director
Planning and Curriculum
New York City Board of Education
New York, New York

TABLE OF CONTENTS

EVERY CHAPTER HAS

Maintenance: Keeping Fits/Basic Skills Checks
Review and Testing: Mid-Chapter Reviews/Chapter Reviews/Chapter Tests
Enrichment: Special Topics/Find Outs!/Activities

At the Shore

Ten wide whales all in a row
Nine swift sharks way down below

Eight diving ducks up in the sky
Seven big boats with sails so high

Six soft seals lying in the sun
Five playful porpoises having some fun

Four gray gulls standing in the sand
Three strong swimmers heading for land

Two cheery children playing with a ball
One crawling crab climbing a wall

Everyone goes to the shore you'll agree
To look at the things that live by the sea.

Addition and Subtraction Facts

CHAPTER 1

ADDITION AND SUBTRACTION FACTS

A. Look at the picture.

1. Find the whales.
   Count them.

2. How many whales are there?

Practice

How many of each are there?

1. ducks

2. swimmers

3. crabs

4. boats

5. gulls

6. children

7. seals

8. sharks

9. porpoises

Addition to Sum 10

$$3 \leftarrow$$
$$\underline{+\,2} \leftarrow \text{Addends}$$
$$5 \leftarrow \text{Sum}$$

$$3 + 2 = 5$$

Read: three plus two equals five

A. Look at the picture.

   1. How many blue fish?

   2. How many red fish?

   3. How many fish in all?

   4. $4 + 3 = \underline{}$

B. Look at $5 + 3$.

   5. What are the addends?

   6. What is the sum?

$$\begin{array}{r} 5 \\ \underline{+\,3} \end{array}$$

C. Add.

   7. $3 + 6$ **8.** $2 + 8$ **9.** $5 + 0$ **10.** $1 + 0$ **11.** $6 + 4$

   12. $\begin{array}{r} 3 \\ \underline{+\,3} \end{array}$ **13.** $\begin{array}{r} 4 \\ \underline{+\,0} \end{array}$ **14.** $\begin{array}{r} 8 \\ \underline{+\,2} \end{array}$ **15.** $\begin{array}{r} 1 \\ \underline{+\,3} \end{array}$ **16.** $\begin{array}{r} 4 \\ \underline{+\,5} \end{array}$

Add.

1. 3 + 7   **2.** 4 + 6   **3.** 2 + 4   **4.** 0 + 6   **5.** 7 + 3

6.   2   **7.**   9   **8.**   4   **9.**   9   **10.**   2
     + 6   + 0   + 4   + 1   + 1

11.   5   **12.**   2   **13.**   5   **14.**   1   **15.**   3
      + 1   + 3   + 2   + 1   + 5

16.   7   **17.**   6   **18.**   5   **19.**   6   **20.**   3
      + 2   + 3   + 4   + 1   + 0

21.   7   **22.**   1   **23.**   3   **24.**   0   **25.**   2
      + 1   + 8   + 4   + 4   + 5

26.   2   **27.**   8   **28.**   0   **29.**   6   **30.**   1
      + 7   + 0   + 5   + 2   + 7

31.   1   **32.**   0   **33.**   2   **34.**   1   **35.**   3
      + 4   + 0   + 2   + 5   + 1

36.   1   **37.**   0   **38.**   1   **39.**   1   **40.**   0
      + 9   + 8   + 6   + 2   + 3

41.   7   **42.**   4   **43.**   8   **44.**   4   **45.**   6
      + 0   + 1   + 1   + 2   + 0

Solve.

46. Found 8 big starfish
Found 2 little starfish
How many starfish in all?

47. Found 4 shells
Found 3 more shells
How many shells in all?

Addition to Sum 18

$$\begin{array}{r} 7 \\ + 6 \\ \hline 13 \end{array}$$

A. Look at the picture.

    1. How many orange balloons?

    2. How many yellow balloons?

    3. How many balloons in all?

    4. $8 + 5 = \underline{\ \ ?\ \ }$

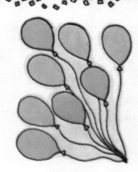
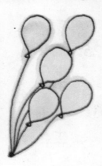

B. Add.

5. $\begin{array}{r}8\\+3\\\hline\end{array}$	**6.** $\begin{array}{r}7\\+4\\\hline\end{array}$	**7.** $\begin{array}{r}9\\+3\\\hline\end{array}$	**8.** $\begin{array}{r}6\\+5\\\hline\end{array}$	**9.** $\begin{array}{r}5\\+9\\\hline\end{array}$	**10.** $\begin{array}{r}6\\+6\\\hline\end{array}$
11. $\begin{array}{r}8\\+8\\\hline\end{array}$	**12.** $\begin{array}{r}9\\+6\\\hline\end{array}$	**13.** $\begin{array}{r}7\\+9\\\hline\end{array}$	**14.** $\begin{array}{r}7\\+7\\\hline\end{array}$	**15.** $\begin{array}{r}6\\+8\\\hline\end{array}$	**16.** $\begin{array}{r}8\\+4\\\hline\end{array}$
17. $\begin{array}{r}7\\+5\\\hline\end{array}$	**18.** $\begin{array}{r}2\\+9\\\hline\end{array}$	**19.** $\begin{array}{r}9\\+8\\\hline\end{array}$	**20.** $\begin{array}{r}7\\+8\\\hline\end{array}$	**21.** $\begin{array}{r}9\\+9\\\hline\end{array}$	**22.** $\begin{array}{r}9\\+4\\\hline\end{array}$

Add.

1. 6 + 5	**2.** 7 + 6	**3.** 8 + 7	**4.** 8 + 5	**5.** 7 + 8	**6.** 9 + 6
7. 8 + 9	**8.** 6 + 7	**9.** 5 + 6	**10.** 4 + 7	**11.** 9 + 4	**12.** 6 + 9
13. 8 + 3	**14.** 7 + 5	**15.** 7 + 7	**16.** 6 + 6	**17.** 7 + 4	**18.** 9 + 7
19. 2 + 9	**20.** 9 + 3	**21.** 5 + 7	**22.** 4 + 8	**23.** 9 + 2	**24.** 9 + 9
25. 8 + 4	**26.** 4 + 9	**27.** 3 + 9	**28.** 3 + 8	**29.** 9 + 8	**30.** 8 + 8

Solve.

31. 6 boys at the party
7 girls at the party
How many children in all?

32. 9 blue paper cups
6 red paper cups
How many cups in all?

Find Out!

Aid to Memory

You can make a ten to help you find a fact.

Example   To add 7 + 8, think: 7 + 3 = 10.

So, 7 + 8 = (7 + 3) + 5 ⟵ Think: 3 + 5 = 8
            = 10 + 5
            = 15

Try these: **1.** 9 + 6   **2.** 8 + 5   **3.** 6 + 8

The Addition Table

Here is how to find
$4 + 5$ in the table.

a. Find 4 on blue.

b. Find 5 on pink.

The sum is where the
yellow paths meet.

$4 + 5 = 9$

+	0	1	2	3	4	5	6	7	8	9
0	0	1	2	3	4	5	6	7	8	9
1	1	2	3	4	5	6	7	8	9	10
2	2	3	4	5	6	7	8	9	10	11
3	3	4	5	6	7	8	9	10	11	12
4	4	5	6	7	8	9	10	11	12	13
5	5	6	7	8	9	10	11	12	13	14
6	6	7	8	9	10	11	12	13	14	15
7	7	8	9	10	11	12	13	14	15	16
8	8	9	10	11	12	13	14	15	16	17
9	9	10	11	12	13	14	15	16	17	18

Practice

Add. Use the table to check.

1. $\begin{array}{r} 9 \\ +5 \end{array}$	**2.** $\begin{array}{r} 7 \\ +8 \end{array}$	**3.** $\begin{array}{r} 6 \\ +9 \end{array}$	**4.** $\begin{array}{r} 9 \\ +8 \end{array}$	**5.** $\begin{array}{r} 8 \\ +6 \end{array}$	**6.** $\begin{array}{r} 6 \\ +6 \end{array}$
7. $\begin{array}{r} 9 \\ +7 \end{array}$	**8.** $\begin{array}{r} 9 \\ +3 \end{array}$	**9.** $\begin{array}{r} 8 \\ +5 \end{array}$	**10.** $\begin{array}{r} 9 \\ +4 \end{array}$	**11.** $\begin{array}{r} 8 \\ +7 \end{array}$	**12.** $\begin{array}{r} 6 \\ +8 \end{array}$
13. $\begin{array}{r} 9 \\ +9 \end{array}$	**14.** $\begin{array}{r} 7 \\ +7 \end{array}$	**15.** $\begin{array}{r} 8 \\ +8 \end{array}$	**16.** $\begin{array}{r} 2 \\ +9 \end{array}$	**17.** $\begin{array}{r} 7 \\ +5 \end{array}$	**18.** $\begin{array}{r} 4 \\ +7 \end{array}$
19. $\begin{array}{r} 8 \\ +3 \end{array}$	**20.** $\begin{array}{r} 6 \\ +7 \end{array}$	**21.** $\begin{array}{r} 9 \\ +6 \end{array}$	**22.** $\begin{array}{r} 8 \\ +9 \end{array}$	**23.** $\begin{array}{r} 4 \\ +8 \end{array}$	**24.** $\begin{array}{r} 5 \\ +9 \end{array}$
25. $\begin{array}{r} 9 \\ +2 \end{array}$	**26.** $\begin{array}{r} 5 \\ +7 \end{array}$	**27.** $\begin{array}{r} 5 \\ +8 \end{array}$	**28.** $\begin{array}{r} 3 \\ +8 \end{array}$	**29.** $\begin{array}{r} 4 \\ +9 \end{array}$	**30.** $\begin{array}{r} 6 \\ +5 \end{array}$

Game Time

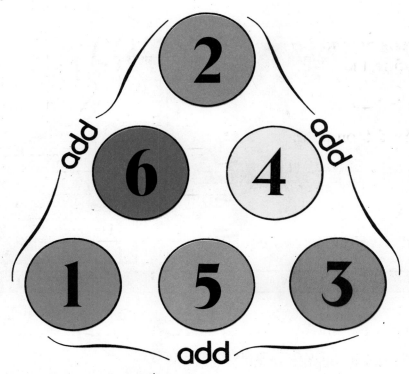

Look at the addition game above.
The sum of each side is 9.

A. Now you play an addition game.

    1. Draw 6 circles as shown.

    2. Use the numbers 1, 2, 3, 4, 5, and 6 only once.

    3. Put a number in each circle to make the sum on each side 10.

    The first one done is the winner!

B. Play the game again.

    4. Make the sum on each side 11.

    5. Make the sum on each side 12.

Subtracting from 10

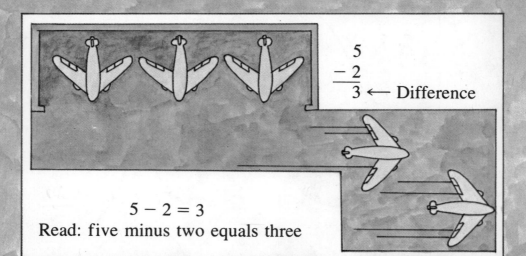

$$5$$
$$\underline{-\ 2}$$
$$3 \leftarrow \text{Difference}$$

$$5 - 2 = 3$$
Read: five minus two equals three

A. Look at the picture.

1. How many people in all?

2. How many people are leaving?

3. How many are staying?

4. $4 - 2 = \underline{\ ?\ }$

B. Subtract.

5. $6 - 4$	**6.** $8 - 8$	**7.** $10 - 2$	**8.** $8 - 0$	**9.** $9 - 5$

10. $\begin{array}{r} 10 \\ -\ 3 \\ \hline \end{array}$	**11.** $\begin{array}{r} 7 \\ -\ 6 \\ \hline \end{array}$	**12.** $\begin{array}{r} 4 \\ -\ 3 \\ \hline \end{array}$	**13.** $\begin{array}{r} 9 \\ -\ 6 \\ \hline \end{array}$	**14.** $\begin{array}{r} 6 \\ -\ 3 \\ \hline \end{array}$

15. $\begin{array}{r} 9 \\ -\ 2 \\ \hline \end{array}$	**16.** $\begin{array}{r} 10 \\ -\ 6 \\ \hline \end{array}$	**17.** $\begin{array}{r} 9 \\ -\ 0 \\ \hline \end{array}$	**18.** $\begin{array}{r} 3 \\ -\ 2 \\ \hline \end{array}$	**19.** $\begin{array}{r} 7 \\ -\ 4 \\ \hline \end{array}$

Subtract.

1. $9 - 1$ **2.** $7 - 2$ **3.** $8 - 3$ **4.** $6 - 0$ **5.** $3 - 1$

6. $\begin{array}{r} 5 \\ -0 \\ \hline \end{array}$ **7.** $\begin{array}{r} 8 \\ -1 \\ \hline \end{array}$ **8.** $\begin{array}{r} 10 \\ -5 \\ \hline \end{array}$ **9.** $\begin{array}{r} 3 \\ -3 \\ \hline \end{array}$ **10.** $\begin{array}{r} 9 \\ -4 \\ \hline \end{array}$

11. $\begin{array}{r} 6 \\ -1 \\ \hline \end{array}$ **12.** $\begin{array}{r} 5 \\ -3 \\ \hline \end{array}$ **13.** $\begin{array}{r} 8 \\ -7 \\ \hline \end{array}$ **14.** $\begin{array}{r} 7 \\ -3 \\ \hline \end{array}$ **15.** $\begin{array}{r} 10 \\ -9 \\ \hline \end{array}$

16. $\begin{array}{r} 8 \\ -2 \\ \hline \end{array}$ **17.** $\begin{array}{r} 10 \\ -1 \\ \hline \end{array}$ **18.** $\begin{array}{r} 4 \\ -0 \\ \hline \end{array}$ **19.** $\begin{array}{r} 6 \\ -2 \\ \hline \end{array}$ **20.** $\begin{array}{r} 2 \\ -0 \\ \hline \end{array}$

21. $\begin{array}{r} 9 \\ -3 \\ \hline \end{array}$ **22.** $\begin{array}{r} 2 \\ -1 \\ \hline \end{array}$ **23.** $\begin{array}{r} 7 \\ -7 \\ \hline \end{array}$ **24.** $\begin{array}{r} 1 \\ -0 \\ \hline \end{array}$ **25.** $\begin{array}{r} 6 \\ -6 \\ \hline \end{array}$

26. $\begin{array}{r} 7 \\ -5 \\ \hline \end{array}$ **27.** $\begin{array}{r} 5 \\ -1 \\ \hline \end{array}$ **28.** $\begin{array}{r} 10 \\ -8 \\ \hline \end{array}$ **29.** $\begin{array}{r} 8 \\ -6 \\ \hline \end{array}$ **30.** $\begin{array}{r} 0 \\ -0 \\ \hline \end{array}$

31. $\begin{array}{r} 4 \\ -1 \\ \hline \end{array}$ **32.** $\begin{array}{r} 9 \\ -7 \\ \hline \end{array}$ **33.** $\begin{array}{r} 2 \\ -2 \\ \hline \end{array}$ **34.** $\begin{array}{r} 7 \\ -0 \\ \hline \end{array}$ **35.** $\begin{array}{r} 9 \\ -9 \\ \hline \end{array}$

36. $\begin{array}{r} 10 \\ -4 \\ \hline \end{array}$ **37.** $\begin{array}{r} 8 \\ -4 \\ \hline \end{array}$ **38.** $\begin{array}{r} 7 \\ -1 \\ \hline \end{array}$ **39.** $\begin{array}{r} 5 \\ -5 \\ \hline \end{array}$ **40.** $\begin{array}{r} 9 \\ -5 \\ \hline \end{array}$

41. $\begin{array}{r} 6 \\ -5 \\ \hline \end{array}$ **42.** $\begin{array}{r} 4 \\ -4 \\ \hline \end{array}$ **43.** $\begin{array}{r} 5 \\ -4 \\ \hline \end{array}$ **44.** $\begin{array}{r} 10 \\ -7 \\ \hline \end{array}$ **45.** $\begin{array}{r} 3 \\ -0 \\ \hline \end{array}$

Solve.

46. 9 boats at the dock
8 boats leave.
How many boats are left?

47. 8 cars in a parking lot
5 cars drive away.
How many cars are left?

Subtracting from 18

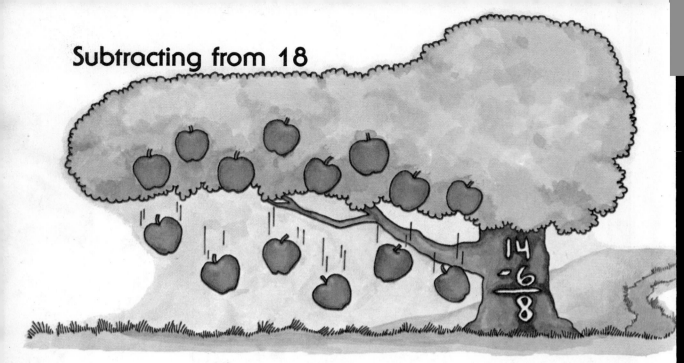

A. Look at the picture.

1. How many apples?

2. How many bananas?

3. How many more apples than bananas?

4. $14 - 8 =$ ___?___

B. Subtract.

5. 16 − 9	**6.** 14 − 7	**7.** 11 − 2	**8.** 12 − 3	**9.** 11 − 6	**10.** 13 − 9
11. 15 − 7	**12.** 13 − 8	**13.** 12 − 8	**14.** 17 − 9	**15.** 15 − 9	**16.** 14 − 9
17. 12 − 5	**18.** 12 − 6	**19.** 18 − 9	**20.** 11 − 7	**21.** 11 − 3	**22.** 16 − 8

Subtract.

1.	18 − 9	**2.**	13 − 6	**3.**	11 − 9	**4.**	17 − 8	**5.**	16 − 7	**6.**	13 − 5
7.	14 − 8	**8.**	11 − 3	**9.**	15 − 7	**10.**	12 − 8	**11.**	11 − 2	**12.**	15 − 9
13.	13 − 4	**14.**	12 − 7	**15.**	11 − 4	**16.**	15 − 8	**17.**	14 − 7	**18.**	11 − 6
19.	12 − 6	**20.**	13 − 9	**21.**	14 − 9	**22.**	13 − 8	**23.**	16 − 8	**24.**	12 − 4
25.	15 − 6	**26.**	13 − 7	**27.**	11 − 5	**28.**	14 − 5	**29.**	17 − 9	**30.**	12 − 9

Solve.

31. 13 large pears
9 small pears
How many more large pears?

32. 16 oranges
8 peaches
How many more oranges than peaches?

Find Out!

Aid to Memory

Here's a way to help you subtract 9.

1 3 ← Add 1 to this number to give you the answer.
− 9
‾‾‾
4

Try these: **1.** 12 − 9   **2.** 18 − 9   **3.** 14 − 9

Number Families

These are number families.

13 Family
9 + 4 = 13
13 - 4 = 9
4 + 9 = 13
13 - 9 = 4

12 Family
7 + 5 = 12
12 - 5 = 7
5 + 7 = 12
12 - 7 = 5

Complete the number families.

1. 5 + 6 = _?_
6 + 5 = _?_
11 − 6 = _?_
11 − 5 = _?_

2. 3 + 9 = _?_
9 + 3 = _?_
12 − 9 = _?_
12 − 3 = _?_

3. 8 + 5 = _?_
5 + 8 = _?_
13 − 5 = _?_
13 − 8 = _?_

Write two subtraction sentences to complete the number families.

4. 7 + 8 = 15
8 + 7 = 15

5. 5 + 7 = 12
7 + 5 = 12

6. 6 + 4 = 10
4 + 6 = 10

7. 5 + 9 = 14
9 + 5 = 14

8. 7 + 4 = 11
4 + 7 = 11

9. 6 + 8 = 14
8 + 6 = 14

Write two addition sentences to complete the number families.

10. 17 − 8 = 9
17 − 9 = 8

11. 13 − 7 = 6
13 − 6 = 7

12. 9 − 4 = 5
9 − 5 = 4

13. 11 − 8 = 3
11 − 3 = 8

14. 10 − 2 = 8
10 − 8 = 2

15. 15 − 6 = 9
15 − 9 = 6

★**16.** Write a number family using the numbers 4, 7, and 11.

Missing Addends

Look at the picture.

1. How many cages?

2. How many more dogs are needed to fill the cages?

3. Solve. $4 + \square = 6$

Still need 2 more dogs.

Solve.

1.

$2 + \square = 3$

2.

$2 + \square = 4$

3.

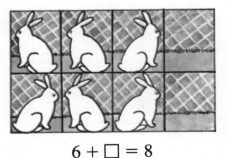

$6 + \square = 8$

4.

$3 + \square = 6$

Add. *(2, 4)*

1. 2 + 3	**2.** 3 + 5	**3.** 4 + 1	**4.** 2 + 2	**5.** 5 + 4	**6.** 2 + 8
7. 9 + 5	**8.** 9 + 9	**9.** 8 + 4	**10.** 7 + 9	**11.** 8 + 8	**12.** 6 + 6

Subtract. *(8, 10)*

13. 9 − 6	**14.** 8 − 3	**15.** 7 − 3	**16.** 5 − 2	**17.** 7 − 1	**18.** 10 − 3
19. 12 − 8	**20.** 15 − 9	**21.** 18 − 9	**22.** 13 − 8	**23.** 16 − 9	**24.** 11 − 6

Write two number sentences to complete the number families. *(12)*

25. 8 + 9 = 17
9 + 8 = 17

26. 6 + 9 = 15
9 + 6 = 15

Find Out! _____

Brainteaser

Choose the figure that completes the pattern.

1.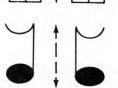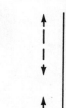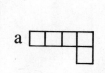

2.

Keeping Fit

Add.

1. 6 +5	2. 2 +3	3. 7 +0	4. 3 +8	5. 9 +4
6. 9 +7	7. 2 +2	8. 9 +5	9. 2 +7	10. 3 +6

11. 4 +8	12. 7 +8	13. 6 +4	14. 9 +9	15. 1 +6	16. 9 +0	17. 1 +4
18. 5 +8	19. 8 +9	20. 6 +2	21. 5 +7	22. 7 +7	23. 0 +2	24. 3 +5
25. 4 +7	26. 3 +3	27. 8 +8	28. 3 +4	29. 7 +5	30. 6 +7	31. 8 +2
32. 1 +0	33. 4 +5	34. 9 +2	35. 0 +8	36. 3 +7	37. 4 +4	38. 4 +2

Subtract.

39. 4 −3	40. 10 −6	41. 9 −5	42. 0 −0	43. 3 −3	44. 7 −4	45. 13 −7
46. 17 −8	47. 6 −6	48. 3 −2	49. 11 −5	50. 9 −2	51. 12 −3	52. 14 −6
53. 10 −9	54. 8 −2	55. 12 −4	56. 8 −3	57. 7 −5	58. 13 −5	59. 16 −9
60. 13 −9	61. 5 −3	62. 9 −0	63. 7 −2	64. 5 −5	65. 11 −2	66. 18 −9
67. 11 −7	68. 14 −5	69. 13 −4	70. 15 −7	71. 2 −1	72. 6 −1	73. 12 −7
74. 7 −6	75. 10 −4	76. 8 −6	77. 6 −5	78. 4 −2	79. 16 −7	80. 15 −9

Problem Solving

6 girls in a pet store
6 boys in a pet store
How many children in all?

Think:

1. What is asked? ⟶ How many in all?

2. Do you add or subtract? ⟶ Add.

▶ To find how many in all, add.

A. Complete.
5 frogs
4 turtles
How many more frogs?

1. What is asked?

2. Do you add or subtract?

▶ To find how many more, subtract.

To find how many are left, subtract.

B. Which operation would you use? Write + or −.

3. 3 small dogs
4 large dogs
How many in all?

4. 6 customers
2 leave
How many are left?

Which operation would you use? Write + or − .

1. 16 packages of bird seed
8 packages sold
How many are left?

2. 11 black kittens
5 grey kittens
How many more black kittens?

3. 14 blue birds
7 green birds
How many birds in all?

4. 17 goldfish in a tank
8 sold
How many are left?

5. 8 hamsters
6 more hamsters born
How many hamsters in all?

6. 6 white puppies
9 brown puppies
How many in all?

7. 18 goldfish
9 turtles
How many more goldfish?

8. 9 grey mice
7 white mice
How many in all?

9. Have 2 turtles
Bought 3 more
How many in all?

10. 10 puppies
3 have bones
How many do not have bones?

Hour and Half Hour

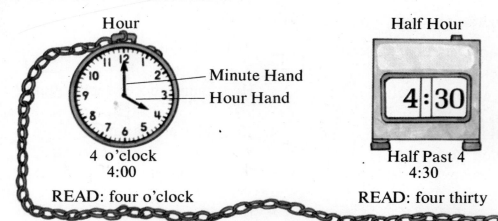

Hour

Minute Hand
Hour Hand

4 o'clock
4:00

READ: four o'clock

Half Hour

Half Past 4
4:30

READ: four thirty

A. Look at the clock.

  1. Where is the hour hand?

  2. Where is the minute hand?

  3. Complete. 1 o'clock or _:00_

B. Look at the clock.

  4. Where is the hour hand?

  5. Where is the minute hand?

  6. What is the time? Half past 2 or _:30_

C. Complete.

  7.

  ____ o'clock
  _:00_

  8.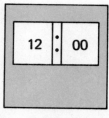

  12 : 00

  ____ o'clock
  ____ : ____

  9.

  half past ____
  ____ : ____

Complete.

1.

half past ____

:____

2.

____ o'clock

:____

3.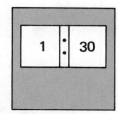

half past ____

:____

4.

half past ____

:____

5.

____ o'clock

:____

6.

____ o'clock

:____

7.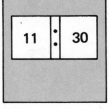

half past ____

:____

8.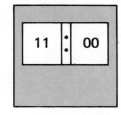

half past ____

:____

9.

____ o'clock

:____

10.

half past ____

:____

11.

____ o'clock

:____

★ **12.**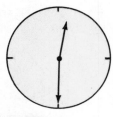

half past ____

:____

Time After the Hour

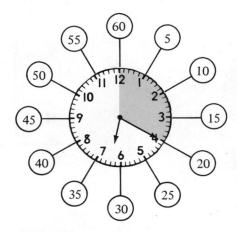

There are 5 minutes between each of the numbers on the clock.
Count by fives to find how many minutes after the hour.

20 minutes after 6
6:20 ← Read: Six twenty

A. Look at the clock.

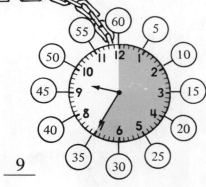

   1. Where is the hour hand?

   2. Where is the minute hand?

   3. How many minutes after the hour?
      [HINT: Count by fives.]

   4. What is the time? ___ minutes after _9_
                   9: __

B. Complete.

5.

___ minutes after _7_
    7: __

6.
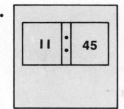

___ minutes after ___
    :05

7.

| 11 | : | 45 |

___ minutes after ___
    : __

Complete.

1.

_____ minutes after _____

_____:_____

2.

_____ minutes after _____

_____:_____

3.

_____ minutes after _____

_____:_____

4.

_____ minutes after _____

_____:_____

5.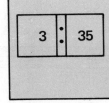

_____ minutes after _____

_____:_____

6.

_____ minutes after _____

_____:_____

7.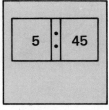

_____ minutes after _____

_____:_____

8.

_____ minutes after _____

_____:_____

9.

_____ minutes after _____

_____:_____

10.

_____ minutes after _____

_____:_____

11.

_____ minutes after _____

_____:_____

★ **12.**

_____ minutes after _____

_____:_____

Time Before the Hour

The green shows 25 more minutes to 10 o'clock.

25 minutes to 10

The pink shows 35 minutes after 9 o'clock.

9:35

Here are two ways to tell the time: 25 minutes to 10 or 9:35

A. Look at the clock.

   1. How many more minutes to 3 o'clock?

   2. How many minutes after 2 o'clock?

   3. What is the time? ____ minutes to 3
                            2:___

B. Complete.

4.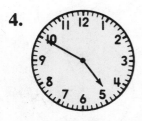

____ minutes to 5
4:___

5.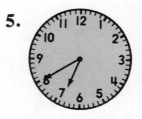

____ minutes to ____
:40

6.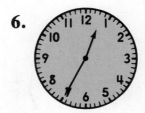

____ minutes to ____
___:___

Complete.

1.

_____ minutes to _____

_____ : _____

2.

_____ minutes to _____

_____ : _____

3.

_____ minutes to _____

_____ : _____

4.

_____ minutes to _____

_____ : _____

5.

_____ minutes to _____

_____ : _____

6.

_____ minutes to _____

_____ : _____

7.

_____ minutes to _____

_____ : _____

8.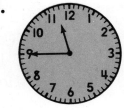

_____ minutes to _____

_____ : _____

9.

_____ minutes to _____

_____ : _____

10.

_____ minutes to _____

_____ : _____

11.

| 9 | : | 40 |

_____ minutes to _____

_____ : _____

★ **12.**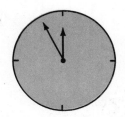

_____ minutes to _____

_____ : _____

Problem Solving

10 children
5 desks
How many more children?
[HINT: $10 - 5 =$ ___?___]
There are 5 more children.

9 crayons
9 pencils
How many in all?

8 children
3 leave
How many are left?

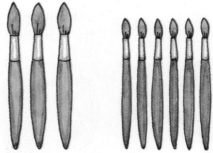

3 large paint brushes
6 small paint brushes
How many in all?

4 green erasers
6 blue erasers
How many more blue erasers?

Add. *(2, 4)*

1.	**2.**	**3.**	**4.**	**5.**	**6.**	**7.**
5	1	2	9	8	7	5
+ 3	+ 9	+ 4	+ 3	+ 9	+ 7	+ 6

Subtract. *(8, 10)*

8.	**9.**	**10.**	**11.**	**12.**	**13.**	**14.**
10	7	9	14	12	18	15
− 6	− 5	− 4	− 8	− 3	− 9	− 7

Write two sentences to complete the number families. *(12)*

15. 7 + 6 = 13
6 + 7 = 13

16. 16 − 7 = 9
16 − 9 = 7

Complete.

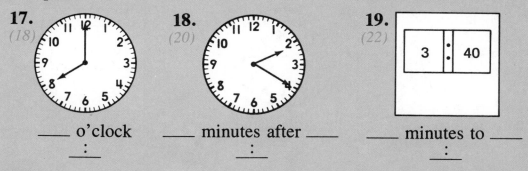

17.
(18)

_____ o'clock
_____:_____

18.
(20)

_____ minutes after _____
_____:_____

19.
(22)

3	:	40

_____ minutes to _____
_____:_____

Which operation would you use? Write + or −. *(16)*

20. 13 people sitting
5 people get up and leave
How many left sitting?

Add. *(2, 4)*

1. 6	**2.** 4	**3.** 3	**4.** 6	**5.** 5	**6.** 9	**7.** 9
+ 3	+ 4	+ 1	+ 9	+ 8	+ 7	+ 9

Subtract. *(8, 10)*

8. 6	**9.** 10	**10.** 8	**11.** 16	**12.** 13	**13.** 17	**14.** 11
− 1	− 5	− 6	− 7	− 9	− 8	− 5

Write two sentences to complete the number families. *(12)*

15. $11 - 6 = 5$
$\quad\ 11 - 5 = 6$

16. $8 + 7 = 15$
$\quad\ 7 + 8 = 15$

Complete.

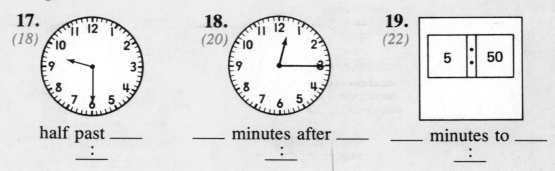

17. *(18)*
half past ____
____ : ____

18. *(20)*
____ minutes after ____
____ : ____

19. *(22)*
5 : 50
____ minutes to ____
____ : ____

Which operation would you use? Write + or − . *(16)*

20. 7 small cars
7 large cars
How many cars in all?

Basic Skills Check

1.

$$15 - 8 = \underline{\quad?\quad}$$

A	B	C	D
1	7	9	10

2.

$$\begin{array}{r} 6 \\ + 3 \\ \hline \end{array}$$

E	F	G	H
7	8	9	10

3.

$$\begin{array}{r} 12 \\ - 6 \\ \hline \end{array}$$

A	B	C	D
6	14	16	18

4.

$$9 - 6 = \underline{\quad?\quad}$$

E	F	G	H
3	4	6	7

5.

$$\begin{array}{r} 5 \\ + 5 \\ \hline \end{array}$$

A	B	C	D
9	10	11	13

6.

$$9 + 8 = \underline{\quad?\quad}$$

E	F	G	H
13	15	17	19

7.

$$\begin{array}{r} 10 \\ - 2 \\ \hline \end{array}$$

A	B	C	D
8	9	10	11

8.

$$14 - 8 = \underline{\quad?\quad}$$

E	F	G	H
3	4	5	6

9.

$$\begin{array}{r} 6 \\ + 7 \\ \hline \end{array}$$

A	B	C	D
10	11	13	16

10.

$$8 - 7 = \underline{\quad?\quad}$$

E	F	G	H
0	1	2	3

11.

$$\begin{array}{r} 18 \\ - 9 \\ \hline \end{array}$$

A	B	C	D
9	10	11	24

12.

$$4 + 2 = \underline{\quad?\quad}$$

E	F	G	H
5	6	7	8

The Calendar

There are seven days in a week.

Sunday, Monday, Tuesday, Wednesday, Thursday, Friday, Saturday.

SEPTEMBER

Sun	Mon	Tue	Wed	Thur	Fri	Sat
		1	2	3	4	5
6	7	8	9	10	11	12
13	14	15	16	17	18	19
20	21	22	23	24	25	26
27	28	29	30			

Use the calendar to answer these questions.

1. How many days in two weeks?

2. Name the days in September.

3. What date is the first Sunday?

4. What day is September third?

5. What date is the fourth Saturday?

6. Put your finger on the first Thursday. Count forward seven days. Name the day and date.

7. What is the date 3 days after September fourth?

Practice

1. Name the days of the week.

Write each date.

2. The second Monday

3. The last Friday

4. The first Wednesday

5. The third Monday

6. The twenty-first

7. The sixteenth

8. The eleventh

9. The twentieth

Months of the Year

JANUARY						
S	M	T	W	T	F	S
				1	2	3
4	5	6	7	8	9	10
11	12	13	14	15	16	17
18	19	20	21	22	23	24
25	26	27	28	29	30	31

FEBRUARY						
S	M	T	W	T	F	S
1	2	3	4	5	6	7
8	9	10	11	12	13	14
15	16	17	18	19	20	21
22	23	24	25	26	27	28

MARCH						
S	M	T	W	T	F	S
1	2	3	4	5	6	7
8	9	10	11	12	13	14
15	16	17	18	19	20	21
22	23	24	25	26	27	28
29	30	31				

APRIL						
S	M	T	W	T	F	S
		1	2	3	4	
5	6	7	8	9	10	11
12	13	14	15	16	17	18
19	20	21	22	23	24	25
26	27	28	29	30		

MAY						
S	M	T	W	T	F	S
					1	2
3	4	5	6	7	8	9
10	11	12	13	14	15	16
17	18	19	20	21	22	23
24	25	26	27	28	29	30
31						

JUNE						
S	M	T	W	T	F	S
	1	2	3	4	5	6
7	8	9	10	11	12	13
14	15	16	17	18	19	20
21	22	23	24	25	26	27
28	29	30				

JULY						
S	M	T	W	T	F	S
		1	2	3	4	
5	6	7	8	9	10	11
12	13	14	15	16	17	18
19	20	21	22	23	24	25
26	27	28	29	30	31	

AUGUST						
S	M	T	W	T	F	S
						1
2	3	4	5	6	7	8
9	10	11	12	13	14	15
16	17	18	19	20	21	22
23	24	25	26	27	28	29
30	31					

SEPTEMBER						
S	M	T	W	T	F	S
		1	2	3	4	5
6	7	8	9	10	11	12
13	14	15	16	17	18	19
20	21	22	23	24	25	26
27	28	29	30			

OCTOBER						
S	M	T	W	T	F	S
				1	2	3
4	5	6	7	8	9	10
11	12	13	14	15	16	17
18	19	20	21	22	23	24
25	26	27	28	29	30	31

NOVEMBER						
S	M	T	W	T	F	S
1	2	3	4	5	6	7
8	9	10	11	12	13	14
15	16	17	18	19	20	21
22	23	24	25	26	27	28
29	30					

DECEMBER						
S	M	T	W	T	F	S
		1	2	3	4	5
6	7	8	9	10	11	12
13	14	15	16	17	18	19
20	21	22	23	24	25	26
27	28	29	30	31		

A. Solve. Use the calendar to help you.

1. How many months are there in one year?

2. Name the months of the year in order.

3. Which months have 31 days?

4. Which is the seventh month of the year?

July 4, 1976, can be written like this: month / day / year   7 / 4 / 76.

B. Write each another way. Use the month/day/year form.

5. February 14, 1983　　**6.** May 2, 1981　　**7.** August 9, 1980

C. Write the month, day, and year.

8. 4/3/82   **9.** 9/2/70   **10.** 12/25/85

_____ Practice

Write the name of each month.

1. Second month   **2.** Fourth month   **3.** Tenth month

4. Third month   **5.** Ninth month   **6.** Sixth month

7. First month   **8.** Fifth month   **9.** Twelfth month

Write the month, day, and year.

10. 3/7/82   **11.** 6/16/79   **12.** 11/11/81

13. 2/24/83   **14.** 10/31/87   **15.** 1/30/92

Write each another way. Use the month/day/year form.

16. June 6, 1992   **17.** April 22, 1977   **18.** November 17, 1953

19. September 8, 1935   **20.** July 4, 1987 ★ **21.** January 1, 2004

— Find Out!

Aid to Memory

Here's a way to remember the number of days in each month.

Thirty days has September,
April, June, and November.
All the rest have thirty-one
Except February which has twenty-eight.

Value of Coins

Penny 1¢	Nickel 5¢	Dime 10¢	Quarter 25¢	Half Dollar 50¢

A. Count by fives.

    1. 5¢, 10¢, 15¢, __?__¢, __?__¢, __?__¢, __?__¢, __?__¢

    2. 40¢, 45¢, 50¢, __?__¢, __?__¢, __?__¢, __?__¢, __?__¢

B. Count by tens.

    3. 10¢, 20¢, 30¢, __?__¢, __?__¢, __?__¢, __?__¢, __?__¢

    4. 30¢, 40¢, 50¢, __?__¢, __?__¢, __?__¢, __?__¢, __?__¢

C. Give the value in cents.

5.    **6.**

D. What is the value in cents?

    Example   2 dimes and 4 pennies = 24¢

    7. 1 quarter and 1 dime   **8.** 1 half dollar and 3 dimes

    9. 1 quarter and 2 nickels   **10.** 4 dimes, 3 nickels, and 6 pennies

E. Which is worth more?

11. 3 dimes or 4 nickels?   **12.** 12 pennies or 5 nickels?

13. 20 pennies or 1 quarter?   **14.** 4 dimes or 5 nickels?

What is the value in cents?

1. 1 quarter and 3 dimes   **2.** 6 dimes and 4 nickels

3. 3 quarters and 4 pennies   **4.** 7 nickels and 3 dimes

5. 1 half dollar and 2 dimes   ★ **6.** 1 half dollar and 4 quarters

Which is worth more?

7. 18 pennies or 3 nickels   **8.** 28 pennies or 6 nickels

9. 4 nickels or 4 dimes   ★ **10.** 10 dimes or 3 half dollars

Use construction paper to make 25 pennies, 1 quarter, 2 dimes, and 5 nickels. Make a chart to show all the different ways you can make 25 cents. The chart shows one way.

Quarters	Dimes	Nickels	Pennies
	2		5

Dollars and Cents

one dollar
$1.00

five dollars
$5.00

or

A. Read each amount.

Example $1.37 is read 1 dollar and 37 cents.

1. $2.45   **2.** $9.05   **3.** $3.23   **4.** $4.60   **5.** $1.39

B. Write using the $ sign.

Example   4 dollars and 6 cents is written $4.06.

6. 2 dollars and 15 cents   **7.** 2 dollars and 30 cents

8. 3 dollars and 12 cents   **9.** 1 dollar and 16 cents

C. Give the value in dollars and cents.

10.

11.

D. What is the value? Write using the $ sign.

12. 4 dollars and 2 dimes   **13.** 1 dollar and 2 quarters

14. 2 dollars, 5 nickels, and
     1 dime

Practice

Read each amount.

1. $7.04   **2.** $9.50   **3.** $4.00

4. $3.15   **5.** $6.08   **6.** $3.74

Write using the $ sign.

7. 99 cents   **8.** 9 dollars and 9 cents

9. 4 dollars and 25 cents   **10.** 3 dollars and 35 cents

11. 8 dollars and 50 cents   **12.** 1 dollar and 46 cents

What is the value? Write using the $ sign.

13. 4 dollars and 4 nickels   **14.** 2 dollars and 1 half dollar

15. 3 dollars and 1 dime   **16.** 1 dollar, 3 quarters, and
     1 nickel

★ **17.** 4 dollars, 3 quarters, and   ★ **18.** 7 half dollars
     7 pennies

Hundreds

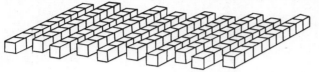 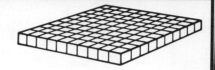

10 tens   =   1 hundred

Hundreds	Tens	Ones
	8	5
3	6	0
2	0	4

Read as:

eighty-five

three hundred sixty

two hundred four

A. Read the number.

1. 30 **2.** 60 **3.** 47 **4.** 98 **5.** 36

6. 400 **7.** 506 **8.** 891 **9.** 650 **10.** 728

B. Write the number.

Example Four hundred six is 406

11. Ninety-four **12.** Fifty-six

13. Two hundred ten **14.** Six hundred

15. Four hundred eighty **16.** Three hundred ninety-two

Write the number.

1. Seventy-seven

2. Fifty-four

3. Ninety

4. Thirty-two

5. Forty-nine

6. Eighty-one

7. Two hundred nine

8. Three hundred ten

9. Eight hundred seventeen

10. Six hundred sixty

11. Five hundred twenty-seven

12. One hundred fifty-nine

13. Two hundred fifty-six

14. Four hundred eighty

Find Out!
Brainteaser

Complete each pattern.

1. 300, 400, 500, __?__ , __?__ , __?__ , __?__

2. 130, 230, __?__ , __?__ , __?__ , __?__ , 730

3. 696, 697, __?__ , __?__ , 700, __?__ , 702

Thousands

Hedges have thousands of leaves.

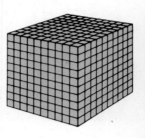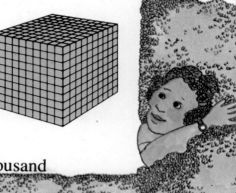

10 hundreds = 1 thousand

A. Read the number.

1. 1,000 **2.** 3,000 **3.** 5,000 **4.** 8,000 **5.** 2,000

B. Write the number.

6. Seven thousand **7.** Three thousand **8.** Six thousand

Thousands	Hundreds	Tens	Ones
2	1	4	6

Read 2,146 as two thousand, one hundred forty-six.

C. Read the number.

9. 5,004 **10.** 7,039 **11.** 6,720 **12.** 2,815 **13.** 3,526

D. Write the number.

14. Three thousand, seven **15.** Two thousand, twenty-three

16. Nine thousand, four hundred sixty-six

Write the number.

1. Three thousand

2. Four thousand, forty

3. Six thousand, six hundred

4. Nine thousand, ninety

5. Five thousand, two hundred fifty-five

6. Seven thousand, four hundred thirty-eight

7. Six thousand, four hundred nineteen

8. One thousand, three hundred four

★ 9. Twelve hundred

★ 10. Twenty-five hundred

★ Complete each pattern.

11. 1,000, 2,000, 3,000, __?__ , __?__ , __?__

12. 1,010, 1,011, 1,012, __?__ , 1,014, __?__

13. 1,100, 1,200, __?__ , 1,400, __?__ , __?__

Place Value

There are 8,653 bees.

A digit's value depends on its place.

Thousands	Hundreds	Tens	Ones
8	6	5	3

8,653 = 8 thousands, 6 hundreds, 5 tens, and 3 ones

8,653 = 8,000 + 600 + 50 + 3

A. Complete, using this chart.

Thousands	Hundreds	Tens	Ones
3	5	0	6

1. The 5 is in the __?__ place. Its value is __?__ .

2. The 0 is in the __?__ place. Its value is __?__ .

3. The 6 is in the __?__ place. Its value is __?__ .

4. The 3 is in the __?__ place. Its value is __?__ .

B. What is the value of each underlined digit?

Example   6,5̲84   500

5. 4̲7   6. 3̲2   7. 64̲7   8. 3̲80   9. 12̲3

10. 3,2̲19   11. 6̲,721   12. 1,20̲3   13. 4,4̲44   14. 9̲,046

C. Write the number.

    Example   4 tens and 3 ones   43

    15. 9 tens and 9 ones   **16.** 6 tens and 0 ones

    17. 40 + 3   **18.** 60 + 8

    19. 2 hundreds, 3 tens, and 8 ones   **20.** 100 + 20 + 1

    21. 4 thousands, 0 hundreds, 6 tens, and 2 ones

Practice

What is the value of each underlined digit?

  1. 2̲7   **2.** 49̲   **3.** 2̲8   **4.** 61̲   **5.** 3̲5

  6. 18̲9   **7.** 8̲42   **8.** 936̲   **9.** 1̲48   **10.** 30̲7

  11. 3̲,972   **12.** 8,03̲6   **13.** 2,7̲84   **14.** 1,86̲2   **15.** 4̲,237

Write the number.

  16. 3 tens and 4 ones   **17.** 6 tens and 6 ones

  18. 10 + 9   **19.** 3 hundreds, 4 tens, and 1 one

  20. 8 hundreds, 9 tens, and 6 ones **21.** 900 + 90 + 9

  22. 1 thousand, 4 hundreds, 6 tens, and 1 one

  23. 6,000 + 100 + 80 + 4

★ **24.** 3 thousands and 1 ten

★ **25.** 18 thousands, 4 hundreds, 1 ten, and 9 ones

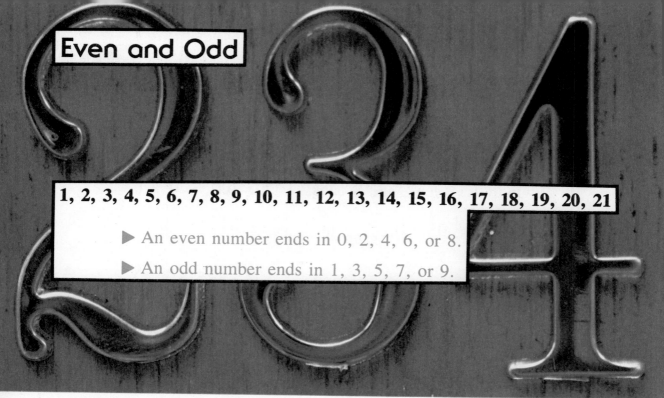

Even and Odd

1, 2, 3, 4, 5, 6, 7, 8, 9, 10, 11, 12, 13, 14, 15, 16, 17, 18, 19, 20, 21

▶ An even number ends in 0, 2, 4, 6, or 8.

▶ An odd number ends in 1, 3, 5, 7, or 9.

A. Write even or odd.

   1. 13   **2.** 16   **3.** 103   **4.** 471   **5.** 3,270

B. Write the next five even numbers.

   6. 30, 32, 34, __?__, __?__, __?__, __?__, __?__

C. Write the next five odd numbers.

   7. 25, 27, 29, __?__, __?__, __?__, __?__, __?__

D. Find the number of each. Is it even or odd?

   8. pennies in a dollar   **9.** days in this month

   10. students in your class   **11.** players on a baseball team

   12. black keys on a piano   **13.** white keys on a piano

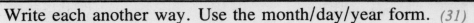

Write each another way. Use the month/day/year form. *(31)*

1. June 16, 1984   **2.** October 11, 1952   **3.** December 15, 1987

What is the value in cents? *(32)*

4. 1 quarter and 3 nickels   **5.** 4 dimes and 4 pennies

What is the value? Write using the $ sign. *(34)*

6. 3 dollars and 12 pennies   **7.** 4 dollars and 1 dime

8. 2 dollars, 2 quarters, and 1 nickel

Write the number. *(36, 38)*

9. 3 tens   **10.** Forty   **11.** Three hundred one   **12.** Six thousand

13. 400 + 20 + 3   **14.** 6,000 + 300 + 30 + 9

What is the value of each underlined digit? *(40)*

15. 3<u>4</u>   **16.** <u>8</u>6   **17.** <u>1</u>42   **18.** <u>3</u>,213   **19.** 6,<u>3</u>41

Find Out!
Calculator Activity

How many ways can you add four odd numbers so that the sum is 16?

Here are a few examples.

1 + 3 + 5 + 7 = 16
7 + 1 + 7 + 1 = 16

Keeping Fit

Add.

1. 2 +3	**2.** 8 +1	**3.** 3 +3	**4.** 0 +4	**5.** 2 +8

| **6.** 5 +3 | **7.** 6 +1 | **8.** 1 +2 | **9.** 4 +6 | **10.** 0 +6 |

| **11.** 3 +6 | **12.** 1 +1 | **13.** 3 +4 | **14.** 9 +0 | **15.** 2 +7 | **16.** 1 +7 | **17.** 2 +4 |

| **18.** 8 +0 | **19.** 9 +1 | **20.** 1 +0 | **21.** 5 +5 | **22.** 6 +7 | **23.** 7 +4 | **24.** 4 +9 |

| **25.** 8 +4 | **26.** 6 +9 | **27.** 7 +7 | **28.** 9 +8 | **29.** 9 +2 | **30.** 8 +8 | **31.** 8 +5 |

| **32.** 9 +3 | **33.** 6 +8 | **34.** 7 +9 | **35.** 9 +9 | **36.** 6 +8 | **37.** 4 +7 | **38.** 7 +8 |

Subtract.

| **39.** 9 −6 | **40.** 5 −4 | **41.** 3 −3 | **42.** 4 −2 | **43.** 10 −5 | **44.** 5 −2 | **45.** 8 −3 |

| **46.** 7 −6 | **47.** 2 −2 | **48.** 6 −3 | **49.** 3 −1 | **50.** 4 −4 | **51.** 10 −8 | **52.** 8 −2 |

| **53.** 9 −0 | **54.** 7 −4 | **55.** 6 −4 | **56.** 8 −7 | **57.** 10 −2 | **58.** 7 −3 | **59.** 6 −1 |

| **60.** 9 −9 | **61.** 5 −1 | **62.** 9 −3 | **63.** 8 −5 | **64.** 7 −0 | **65.** 12 −5 | **66.** 17 −8 |

| **67.** 13 −4 | **68.** 15 −7 | **69.** 11 −4 | **70.** 16 −9 | **71.** 18 −9 | **72.** 13 −5 | **73.** 14 −9 |

| **74.** 11 −7 | **75.** 11 −9 | **76.** 14 −6 | **77.** 12 −7 | **78.** 16 −7 | **79.** 13 −8 | **80.** 15 −8 |

Check It Out

Name the fewest number of coins needed
to buy each item shown.

Example   Cost is 37¢. The fewest coins you need are
a quarter, dime, and 2 pennies.

Problem Solving

10 squirrels
5 acorns
How many more squirrels than acorns?

Think:

What is asked? ⟶ How many more squirrels?
What do you know? ⟶ 10 squirrels, 5 acorns
Do you add or subtract? ⟶ Subtract.

This number sentence fits the story.

10 − 5 = ___?___

squirrels   acorns   how many more squirrels

A. 9 big pumpkins
7 small pumpkins
How many in all?

   1. What is asked?

   2. What do you know?

   3. Do you add or subtract?

   4. Which number sentence fits the story?

     9 − 7 = __?__   9 + 7 = __?__   9 − 2 = __?__

B. Which number sentence fits the story?

5. 13 bushes
7 trees
How many more bushes?

$13 - 7 = \underline{\ ?\ }$
$13 + 7 = \underline{\ ?\ }$
$20 - 13 = \underline{\ ?\ }$

6. 9 oak leaves
8 maple leaves
How many in all?

$9 - 8 = \underline{\ ?\ }$
$9 - 1 = \underline{\ ?\ }$
$9 + 8 = \underline{\ ?\ }$

Practice

Which number sentence fits the story?

1. 8 yellow leaves
3 red leaves
How many in all?

$8 - 3 = \underline{\ ?\ }$
$8 + 3 = \underline{\ ?\ }$
$8 - 5 = \underline{\ ?\ }$

2. 9 rakes
6 baskets
How many more rakes?

$9 - 6 = \underline{\ ?\ }$
$15 - 9 = \underline{\ ?\ }$
$9 + 6 = \underline{\ ?\ }$

3. 4 big logs
6 small logs
How many in all?

$4 + 6 = \underline{\ ?\ }$
$6 - 2 = \underline{\ ?\ }$
$6 - 4 = \underline{\ ?\ }$

4. 12 red apples
5 yellow apples
How many more red apples?

$17 - 12 = \underline{\ ?\ }$
$12 - 5 = \underline{\ ?\ }$
$12 + 5 = \underline{\ ?\ }$

Comparing Numbers

Compare 23 and 21.

Step 1 Compare tens.

2 3
2 1
Same

Step 2 Compare ones.

2 3
2 1
3 > 1
↑
3 is greater than 1

So, 23 is greater than 21.
Write as 23 > 21.

A. Compare 133 and 136.

  1. Are the hundreds the same?

  2. Are the tens the same?

  3. Are the ones the same?

     3 < 6
      ↑
  3 is less than 6
  So, 133 < 136

B. Compare. Replace ≡ with > or <.

  4. 98 ≡ 88   **5.** 67 ≡ 68   **6.** 36 ≡ 31

  7. 104 ≡ 108   **8.** 212 ≡ 121   **9.** 642 ≡ 612

C. Compare 6,541 and 6,324.

    10. Are the thousands the same?

    11. Are the hundreds the same?

    12. 5 ≡ 3

    13. So, 6,541 ≡ 6,324

D. Compare. Use > or <.

    14. 5,496 ≡ 6,694   **15.** 3,485 ≡ 3,483

    16. 6,853 ≡ 6,841   **17.** 4,412 ≡ 4,512

Practice

Compare. Use > or <.

  1. 33 ≡ 43   **2.** 21 ≡ 11   **3.** 46 ≡ 47

  4. 82 ≡ 71   **5.** 75 ≡ 85   **6.** 91 ≡ 90

  7. 126 ≡ 127   **8.** 340 ≡ 339   **9.** 421 ≡ 431

10. 670 ≡ 570   **11.** 386 ≡ 396   **12.** 842 ≡ 986

13. 6,421 ≡ 6,321   **14.** 1,298 ≡ 1,290

15. 4,212 ≡ 5,212   **16.** 7,387 ≡ 7,377

★**17.** 35,126 ≡ 34,126   ★**18.** 12,106 ≡ 12,108

Rounding Numbers

John's pig weighs 32 pounds.
What is 32 to the nearest ten?

▶ To round to the nearest ten, look at the ones place.

Round 32 to the nearest ten.
└── less than 5, so round down to 30

32 rounded to the nearest ten is 30.

Round 35 to the nearest ten.
└── 5 or more, so round up to 40

35 rounded to the nearest ten is 40.

A. Round each to the nearest ten.

1. 82	**2.** 87	**3.** 63	**4.** 85	**5.** 41
6. 65	**7.** 89	**8.** 66	**9.** 23	**10.** 58

▶ To round to the nearest hundred, look at the tens place.

348
└── less than 5, so round down to 300

368
└── 5 or more, so round up to 400.

B. Round each to the nearest hundred.

11. 187	**12.** 236	**13.** 412	**14.** 651	**15.** 138
16. 276	**17.** 493	**18.** 819	**19.** 333	**20.** 256

▶ To round to the nearest dollar, look at the tens place.

$1.42

⎿— less than 5, so round down to $1.00

$1.52

⎿— 5 or more, so round up to $2.00

C. Round each to the nearest dollar.

21. $1.76   **22.** $3.42   **23.** $2.86   **24.** $1.32   **25.** $4.56

26. $2.14   **27.** $7.25   **28.** $1.61   **29.** $4.72   **30.** $6.42

_____ Practice

Round each to the nearest ten.

1. 73   **2.** 25   **3.** 46   **4.** 82   **5.** 79

6. 41   **7.** 33   **8.** 27   **9.** 44   ★ **10.** 137

Round each to the nearest hundred.

11. 142   **12.** 632   **13.** 283   **14.** 452   **15.** 672

16. 314   **17.** 852   **18.** 412   **19.** 234   ★ **20.** 3,250

Round each to the nearest dollar.

21. $2.58   **22.** $3.30   **23.** $6.72   **24.** $1.15   **25.** $1.98

26. $7.81   **27.** $5.35   **28.** $4.63   **29.** $6.10   **30.** $3.91

★ **31.** $9.89   ★ **32.** $11.46   ★ **33.** $126.75   ★ **34.** $187.56

Larger Numbers

146,502 people watched the parade.

Hundred Thousands	Ten Thousands	One Thousands	Hundreds	Tens	Ones
1	4	6	5	0	2

Read as one hundred forty-six thousand, five hundred two.

A. To read large numbers:

   1. Read the digits to the left of the comma.

   2. Say thousand.

   3. Read the digits to the right of the comma.

Example 26,216

twenty-six

thousand

two hundred sixteen

26,216 is read twenty-six thousand, two hundred sixteen.

B. Read the number.

   4. 57,122

   5. 36,480

   6. 86,302

   7. 436,981

   8. 630,464

   9. 904,746

C. What is the value of each underlined digit?

   10. 1<u>6</u>,438

   11. <u>1</u>3,190

   12. 27,<u>1</u>80

   13. 7<u>8</u>7,412

   14. 49<u>3</u>,851

   15. <u>8</u>50,417

What is the value of each underlined digit?

1. 14,<u>1</u>08   **2.** 4<u>4</u>,787   **3.** <u>8</u>6,390

4. 3<u>8</u>,479   **5.** 26,3<u>8</u>7   **6.** <u>2</u>0,645

7. 8<u>9</u>5,302   **8.** 6<u>2</u>0,004   **9.** <u>7</u>15,850

10. 376,<u>8</u>95   **11.** 9<u>6</u>7,543   **12.** <u>1</u>72,275

★ Complete each pattern.

13. 99,600, 99,700, ___?___, ___?___, 100,000

14. 96,000, 97,000, ___?___, ___?___, ___?___

15. 99,910, 99,920, ___?___, ___?___, ___?___

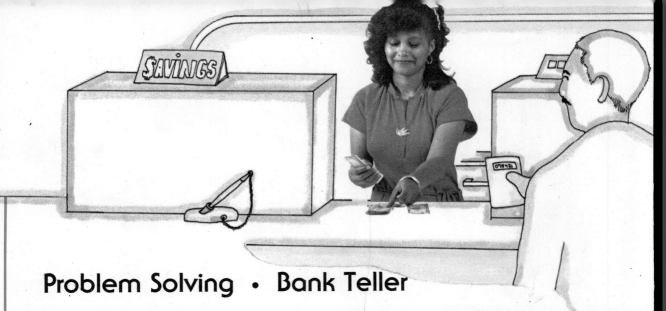

Problem Solving • Bank Teller

NUMBER OF CUSTOMERS

	Savings	Checking	Loans
Monday	113	68	18
Tuesday	89	137	6
Wednesday	160	98	9
Thursday	77	210	26
Friday	256	396	43

1. On which day did the bank have 113 savings customers?

2. How many loan customers were there on Friday?

3. On Monday, were there more customers for savings or checking?

4. On Thursday, were there fewer customers for savings or loans?

5. On Tuesday, how many customers were there for savings?

★ 6. Which day had the fewest customers for loans?

Write another way. Use the month/day/year form. *(30)*

1. April 27, 1983

What is the value of each? *(32, 34)*

2. 1 quarter and 1 dime

3. 1 dollar and 3 nickels

Write the number. *(36, 38, 40)*

4. Sixty-eight

5. Six hundred twelve

6. Eight thousand, four hundred eighty-three

7. 4,000 + 600 + 70 + 6

What is the value of each underlined digit? *(40)*

8. <u>8</u>7

9. <u>1</u>87

10. <u>7</u>,621

Compare. Use < or >. *(48)*

11. 46 ⬛ 56

12. 109 ⬛ 108

13. 7,377 ⬛ 7,477

Round each to the nearest ten. *(50)*

14. 68

15. 45

16. 33

Round each to the nearest hundred or dollar. *(51)*

17. 121

18. 486

19. $3.25

Which number sentence fits the story? *(46)*

20. There were 12 apples. 6 apples were eaten.
How many apples are left?

12 + 6 = __?__   12 − 6 = __?__   18 − 6 = __?__

Write another way. Use the month/day/year form. *(30)*

1. March 9, 1980

What is the value of each? *(32, 34)*

2. 1 half dollar and 1 nickel   **3.** 1 dollar and 3 quarters

Write the number. *(36, 38, 40)*

4. Two hundred   **5.** 50 + 7

6. Nine hundred fifty-six

7. Three thousand, two hundred ninety-five

What is the value of each underlined digit? *(40)*

8. 7<u>3</u>   **9.** 2<u>64</u>   **10.** <u>9</u>,861

Compare. Use < or >. *(48)*

11. 34 ≡ 43   **12.** 162 ≡ 262   **13.** 8,406 ≡ 7,406

Round each to the nearest ten. *(50)*

14. 36   **15.** 81   **16.** 15

Round each to the nearest hundred or dollar. *(51)*

17. 130   **18.** 186   **19.** $2.87

Which number sentence fits the story? *(46)*

20. 8 red pens and 7 blue pens
How many pens in all?

$8 - 7 = \underline{\quad?\quad}$ $8 + 7 = \underline{\quad?\quad}$ $15 - 8 = \underline{\quad?\quad}$

1. What time is it?

A 4:00   B 3:00

C 12:00   D 6:00

2. Find the third tepee.

E   F   G   H

3. How many ❉ ?

❉ ❉ ❉   ❉ ❉ ❉

❉ ❉ ❉   ❉ ❉ ❉ ❉

A 11   B 13

C 12   D 14

4. What is a name for 73?

E Seven-three   F Thirty-seven

G Seven-thirty   H Seventy-three

5. Which is not a rectangle?

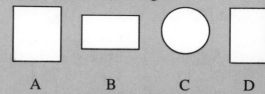

A   B   C   D

6. Count by ones. What number is mssing?

21   22   __   24   25

E 19   F 20

G 23   H 28

7. What time is it?

A 9:30   B 10:30

C 11:30   D 12:30

8. Which coin is a nickel?

E   F   G   H

Up and Down

Add Down.

```
  5      Think:
  7  12 ←  5 + 7 = 12
+ 3   ↓   12 + 3 = 15
 15
```

Add Up

```
  5      Think:
  7  10 ←  3 + 7 = 10
+ 3       10 + 5 = 15
 15
```

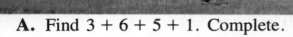

A. Find 3 + 6 + 5 + 1. Complete.

1. Add down. 3 + 6 = __?__   WRITE

2. 9 + 5 = __?__   3

3. 14 + 1 = __?__   6
                                        5
4. Now add up.   + 1

5. Is the sum the same?

▶ Add up to check addition.

B. Add.

6.	7.	8.	9.	10.	11.
4	6	2	5	7	3
2	8	9	1	2	2
+ 7	+ 2	+ 3	+ 9	5	6
				+ 4	+ 2

Practice

Add.

	1.	**2.**	**3.**	**4.**	**5.**	★**6.**	★**7.**
	8	5	2	7	3	5	9
	3	7	9	6	7	9	4
	+5	+2	+6	+5	1	8	7
					+8	6	9
						+2	+4

RACE TIME

Add.

1. 4
   9

2. 6
   8

3. 7
   6

4. 5
   1

5. 9
   4

6. 0
   8

7. 5
   5

8. 8
   6

9. 8
   3

10. 6
    4

11. 9
    8

12. 7
    4

13. 0
    3

14. 8
    7

15. 6
    6

16. 7
    9

17. 1
    6

18. 6
    5

19. 8
    4

20. 1
    2

21. 1
    9

22. 9
    9

23. 3
    9

24. 6
    7

25. 3
    1

26. 1
    7

27. 5
    3

28. 9
    7

29. 9
    0

30. 8
    8

31. 7
    3

32. 2
    8

33. 9
    5

34. 2
    2

35. 5
    2

36. 8
    5

37. 1
    8

38. 2
    5

39. 7
    8

40. 4
    6

41. 3
    8

42. 4
    2

43. 7
    0

44. 9
    3

45. 3
    3

46. 8
    2

47. 3
    2

48. 3
    4

49. 6
    4

50. 9
    6

51. 3
    6

52. 7
    5

53. 5
    6

54. 7
    7

55. 2
    6

56. 4
    8

57. 7
    2

58. 5
    4

59. 4
    4

60. 2
    4

61. 9
    1

62. 6
    0

63. 3
    7

64. 9
    2

65. 6
    3

66. 8
    9

67. 5
    9

68. 4
    5

69. 5
    7

70. 6
    9

Patterns

A, 1, B, 2, C, 3, D, 4, __?__ , __?__ , __?__ , __?__

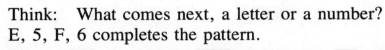

Say the letters.
Say the numbers.

Think: What comes next, a letter or a number?
E, 5, F, 6 completes the pattern.

Complete the patterns.

Example A, B, 1, 2, C, D, 3, 4, __E__ , __F__ , __5__ , __6__

1. A, 1, 2, C, 3, 4, E, 5, 6, __?__ , __?__ , __?__

2. A, 10, B, 20, C, 30, __?__ , __?__ , __?__ , __?__

3. A, B, 15, C, D, 25, E, F, 35, __?__ , __?__ , __?__

4. Z, Y, 26, 25, X, W, 24, 23, __?__ , __?__ , __?__ , __?__

_____ Practice

Complete the patterns.

1. A, 11, B, 12, C, 13, __?__ , __?__ , __?__ , __?__

2. A, 10, 20, B, 30, 40, __?__ , __?__ , __?__

3. A, B, 25, 35, C, D, 45, 55, __?__ , __?__ , __?__ , __?__

4. Q, 100, R, 110, S, 120, __?__ , __?__ , __?__ , __?__

★**5.** Z, 260, Y, 250, X, 240, __?__ , __?__ , __?__ , __?__

★**6.** A, B, 3, 4, E, F, 7, 8, I, J, 11, 12, __?__ , __?__ , __?__ , __?__

Addition

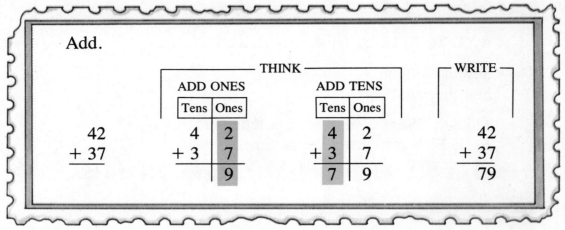

Add.

	THINK		WRITE

ADD ONES

Tens	Ones
4	2
+ 3	7
	9

ADD TENS

Tens	Ones
4	2
+ 3	7
7	9

```
  42
+ 37
```

```
  42
+ 37
  79
```

A. Add.

1. 75
     + 1

2. 13
     + 30

3. 72
     + 25

4. 40
     + 39

5. 21
     + 65

B. Find 135 + 432. Complete.

6. Add ones. 5 + 2 = ___?___

7. Add tens. 3 + 3 = ___?___

8. Add hundreds. 1 + 4 = ___?___

9. What is the sum?

WRITE

```
  135
+ 432
  567
```

C. Add.

10. 525
      + 60

11. 452
      + 15

12. 380
      + 214

13. 607
      + 181

14. 732
      + 224

15. 238
      + 111

16. 623
      + 224

17. 561
      + 101

18. 470
      + 109

19. 613
      + 366

Add.

1. 43 + 6	**2.** 72 + 1	**3.** 54 + 3	**4.** 313 + 6	**5.** 876 + 2
6. 54 + 32	**7.** 26 + 71	**8.** 40 + 24	**9.** 932 + 53	**10.** 552 + 11
11. 370 + 419	**12.** 643 + 253	**13.** 101 + 572	**14.** 214 + 324	**15.** 423 + 501
16. 422 + 34	**17.** 574 + 204	**18.** 12 + 32	**19.** 31 + 7	**20.** 740 + 10
21. 326 + 641	**22.** 73 + 25	**23.** 810 + 126	★ **24.** 995 + 5	★ **25.** 675 + 523

Solve.

26. Manuel has 142 stamps. Elena has 215 stamps. How many stamps in all?

27. 113 pages in Elena's stamp album 82 pages in Manuel's stamp album How many pages in all?

Keeping Fit

What is the value of each?

1. 4 nickels

2. 5 dimes

Write the number.

3. sixty-eight

4. 100 + 30 + 9

What is the value of each underlined digit?

5. 8̲7

6. 1̲07

7. 3̲,472

Renaming Ones

Add.

THINK

ADD ONES		ADD TENS		WRITE

24
+ 19

ADD ONES
Tens | Ones
1
2 | 4
+ 1 | 9
| 3

13 is 1 ten and 3 ones

ADD TENS
Tens | Ones
1
2 | 4
+ 1 | 9
4 |

WRITE
1
24
+ 19
43

How many ones? How many tens?

A. Find 57 + 7. Complete.

   1. Add ones. $7 + 7 = $ __?__

   2. How is 14 written?

   3. Add tens. $1 + 5 = $ __?__

   4. What is the sum?

WRITE
1
57
+ 7
64

B. Complete.

   5.   1
       59
     + 8
       7

   6.   1
       35
     + 6
       1

   7.   73
     + 19

   8.   16
     + 24

   9.   68
     + 25

C. Add.

   10.   24
      + 8

   11.   75
      + 7

   12.   45
      + 27

   13.   19
      + 64

   14.   37
      + 26

Add.

1.   87
   + 6

2.   44
   + 8

3.   19
   + 6

4.   78
   + 3

5.   25
   + 5

6.   36
   + 48

7.   62
   + 29

8.   13
   + 27

9.   58
   + 18

10.   39
   + 21

11.   16
   + 48

12.   34
   + 7

13.   42
   + 28

14.   79
   + 5

15.   57
   + 19

16.   49
   + 38

17.   23
   + 28

18.   85
   + 7

★ **19.** 27 + □ = 70

Keeping Fit

Subtract.

1.   2
   − 1

2.   5
   − 2

3.   8
   − 2

4.   9
   − 0

5.   10
   − 1

6.   7
   − 7

7.   10
   − 3

8.   8
   − 5

9.   3
   − 1

10.   9
   − 4

11.   14
   − 5

12.   11
   − 2

13.   13
   − 5

14.   12
   − 4

15.   16
   − 9

16.   11
   − 6

17.   14
   − 8

18.   16
   − 7

19.   15
   − 8

20.   18
   − 9

21.   13
   − 9

22.   17
   − 8

23.   15
   − 9

24.   12
   − 3

25.   15
   − 6

26.   17
   − 9

27.   16
   − 8

28.   12
   − 7

29.   11
   − 8

30.   14
   − 7

31.   13
   − 7

32.   6
   − 4

33.   9
   − 2

34.   10
   − 6

35.   7
   − 3

36.   10
   − 5

37.   11
   − 3

38.   13
   − 6

Adding Hundreds

Add 426 + 259.
Follow these steps.

ADD ONES	ADD TENS	ADD HUNDREDS
$\begin{array}{r}1\\ 4\,2\,6\\ +\,2\,5\,9\\ \hline 5\end{array}$	$\begin{array}{r}1\\ 4\,2\,6\\ +\,2\,5\,9\\ \hline 8\,5\end{array}$	$\begin{array}{r}1\\ 4\,2\,6\\ +\,2\,5\,9\\ \hline 6\,8\,5\end{array}$
15 is 1 ten and 5 ones		

A. Find 256 + 26. Complete.

1. Add ones. $6 + 6 =$ ___?___

2. How is 12 written?

3. Add tens. $1 + 5 + 2 =$ ___?___

4. Bring down the hundreds.

5. What is the sum?

WRITE

$\begin{array}{r}1\\ 256\\ +\ \ 26\\ \hline 282\end{array}$

B. Complete.

6. $\begin{array}{r}1\\ 718\\ +\ \ \ 9\\ \hline 27\end{array}$
7. $\begin{array}{r}1\\ 906\\ +\ \ 54\\ \hline 60\end{array}$
8. $\begin{array}{r}649\\ +\,338\\ \hline \end{array}$
9. $\begin{array}{r}267\\ +\,216\\ \hline \end{array}$
10. $\begin{array}{r}807\\ +\,188\\ \hline \end{array}$

C. Add.

11. $\begin{array}{r}731\\ +\ \ \ 9\\ \hline \end{array}$
12. $\begin{array}{r}432\\ +\ \ 29\\ \hline \end{array}$
13. $\begin{array}{r}545\\ +\ \ 49\\ \hline \end{array}$
14. $\begin{array}{r}134\\ +\,347\\ \hline \end{array}$
15. $\begin{array}{r}327\\ +\,315\\ \hline \end{array}$

Add.

1. 278
   + 4

2. 539
   + 2

3. 708
   + 8

4. 948
   + 6

5. 389
   + 1

6. 153
   + 7

7. 427
   + 5

8. 868
   + 3

9. 616
   + 9

10. 579
    + 8

11. 632
    + 29

12. 505
    + 85

13. 336
    + 17

14. 918
    + 54

15. 819
    + 71

16. 448
    + 38

17. 729
    + 16

18. 127
    + 66

19. 507
    + 29

20. 224
    + 47

21. 515
    + 325

22. 238
    + 437

23. 746
    + 104

24. 547
    + 239

25. 209
    + 362

26. 354
    + 138

27. 401
    + 529

28. 817
    + 147

29. 109
    + 619

30. 236
    + 245

31. 309
    + 438

32. 817
    + 64

33. 145
    + 415

34. 476
    + 7

35. 503
    + 408

36. 954
    + 19

37. 248
    + 104

38. 629
    + 5

★ 39. 708
      + 392

★ 40. 879
      + 523

Solve.

41. 346 people upstairs
    147 people downstairs
    How many people in all?

42. 318 people buy tickets.
    204 more people buy tickets.
    How many tickets in all?

Renaming Tens

Add 131 + 674.
Follow these steps.

ADD ONES   ADD TENS   ADD HUNDREDS

```
     1              1            1
 1 3 1          1 3 1        1 3 1
+6 7 4         +6 7 4       +6 7 4
─────          ─────        ─────
     5            0 5        8 0 5
```

10 tens is 1 hundred

A. Find 538 + 91. Complete.

    1. Add ones. 8 + 1 = ___?___   WRITE

    2. Add tens. 3 + 9 = ___?___

    3. How is 12 tens written?

    4. Add hundreds. 1 + 5 = ___?___

    5. What is the sum?

```
   1
 538
+ 91
────
 629
```

B. Complete.

```
      1               1
 6.    393    7.    860    8.    794    9.    487   10.    271
     + 74         + 42        + 181        + 262        + 355
     ────         ────
       67           02
```

C. Add.

```
 11.    825   12.    182   13.    361   14.    494   15.    556
      + 83        + 71        + 456        + 190        + 192
```

Add.

1.	492 + 24	**2.**	875 + 53	**3.**	361 + 81	**4.**	634 + 75	**5.**	480 + 83
6.	783 + 92	**7.**	190 + 30	**8.**	814 + 91	**9.**	295 + 62	**10.**	563 + 41
11.	683 + 241	**12.**	355 + 153	**13.**	496 + 391	**14.**	270 + 564	**15.**	763 + 186
16.	574 + 392	**17.**	121 + 294	**18.**	283 + 370	**19.**	692 + 187	**20.**	262 + 452
21.	251 + 68	**22.**	576 + 292	**23.**	774 + 134	**24.**	496 + 91	**25.**	183 + 472
26.	393 + 383	**27.**	842 + 80	**28.**	360 + 172	**29.**	171 + 662	**30.**	425 + 82
31.	382 + 532	**32.**	440 + 86	★ **33.**	911 + 94	★ **34.**	684 + 563	★ **35.**	952 + 77

Solve.

36. 141 third graders in the parade
76 fourth graders in the parade
How many children in the parade?

37. 584 people marching in green uniforms
150 people marching in blue uniforms
How many people marching in all?

Add.

1.   3
(59)   5
   + 8

2.   2
(59)   9
   6
   + 1

3.   31
(62) + 48

4. 604
(62) + 172

5. 523
(62) + 75

6. 55
(64) + 27

7. 46
(64) + 9

8. 249
(66) + 409

9. 768
(66) + 212

10. 536
(66) + 58

11. 429
(66) + 3

12. 398
(68) + 440

13. 264
(68) + 361

14. 633
(68) + 176

15. 742
(68) + 75

Find Out!
Activity

Across

a.   7
   + 6

c. 49
  + 8

e. 49
  + 49

f. 33
  + 31

g. 18
  + 9

i. 18
  + 6

j. 49
  + 19

l. 58
  + 39

n. 26
  + 27

o. 37
  + 53

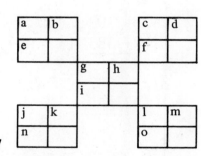

Down

a 13
  + 6

b. 19
  + 19

c. 28
  + 28

d. 65
  + 9

g. 14
  + 8

h. 28
  + 46

j. 20
  + 45

k. 67
  + 16

l. 62
  + 37

m. 35
  + 35

Adding 9

A. Here is a way to remember adding 9 to a number.

Start	→	Add 10	→	Subtract 1	→	Answer
1. 52		62		61		61
2. 36		46		45		45
3. 41		51		?		?
4. 25		?		?		?
5. 87		?		?		?

B. Add 9 to each.

6. 38   **7.** 68   **8.** 19   **9.** 42   **10.** 66

Practice

Add 9 to each.

1. 62   **2.** 27   **3.** 47   **4.** 53   **5.** 81

6. 18   **7.** 75   **8.** 26   ★**9.** 999   ★**10.** 1,025

Problem Solving

East side: 34 office buildings
West side: 63 apartment buildings
How many in all?

Think:

What is asked? ————→ How many in all?

What do you know? ———→ 34 office buildings, 63 apartment buildings

Do you add or subtract? → Add.

This number sentence fits the story.

    34   +   63   =   ?
     ↑   ↑   ↑
  offices apartments how many in all

A. 135 buildings
   14 are stores
   How many are not stores?

   1. What is asked?

   2. What do you know?

   3. Do you add or subtract?

   4. Write the number sentence that fits the story.

B. Write the number sentence that fits the story.

5. 252 people on South Street
108 people on Main Street
How many people in all?

6. 13 street signs
5 mailboxes
How many more street signs?

Practice

Write the number sentence that fits the story.

1. 14 fire fighters
6 went to a fire
How many were left?

2. 16 stop signs
9 traffic lights
How many more stop signs?

3. 24 police cars
19 police trucks
How many in all?

4. 17 park benches
8 fountains
How many more park benches?

5. Monthly rent:
2-family house $765
1-family house $572
How much more for
the 2-family house?

★ 6. 146 patients
32 nurses
18 doctors
How many people in all?

Renaming Ones and Tens

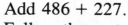

Add 486 + 227.
Follow these steps.

ADD ONES

```
  1
 4 8 6
+ 2 2 7
     3
```

13 is 1 ten and
3 ones

ADD TENS

```
 1 1
 4 8 6
+ 2 2 7
   1 3
```

11 tens is 1 hundred
and 1 ten

ADD HUNDREDS

```
 1 1
 4 8 6
+ 2 2 7
 7 1 3
```

A. Add 189 + 43. Complete.

    1. Add ones. 9 + 3 = ___?___

    2. How is 12 written?

    3. Add tens. 1 + 8 + 4 = ___?___

    4. How is 13 tens written?

    5. Complete the addition.

WRITE

```
   1
  189
+  43
    2
```

B. Complete.

6. $\begin{array}{r} \overset{1\,1}{697} \\ +\ \ \ 4 \\ \hline 01 \end{array}$	**7.** $\begin{array}{r} \overset{1\,1}{494} \\ +\ \ 38 \\ \hline 32 \end{array}$	**8.** $\begin{array}{r} 228 \\ +\ 387 \\ \hline \end{array}$	**9.** $\begin{array}{r} 365 \\ +\ 195 \\ \hline \end{array}$	**10.** $\begin{array}{r} 156 \\ +\ 279 \\ \hline \end{array}$

C. Add.

11. $\begin{array}{r} 498 \\ +\ \ \ 5 \\ \hline \end{array}$	**12.** $\begin{array}{r} 276 \\ +\ \ 74 \\ \hline \end{array}$	**13.** $\begin{array}{r} 347 \\ +\ 559 \\ \hline \end{array}$	**14.** $\begin{array}{r} 592 \\ +\ 289 \\ \hline \end{array}$	**15.** $\begin{array}{r} 655 \\ +\ 267 \\ \hline \end{array}$

Add.

1. 96
    + 7

2. 37
    + 73

3. 89
    + 63

4. 58
    + 59

5. 14
    + 98

6. 47
    + 79

7. 97
    + 87

8. 69
    + 35

9. 88
    + 72

10. 76
    + 65

11. 498
    + 5

12. 497
    + 34

13. 576
    + 25

14. 168
    + 48

15. 343
    + 97

16. 758
    + 56

17. 689
    + 39

18. 276
    + 89

19. 735
    + 65

20. 875
    + 77

21. 249
    + 257

22. 487
    + 386

23. 138
    + 162

24. 453
    + 468

25. 376
    + 586

26. 168
    + 449

27. 597
    + 233

28. 735
    + 197

29. 288
    + 316

30. 674
    + 279

31. 68
    + 57

32. 92
    + 8

33. 397
    + 596

34. 146
    + 88

35. 684
    + 167

36. 397
    + 73

37. 459
    + 276

38. 83
    + 98

★ 39. 997
    + 9

★ 40. 746
    + 356

Solve.

41. Ella picked 357 tomatoes. Sam picked 259 tomatoes. How many tomatoes were picked in all?

42. Ella gathered 184 eggs. Sam gathered 98 eggs. How many eggs were gathered in all?

Column Addition

Add.

Follow these steps.

	ADD ONES	ADD TENS
3 4	¹ 3 4	¹ 3 4
2 7	2 7	2 7
+ 3 1	+ 3 1	+ 3 1
	2	9 2

12 is 1 ten and 2 ones

A. Find 242 + 195 + 464. Complete.

   1. Add ones. 2 + 5 + 4 = ___?___   Write

   2. How is 11 written?

   3. Add tens. 1 + 4 + 9 + 6 = ___?___

   4. Complete the addition.

$$\begin{array}{r} \overset{2\,1}{242} \\ 195 \\ + 464 \\ \hline 01 \end{array}$$

B. Complete.

5.	**6.**	**7.**	**8.**	**9.**
¹ 29	² 86	391	107	181
33	67	263	451	620
+ 14	+ 49	+ 184	+ 416	+ 148
6	2			

C. Add.

10.	**11.**	**12.**	**13.**	**14.**
51	47	235	300	418
25	83	483	246	139
+ 62	+ 90	+ 187	+ 375	+ 244

Add.

1.	42 5 + 24	2.	63 40 + 6	3.	38 8 + 36	4.	84 91 + 4	5.	84 62 + 1
6.	34 26 + 47	7.	58 43 + 75	8.	96 60 + 85	9.	68 97 + 59	10.	85 78 + 87
11.	352 42 + 380	12.	217 705 + 23	13.	149 316 + 128	14.	263 231 + 434	15.	584 165 + 190
16.	206 394 + 65	17.	698 47 + 221	18.	284 341 + 125	19.	237 267 + 478	20.	320 189 + 305
21.	142 280 + 257	22.	459 169 + 156	23.	54 82 + 93	24.	362 177 + 385	25.	16 28 + 39
26.	27 13 + 64	27.	346 415 + 129	28.	255 144 + 384	★29.	427 9 787 + 44	★30.	368 549 29 + 56

Solve.

31. 147 third graders
219 fourth graders
197 fifth graders
How many students in all?

32. 34 music students
51 science students
40 art students
How many students in all?

Adding Money

Adding amounts of money is the same as adding numbers.
Beatrice bought one record for
$3.35 and another record for $4.80.
How much did she spend in all?

$$\begin{array}{r} 335 \\ +\ 480 \\ \hline 815 \end{array} \qquad \begin{array}{r} \$\ 3.35 \\ +\ 4.80 \\ \hline \$\ 8.15 \end{array}$$

dollar sign
decimal point

She spent $8.15 in all.

A. Find $2.42 + $0.89 + $4.96. Complete.

1. Add ones. $2 + 9 + 6 =$ __?__

2. How is 17 written?

3. Add tens. $1 + 4 + 8 + 9 =$ __?__

4. Complete the addition.

Write

$$\begin{array}{r} \overset{2}{\ }\ \overset{1}{\ } \\ \$\ 2.42 \\ 0.89 \\ +\ 4.96 \\ \hline .27 \end{array}$$

B. Complete.

5. $\begin{array}{r} \overset{1}{\ } \\ \$\ 1.09 \\ +\ 0.77 \\ \hline 86 \end{array}$

6. $\begin{array}{r} \overset{1}{\ } \\ \$\ 3.45 \\ +\ 6.35 \\ \hline 0 \end{array}$

7. $\begin{array}{r} \$\ 3.24 \\ 3.11 \\ +\ 0.32 \\ \hline \end{array}$

8. $\begin{array}{r} \$\ 5.40 \\ 1.43 \\ +\ 2.25 \\ \hline \end{array}$

9. $\begin{array}{r} \$\ 2.87 \\ 2.52 \\ +\ 1.24 \\ \hline \end{array}$

C. Add.

10. $\begin{array}{r} \$\ 2.15 \\ +\ 5.48 \\ \hline \end{array}$

11. $\begin{array}{r} \$\ 3.32 \\ +\ 2.07 \\ \hline \end{array}$

12. $\begin{array}{r} \$\ 2.81 \\ 2.43 \\ +\ 0.94 \\ \hline \end{array}$

13. $\begin{array}{r} \$\ 1.66 \\ 4.08 \\ +\ 3.27 \\ \hline \end{array}$

14. $\begin{array}{r} \$\ 4.30 \\ 1.76 \\ +\ 2.48 \\ \hline \end{array}$

Add.

1. $ 2.24
+ 0.51

2. $ 9.72
+ 0.14

3. $ 6.23
+ 2.45

4. $ 4.57
+ 3.42

5. $ 1.30
+ 5.27

6. $ 5.27
+ 0.39

7. $ 7.54
+ 0.53

8. $ 7.05
+ 2.48

9. $ 3.91
+ 3.63

10. $ 2.72
+ 1.70

11. $ 7.32
+ 0.99

12. $ 5.79
+ 0.63

13. $ 4.16
+ 1.87

14. $ 3.59
+ 5.98

15. $ 6.86
+ 2.84

16. $ 6.08
1.16
+ 0.46

17. $ 4.80
2.52
+ 0.81

18. $ 2.65
1.31
+ 5.22

19. $ 1.43
4.08
+ 2.36

20. $ 3.92
1.70
+ 1.92

21. $ 4.34
0.27
+ 1.59

22. $ 1.82
3.19
+ 0.36

23. $ 3.56
1.24
+ 4.46

24. $ 5.77
1.58
+ 1.67

25. $ 2.65
3.82
+ 2.08

26. $ 6.84
+ 1.92

27. $ 2.98
+ 0.66

28. $ 4.27
+ 2.31

29. $ 3.22
3.36
+ 1.79

30. $ 5.82
+ 3.09

31. $ 4.33
1.72
+ 0.92

32. $ 3.47
+ 0.42

33. $ 2.16
1.69
+ 4.03

★ 34. $ 5.87
+ 4.65

★ 35. $ 4.95
5.98
+ 0.09

Solve.

36. A music book cost $2.25.
A record cost $4.95.
A tape cost $1.75.
How much in all?

★ 37. Spent $4.49 for a record
Spent $5.98 for another record
How much spent for both
records?

Estimating Sums

Sold 42 glasses of lemonade
Sold 27 more glasses of lemonade
About how many glasses sold in all?

Round to the nearest ten, then add.

$$42 \longrightarrow 40$$
$$+ 27 \longrightarrow + 30$$
$$\overline{ \quad 70}$$

About 70 glasses were sold.

Estimate the sum to find **about** how many or how much.

A. Estimate the sums.

1.	2.	3.	4.	5.
36	25	58	29	71
+ 19	+ 31	+ 17	+ 35	+ 12

B. Estimate 236 + 113.
Round to the nearest hundred.

6. Round 236.

7. Round 113.

8. Add. 200 + 100 = __?__

9. What is the estimated sum?

	EXACT	ROUNDED
	236 $\longrightarrow$	200
	+ 113 $\longrightarrow$	+ 100

C. Estimate $1.85 + $2.12.
Round to the nearest dollar.

10. Round $1.85.

11. Round $2.12.

12. Add. $2.00 + $2.00 = __?__

13. What is the estimated sum?

	EXACT	ROUNDED
	$ 1.85 $\longrightarrow$	$ 2.00
	+ 2.12 $\longrightarrow$	+ 2.00

D. Estimate to solve.

14.	15.	16.	17.	18.
514	183	480	$ 1.95	$ 3.13
+ 297	+ 342	+ 416	+ 2.48	+ 4.90

Estimate the sums. Round to the nearest ten.

1.	47 + 21	**2.**	34 + 62	**3.**	51 + 18	**4.**	37 + 38	**5.**	42 + 44
6.	55 + 33	**7.**	52 + 17	**8.**	71 + 14	**9.**	25 + 48	**10.**	29 + 41

Estimate the sums. Round to the nearest hundred or dollar.

11.	364 + 108	**12.**	214 + 283	**13.**	121 + 615	**14.**	328 + 467	**15.**	250 + 472
16.	520 + 146	**17.**	392 + 180	**18.**	450 + 235	**19.**	219 + 507	**20.**	373 + 389
21.	$ 2.26 + 1.21	**22.**	$ 4.94 + 3.30	**23.**	$ 5.02 + 1.64	**24.**	$ 3.86 + 2.70	**25.**	$ 2.82 + 6.13
26.	$ 7.14 + 1.85	**27.**	$ 1.99 + 4.61	**28.**	$ 4.11 + 4.04	**29.**	$ 5.92 + 3.47	**30.**	$ 2.40 + 1.16

Estimate the sums.

31.	423 + 293	**32.**	65 + 16	**33.**	$ 3.50 + 3.74	**34.**	317 + 130	**35.**	$ 6.19 + 1.48
36.	39 + 43	**37.**	$ 1.63 + 4.09	**38.**	284 + 572	★ **39.**	$ 12.31 + 13.07	★ **40.**	880 + 310

Estimate to solve.

41. Spent $6.85 for lemons
Spent $2.25 for ice
About how much was spent in all?

42. Sold 31 glasses of lemonade
Sold 47 more glasses
About how many sold in all?

Adding Thousands

Add 4,157 + 3,668.
Follow these steps.

ADD ONES	ADD TENS	ADD HUNDREDS	ADD THOUSANDS
1	1 1	1	
4,1 5 7	4,1 5 7	4,1 5 7	4,1 5 7
+ 3,6 6 8	+ 3,6 6 8	+ 3,6 6 8	+ 3,6 6 8
5	2 5	8 2 5	7,8 2 5

15 is 1 ten and 5 ones

A. Find 2,637 + 5,395. Complete.

1. Add ones. 7 + 5 = ___?___

2. How is 12 written?

3. Add tens. 1 + 3 + 9 = ___?___

4. How is 13 tens written?

5. Complete the addition.

WRITE

$$\begin{array}{r} 1\ 1 \\ 2,6\ 3\ 7 \\ +\ 5,3\ 9\ 5 \\ \hline 3\ 2 \end{array}$$

B. Complete.

6.
$$\begin{array}{r} 1 \\ 6,039 \\ +\ 2,141 \\ \hline 80 \end{array}$$

7.
$$\begin{array}{r} 1,385 \\ +\ 4,291 \\ \hline 6 \end{array}$$

8.
$$\begin{array}{r} 3,566 \\ +\ 3,019 \\ \hline \end{array}$$

9.
$$\begin{array}{r} 5,148 \\ +\ 2,706 \\ \hline \end{array}$$

C. Add.

10.
$$\begin{array}{r} 4,327 \\ +\ 3,243 \\ \hline \end{array}$$

11.
$$\begin{array}{r} 1,295 \\ +\ 2,266 \\ \hline \end{array}$$

12.
$$\begin{array}{r} 7,609 \\ +\ 1,869 \\ \hline \end{array}$$

13.
$$\begin{array}{r} 5,795 \\ +\ 1,408 \\ \hline \end{array}$$

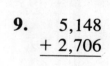

Add.

1.	3,265 + 2,614	**2.**	6,807 + 3,151	**3.**	4,136 + 4,210	**4.**	2,021 + 5,466	**5.**	5,173 + 1,523
6.	2,357 + 2,151	**7.**	6,248 + 3,408	**8.**	3,021 + 2,192	**9.**	7,308 + 1,229	**10.**	4,190 + 5,661
11.	1,349 + 6,733	**12.**	2,970 + 6,574	**13.**	3,819 + 2,546	**14.**	4,697 + 3,284	**15.**	3,618 + 1,852
16.	5,937 + 3,285	**17.**	3,768 + 4,552	**18.**	1,645 + 2,368	**19.**	3,973 + 4,979	**20.**	2,686 + 4,877
21.	4,858 + 1,386	**22.**	3,796 + 5,556	**23.**	2,637 + 3,768	**24.**	4,952 + 4,689	**25.**	6,839 + 1,279
26.	2,275 + 6,243	**27.**	1,549 + 4,151	**28.**	3,572 + 3,679	**29.**	3,695 + 2,715	**30.**	1,366 + 1,087
31.	7,590 + 1,034	**32.**	6,142 + 3,115	**33.**	5,998 + 2,474	★**34.**	9,999 + 7	★**35.**	6,827 + 3,294

Solve.

36. 3,291 people at the game on Saturday
3,143 people at the game on Sunday
How many people in all?

 37. 9,657 football tickets sold
5,186 basketball tickets sold
How many tickets sold in all?

TODAY'S SPECIALS

Honey	$ 3.12	jar
Rolled Oats	$ 2.07	box
Peanut Butter	$ 1.53	jar
Wheat Bread	$ 0.75	loaf
Granola	$ 1.16	box

Problem Solving

Use the chart to solve these problems.

1. A jar of honey
   A box of rolled oats
   How much spent in all?
   [HINT: $3.12 + $2.07 = ___?___]

2. A loaf of bread
   A box of granola
   How much spent in all?

3. A jar of peanut butter
   A loaf of bread
   How much spent in all?

4. 2 jars of honey
   1 jar of peanut butter
   How much spent in all?

5. A jar of honey
   A box of oats
   A box of granola
   How much spent in all?

6. A jar of peanut butter
   A jar of honey
   A loaf of bread
   How much spent in all?

★7. Joan bought 2 of each item on special in the health food
   store. How much spent in all?

Add.

1. 6
(59) 8
    + 3

2. 9
(59) 4
    + 6

3. 1
(59) 8
    7
  + 8

4. 53
(62) + 44

5. 307
(62) + 261

6. 425
(62) + 34

7. 49
(64) + 12

8. 35
(64) + 8

9. 57
(64) + 23

10. 227
(66) + 4

11. 115
(66) + 535

12. 519
(66) + 403

13. 382
(68) + 160

14. 595
(68) + 292

15. 626
(68) + 83

16. 268
(74) + 453

17. 482
(74) + 78

18. 194
(74) + 547

19. 396
(74) + 6

20. 271
(74) + 399

21. 36
(76) 12
   + 28

22. 136
(76) 329
   + 482

23. $ 6.49
(78) + 1.85

24. $ 2.04
(78) 2.57
   + 3.18

25. $ 5.37
(78) + 4.28

Estimate the sums. (80)

26. 48
   + 17

27. 220
   + 693

28. 71
   + 13

29. 389
   + 412

30. 24
   + 66

31. $ 2.78
   + 2.81

Write the number sentence that fits the story. (72)

32. Billy counted 26 oak trees.
Simon counted 19 maple trees.
How many trees did they count in all?

33. Karla had 13 acorns.
Nancy had 8 acorns.
How many more acorns did Karla have?

Add.

1. (59)	4 6 + 5	**2.** (59)	7 9 8 + 2	**3.** (59)	9 1 + 6	**4.** (62)	133 + 403	**5.** (62)	41 + 28

6. (62)	742 + 5	**7.** (64)	59 + 25	**8.** (64)	24 + 16	**9.** (64)	67 + 9	**10.** (66)	407 + 468

11. (66)	241 + 29	**12.** (66)	319 + 645	**13.** (68)	148 + 471	**14.** (68)	470 + 386	**15.** (68)	324 + 82

16. (68)	558 + 171	**17.** (74)	492 + 9	**18.** (74)	387 + 213	**19.** (74)	775 + 46	**20.** (74)	445 + 165

21. (76)	45 20 + 15	**22.** (76)	44 97 + 65	**23.** (78)	$ 1.36 4.26 + 1.64	**24.** (78)	$ 4.92 + 3.18	**25.** (78)	$ 3.79 + 1.95

Estimate the sums. *(80)*

26.	19 + 63	**27.**	$ 3.11 + 5.86	**28.**	492 + 223	**29.**	42 + 11	**30.**	372 + 198	**31.**	72 + 16

Write the number sentence that fits the story. *(72)*

32. There were 10 children.
There were 6 baseball caps.
How many more caps were needed?

33. The coach had 18 baseballs.
He bought 12 more baseballs.
How many baseballs in all?

1. How many centimeters long is the paper clip?

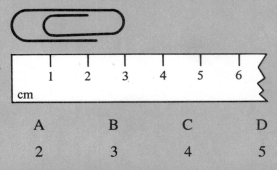

A	B	C	D
2	3	4	5

2. Justin had 25¢. His sister gave him 44¢. How much does he have in all?

E	F	G	H
29¢	52¢	65¢	69¢

3. How many days are there in a week?

A	B	C	D
6	7	8	10

4. Eliot took 1 quarter, 4 dimes, and 5 pennies from his piggy bank. How much does he have to spend?

E	F	G	H
70¢	75¢	83¢	90¢

5. The grocer placed the plump chicken on the scale. What did the scale read?

A	B	C
3 liters	3 kilograms	10 centimeters

6. Maurice wants to buy a book that cost 98¢. He has 53¢. How much more does he need?

D	E	F	G
40¢	45¢	46¢	50¢

At the Park

Subtract when you need to know:
How many more?
How many are left?

A. Look at the picture.

    1. How many girls?

    2. How many girls leaving?

    3. How many girls are left?

B. Look at the picture.

    4. How many boys near the tree?

    5. How many bicycles?

    6. How many more boys than bicycles?

    7. How many more bicycles are needed?

CHAPTER
SUBTRACTION 4

Practice

Subtract.

1. 14 children at the park
   9 children leave
   How many children are left?

2. 17 children
   9 pairs of roller skates
   How many more pairs of roller skates are needed?

3. 12 children
   6 swings
   How many more children than swings?

No Renaming

Subtract.

		THINK			WRITE

SUBTRACT ONES

	Tens	Ones
	4	6
−	3	2
		4

SUBTRACT TENS

	Tens	Ones
	4	6
−	3	2
	1	4

$$46 \atop \underline{-32}$$

WRITE

46
− 32
14

A. Find 598 − 257. Complete.

1. Subtract ones. 8 − 7 = __?__
2. Subtract tens. 9 − 5 = __?__
3. Subtract hundreds. 5 − 2 = __?__
4. What is the difference?

WRITE

598
− 257
341

B. Subtract.

5. 67 − 4	6. 89 − 51	7. 965 − 64	8. 698 − 623	9. 854 − 624

Practice

Subtract.

1. 48 − 6	2. 23 − 1	3. 32 − 12	4. 85 − 82	5. 98 − 23
6. 768 − 7	7. 656 − 3	8. 371 − 21	9. 289 − 42	10. 639 − 14

11. 468 − 254	12. 793 − 240	13. 925 − 321	14. 684 − 132	15. 566 − 532
16. 851 − 310	17. 439 − 226	18. 247 − 243	19. 715 − 604	20. 370 − 120
21. 542 − 131	22. 39 − 6	23. 764 − 432	24. 686 − 14	25. 48 − 18
26. 84 − 61	27. 897 − 813	28. 479 − 73	29. 95 − 20	★ 30. 1,426 − 304

Solve.

31. Herb has $85.
    He spent $41.
    How much left?

32. A dress costs $28.
    Jeannette has $16.
    How much more needed?

Find Out!
Brainteaser

Which shape is like the first one?

Example 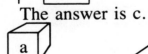 a   b c   d

The answer is c.

1.   a   b c   d

2.   a b   c d

3.   a   b   c   d

RACE TIME

Subtract.

1. 7
  2
	2. 8
	  6
		3. 10
		  1
			4. 9
			  9
				5. 7
				  7
					6. 10
					  4
						7. 12
						  9

8. 10
  8
	9. 13
	  9
		10. 15
		  9
			11. 14
			  5
				12. 17
				  9
					13. 10
					  3
						14. 14
						  9

15. 12
  7
	16. 7
	  4
		17. 13
		  8
			18. 11
			  5
				19. 16
				  9
					20. 12
					  4
						21. 9
						  8

22. 11
  9
	23. 8
	  2
		24. 11
		  3
			25. 9
			  6
				26. 15
				  8
					27. 7
					  6
						28. 9
						  2

29. 13
  5
	30. 7
	  3
		31. 10
		  5
			32. 11
			  8
				33. 13
				  4
					34. 8
					  4
						35. 16
						  8

36. 8
  7
	37. 12
	  8
		38. 14
		  7
			39. 15
			  7
				40. 7
				  5
					41. 11
					  2
						42. 18
						  9

43. 6
  4
	44. 11
	  6
		45. 12
		  3
			46. 8
			  3
				47. 10
				  6
					48. 9
					  7
						49. 7
						  1

50. 10
  9
	51. 13
	  7
		52. 14
		  6
			53. 12
			  6
				54. 16
				  7
					55. 9
					  4
						56. 6
						  3

57. 17
  8
	58. 8
	  5
		59. 9
		  3
			60. 13
			  6
				61. 6
				  2
					62. 11
					  7
						63. 10
						  7

64. 11
  4
	65. 14
	  8
		66. 15
		  6
			67. 9
			  1
				68. 8
				  8
					69. 12
					  5
						70. 9
						  5

Renaming

You can rename the tens in 23.

Take 1 ten.  → Make 10 ones.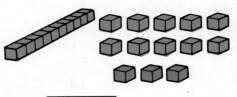

Tens	Ones
2	3

→

Tens	Ones
1 2	13 3

23 can be renamed as 1 ten and 13 ones.

A. Rename 48.

48 →

Tens	Ones
4	8

Rename 1 ten. →

Tens	Ones
4	18 8

1. How many tens left?

2. How many ones now?

B. Rename tens. *Example*   4 17 / 5 7

3. 47   **4.** 61   **5.** 77   **6.** 40   **7.** 286

Practice

Rename tens.

1. 28   **2.** 53   **3.** 92   **4.** 81   **5.** 58

6. 84   **7.** 70   **8.** 145   **9.** 130   **10.** 165

Renaming Tens

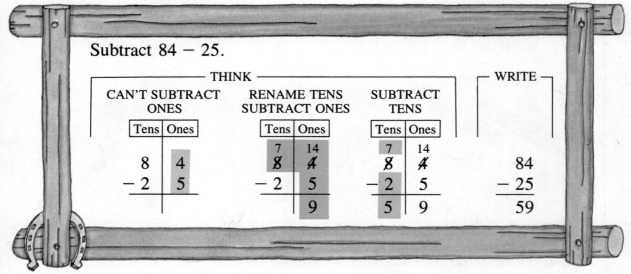

Subtract 84 − 25.

THINK

CAN'T SUBTRACT ONES

Tens	Ones
8	4
− 2	5

RENAME TENS SUBTRACT ONES

Tens	Ones
7	14
8̸	4̸
− 2	5
	9

SUBTRACT TENS

Tens	Ones
7	14
8̸	4̸
− 2	5
5	9

WRITE

$$\begin{array}{r} 84 \\ -25 \\ \hline 59 \end{array}$$

A. Complete.

1. $\overset{7\ 11}{8\ 1}$
    $\underline{-\quad 3}$
    $\ 8$

2. $\overset{4\ 13}{5\ 3}$
    $\underline{-1\ 9}$

3. 72
    $\underline{-36}$

4. 92
    $\underline{-47}$

5. 61
    $\underline{-49}$

B. Find 363 − 106. Complete.

6. Rename tens and subtract ones.
   13 − 6 = ___?___

   WRITE

   $$\begin{array}{r} \overset{5\ 13}{3\ 6\ 3} \\ -1\ 0\ 6 \\ \hline 2\ 5\ 7 \end{array}$$

7. Subtract tens. 5 − 0 = ___?___

8. Subtract hundreds. 3 − 1 = ___?___

9. What is the difference?

C. Subtract.

10. 554
    $\underline{-\ 26}$

11. 181
    $\underline{-\ 78}$

12. 747
    $\underline{-229}$

13. 676
    $\underline{-407}$

14. 232
    $\underline{-108}$

Subtract.

1. 75
    − 9

2. 46
    − 7

3. 84
    − 6

4. 35
    − 8

5. 91
    − 5

6. 67
    − 18

7. 52
    − 29

8. 83
    − 48

9. 28
    − 19

10. 42
    − 23

11. 554
    − 8

12. 872
    − 5

13. 631
    − 7

14. 943
    − 6

15. 293
    − 87

16. 785
    − 26

17. 168
    − 29

18. 951
    − 16

19. 396
    − 48

20. 494
    − 39

21. 766
    − 108

22. 523
    − 319

23. 942
    − 527

24. 371
    − 145

25. 858
    − 209

26. 934
    − 217

27. 497
    − 408

28. 281
    − 149

29. 653
    − 326

30. 725
    − 417

31. 762
    − 207

32. 51
    − 24

33. 354
    − 6

34. 76
    − 39

35. 62
    − 8

36. 581
    − 49

37. 433
    − 308

38. 95
    − 77

39. 872
    − 844

40. 673
    − 57

★ 41. $385 - \square = 147$

★ 42. $843 - \square = 408$

Solve.

43. A ranch had 142 horses.
    It had 37 saddles.
    How many more horses?

44. A ranch had 71 cattle.
    It had 18 horses.
    How many more cattle?

Checking Subtraction

Check subtraction by adding.

$$\begin{array}{r} 59 \\ -\ 26 \\ \hline 33 \end{array} \qquad \begin{array}{r} 33 \\ +\ 26 \\ \hline 59 \end{array}$$

A. Check $439 - 113$.

1. What is $439 - 113$?

2. What number is added to 326?

3. What is the sum?

4. Does $439 - 113 = 326$?

Subtract   Add to check

$$\begin{array}{r} 439 \\ -\ 113 \\ \hline 326 \end{array} \qquad \begin{array}{r} 326 \\ +\ 113 \\ \hline 439 \end{array}$$

B. Subtract and check by adding.

| **5.** $\begin{array}{r} 95 \\ -\ 8 \\ \hline \end{array}$ | **6.** $\begin{array}{r} 68 \\ -\ 36 \\ \hline \end{array}$ | **7.** $\begin{array}{r} 372 \\ -\ 38 \\ \hline \end{array}$ | **8.** $\begin{array}{r} 467 \\ -\ 124 \\ \hline \end{array}$ | **9.** $\begin{array}{r} 635 \\ -\ 209 \\ \hline \end{array}$ |

─────────────────────────────────── Practice

Subtract.

| **1.** $\begin{array}{r} 56 \\ -\ 4 \\ \hline \end{array}$ | **2.** $\begin{array}{r} 94 \\ -\ 9 \\ \hline \end{array}$ | **3.** $\begin{array}{r} 73 \\ -\ 20 \\ \hline \end{array}$ | **4.** $\begin{array}{r} 47 \\ -\ 18 \\ \hline \end{array}$ | **5.** $\begin{array}{r} 66 \\ -\ 52 \\ \hline \end{array}$ |

| **6.** $\begin{array}{r} 293 \\ -\ 37 \\ \hline \end{array}$ | **7.** $\begin{array}{r} 422 \\ -\ 19 \\ \hline \end{array}$ | **8.** $\begin{array}{r} 563 \\ -\ 12 \\ \hline \end{array}$ | **9.** $\begin{array}{r} 974 \\ -\ 26 \\ \hline \end{array}$ | **10.** $\begin{array}{r} 371 \\ -\ 41 \\ \hline \end{array}$ |

| **11.** $\begin{array}{r} 489 \\ -\ 403 \\ \hline \end{array}$ | **12.** $\begin{array}{r} 756 \\ -\ 234 \\ \hline \end{array}$ | **13.** $\begin{array}{r} 685 \\ -\ 416 \\ \hline \end{array}$ | **14.** $\begin{array}{r} 312 \\ -\ 205 \\ \hline \end{array}$ | **15.** $\begin{array}{r} 887 \\ -\ 127 \\ \hline \end{array}$ |

Renaming Hundreds

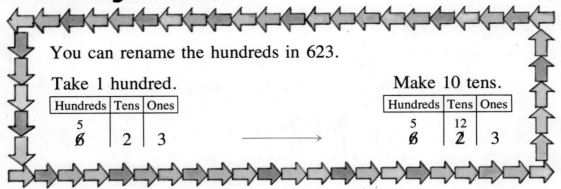

You can rename the hundreds in 623.

Take 1 hundred.

Hundreds	Tens	Ones
5̸	2	3

Make 10 tens.

Hundreds	Tens	Ones
5̸	12̸	3

A. Rename 458.

458 ⟶

H	T	O
4	5	8

Rename 1 hundred.

H	T	O
3		
4̸	5̸	8

1. How many hundreds are left?

2. How many tens now?

3. How many ones?

B. Rename hundreds. *Example*
$$\overset{7\ 14}{8\!\!\!/\,4\!\!\!/\,6}$$

4. 863   **5.** 244   **6.** 782   **7.** 611   **8.** 478

Practice

Rename hundreds.

1. 317   **2.** 643   **3.** 509   **4.** 942   **5.** 256

6. 574   **7.** 709   **8.** 845   **9.** 468   **10.** 351

11. 913   **12.** 356   **13.** 288   **14.** 682   **15.** 207

Renaming Hundreds

Subtract 437 − 172.
Follow these steps.

SUBTRACT ONES	CAN'T SUBTRACT TENS	RENAME HUNDREDS SUBTRACT TENS	SUBTRACT HUNDREDS
4 3 7	4 3 7	³⁄ ¹³⁄ 7	³⁄ ¹³⁄ 7
− 1 7 2	− 1 7 2	− 1 7 2	− 1 7 2
5	5	6 5	2 6 5

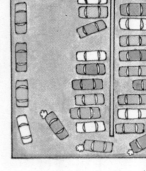

A. Find 349 − 53. Complete.

   1. Subtract ones. $9 - 3 =$ ___?___

   2. Rename hundreds and subtract tens.
     $14 - 5 =$ ___?___

   3. Bring down the hundreds.

   4. What is the difference?

WRITE

$$\begin{array}{r} {}^{2}\cancel{3}\,{}^{14}\cancel{4}\,9 \\ -\ \ 5\,3 \\ \hline 2\,9\,6 \end{array}$$

B. Complete.

   5. ⁶ ¹⁶
     7 6 3
     − 9 1
     ———
       7 2

   6. ⁵ ¹⁰
     6 0 9
     − 7 3
     ———
        6

   7. 857
     − 82

   8. 408
     − 130

   9. 536
     − 294

C. Subtract.

   10. 415
      − 42

   11. 906
      − 80

   12. 836
      − 352

   13. 365
      − 284

   14. 607
      − 361

Subtract.

1. 739 − 67	**2.** 305 − 95	**3.** 543 − 61	**4.** 124 − 43	**5.** 907 − 85
6. 652 − 91	**7.** 439 − 53	**8.** 207 − 74	**9.** 876 − 80	**10.** 525 − 63
11. 418 − 251	**12.** 646 − 593	**13.** 769 − 375	**14.** 508 − 184	**15.** 853 − 480
16. 924 − 453	**17.** 204 − 160	**18.** 677 − 281	**19.** 342 − 192	**20.** 416 − 236
21. 702 − 380	**22.** 474 − 391	**23.** 538 − 272	**24.** 809 − 684	**25.** 627 − 335
26. 886 − 495	**27.** 651 − 70	**28.** 309 − 247	**29.** 428 − 68	**30.** 544 − 291
31. 317 − 93	**32.** 266 − 175	**33.** 901 − 71	**34.** 734 − 450	**35.** 589 − 392

★ **36.** $717 - \square = 253$ ★ **37.** $936 - \square = 83$

Solve.

38. 257 cars
95 buses
How many more cars than buses?

39. 257 cars
160 trucks
How many more cars than trucks?

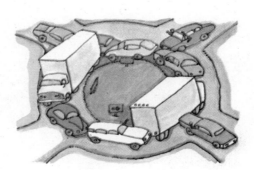

Subtract.

1. 68 (90) − 45	**2.** 46 (90) − 4	**3.** 894 (90) − 623	**4.** 687 (90) − 47	**5.** 359 (90) − 106
6. 54 (94) − 18	**7.** 42 (94) − 35	**8.** 61 (94) − 6	**9.** 564 (94) − 27	**10.** 787 (94) − 348
11. 435 (94) − 119	**12.** 292 (94) − 66	**13.** 728 (98) − 168	**14.** 734 (98) − 83	**15.** 582 (98) − 490

Find Out! _____
Aid to Memory

Here's a way to subtract 9 from a number.

START	SUBTRACT 10	ADD 1	ANSWER
1. 38	28	29	29
2. 72	62	?	?
3. 124	?	?	?
4. 236	?	?	?

Subtract 9 from each number.

5. 27　　　**6.** 77　　　**7.** 34　　　**8.** 55　　　**9.** 81

10. 35　　　**11.** 33　　　**12.** 85　　　**13.** 456　　　**14.** 126

Keeping Fit

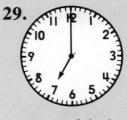

Add.

1. 32
   + 45

2. 643
   + 46

3. 425
   + 263

4. 37
   + 9

5. 564
   + 27

6. 288
   + 105

7. 242
   + 74

8. 483
   + 23

9. 356
   + 481

10. 570
   + 199

11. 464
   + 264

12. 569
   + 53

13. 884
   + 46

14. 768
   + 176

15. 342
   + 358

16. 476
   + 359

Estimate the sums.

17. 34
   + 28

18. 59
   + 17

19. 84
   + 35

20. 27
   + 48

21. 121
   + 280

22. 411
   + 284

23. 625
   + 319

24. $ 8.27
   + 1.06

25. $ 1.85
   + 3.16

26. $ 2.92
   + 4.07

Complete.

27.

_____ minutes to _____

_____ : _____

28.

_____ minutes after _____

_____ : _____

29.

_____ o'clock

_____ : _____

30.

half past _____

_____ : _____

31.

_____ minutes to _____

_____ : _____

32.

half past _____

_____ : _____

Problem-Solving Steps

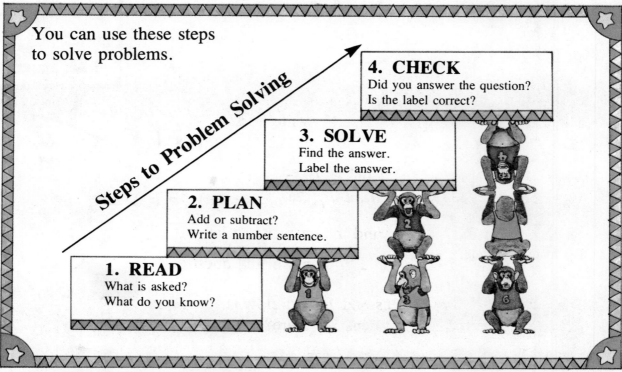

You can use these steps
to solve problems.

Steps to Problem Solving

4. CHECK
Did you answer the question?
Is the label correct?

3. SOLVE
Find the answer.
Label the answer.

2. PLAN
Add or subtract?
Write a number sentence.

1. READ
What is asked?
What do you know?

Use the four steps to solve.

Step 1. **READ**
There are 8 brown monkeys.
There are 2 gray monkeys.
How many monkeys in all?

Step 2. **PLAN**
Will you add or subtract?

Step 3. **SOLVE**
$8 + 2 = $ _____?_____

Step 4. **CHECK**
$8 + 2 = 10$
There are 10 monkeys in all.

Practice

Use the four steps to solve.

There are 16 brown horses and 12 white horses.
How many horses in all?

1. Step 1.   **READ**   What is asked?

2. Step 2.   **PLAN**   Write a number sentence.

3. Step 3.   **SOLVE**   Find the answer and label it.

4. Step 4.   **CHECK**   Did you answer the question?

There are 24 happy clowns and 16 sad clowns.
How many more happy clowns are there?

5. Step 1.   **READ**   What is asked?

6. Step 2.   **PLAN**   Write a number sentence.

7. Step 3.   **SOLVE**   Find the answer and label it.

8. Step 4.   **CHECK**   Did you answer the question?

There are 6 elephants dancing.
There are 7 elephants sitting.
How many elephants in all?

9. Step 1.   **READ**   What is asked?

10. Step 2.   **PLAN**   Write a number sentence.

11. Step 3.   **SOLVE**   Find the answer and label it.

12. Step 4.   **CHECK**   Did you answer the question?

Renaming Twice

Subtract 724 − 286.
Follow these steps.

RENAME TENS SUBTRACT ONES	CAN'T SUBTRACT TENS	RENAME HUNDREDS SUBTRACT TENS	SUBTRACT HUNDREDS
$\begin{array}{r}\overset{1\ 14}{7\,2\,4}\\-2\,8\,6\\\hline 8\end{array}$	$\begin{array}{r}\overset{1\ 14}{7\,2\,4}\\-2\,8\,6\\\hline 8\end{array}$	$\begin{array}{r}\overset{6\ 11\,14}{7\,2\,4}\\-2\,8\,6\\\hline 3\,8\end{array}$	$\begin{array}{r}\overset{6\ 11\,14}{7\,2\,4}\\-2\,8\,6\\\hline 4\,3\,8\end{array}$

A. Find 743 − 86. Complete.

WRITE

1. Rename tens and subtract ones.
   13 − 6 = ___?___

   $\begin{array}{r}\overset{3\ 13}{7\,4\,3}\\-\ \ 8\,6\end{array}$

2. Rename hundreds and subtract tens.
   13 − 8 = ___?___

   $\begin{array}{r}\overset{13}{}\\\overset{6\ 3\ 13}{7\,4\,3}\\-\ \ 8\,6\\\hline 6\,5\,7\end{array}$

3. Bring down the hundreds.

4. What is the difference?

B. Complete.

5. $\begin{array}{r}\overset{\ \ 12}{\overset{1\ 2\ 10}{2\,3\,0}}\\-\ \ 5\,9\\\hline 7\,1\end{array}$

6. $\begin{array}{r}\overset{\ \ 15}{\overset{4\ 5\ 14}{5\,6\,4}}\\-\ \ 7\,6\\\hline 8\end{array}$

7. $\begin{array}{r}8\,2\,3\\-\ \ 8\,7\\\hline\end{array}$

8. $\begin{array}{r}4\,6\,0\\-1\,9\,6\\\hline\end{array}$

9. $\begin{array}{r}2\,5\,6\\-\ \ 5\,8\\\hline\end{array}$

C. Subtract.

10. $\begin{array}{r}3\,6\,2\\-\ \ 8\,7\\\hline\end{array}$

11. $\begin{array}{r}9\,8\,5\\-\ \ 9\,6\\\hline\end{array}$

12. $\begin{array}{r}6\,3\,0\\-1\,3\,9\\\hline\end{array}$

13. $\begin{array}{r}7\,2\,3\\-1\,6\,8\\\hline\end{array}$

14. $\begin{array}{r}5\,1\,4\\-1\,7\,9\\\hline\end{array}$

Subtract.

1. 443
    − 38

2. 964
    − 37

3. 180
    − 29

4. 373
    − 55

5. 596
    − 37

6. 825
    − 218

7. 781
    − 727

8. 348
    − 309

9. 630
    − 116

10. 257
    − 238

11. 955
    − 92

12. 642
    − 81

13. 613
    − 63

14. 726
    − 83

15. 307
    − 72

16. 648
    − 460

17. 511
    − 370

18. 409
    − 193

19. 874
    − 792

20. 935
    − 241

21. 515
    − 67

22. 170
    − 76

23. 421
    − 98

24. 946
    − 49

25. 634
    − 77

26. 787
    − 599

27. 530
    − 253

28. 362
    − 286

29. 833
    − 259

30. 250
    − 185

31. 971
    − 76

32. 327
    − 109

33. 542
    − 155

34. 714
    − 356

35. 449
    − 94

36. 626
    − 587

37. 235
    − 69

38. 540
    − 380

39. 410
    − 408

40. 103
    − 5

★ 41. $734 - \square = 198$

★ 42. $916 - \square = 749$

Solve.

43. 432 girls at King School
    375 boys at King School
    How many more girls?

44. 243 adults at the school play
    156 children at the school play
    How many more adults?

Zeros in Subtraction

Subtract 400 − 254.
Follow these steps.

CAN'T SUBTRACT ONES CAN'T RENAME TENS	RENAME HUNDREDS	RENAME TENS	SUBTRACT
400 − 254	3 10 4̸ 0̸ 0 − 2 5 4	9 3 10̸ 10 4̸ 0̸ 0̸ − 2 5 4	9 3 10̸ 10 4̸ 0̸ 0̸ − 2 5 4 1 4 6

A. Rename 300.

300 ⟶

H	T	O
3	0	0

Rename 1 hundred. ⟶

H	T	O
2	10	
3̸	0̸	0

Rename 1 ten. ⟶

H	T	O
	9	
2	10̸	10
3̸	0̸	0̸

1. How many hundreds left?
2. How many tens now?
3. How many ones now?

B. Find 500 − 126. Complete.

4. Rename hundreds.

5. Rename tens.

6. Complete the subtraction.

7. What is the difference?

WRITE

9
4 10̸ 10
5̸ 0̸ 0̸
− 1 2 6

C. Subtract.

8.　400
　　−　 7

9.　906
　　− 458

10.　700
　　− 165

11.　400
　　− 228

12.　630
　　− 346

Subtract.

1. 204
  − 6

2. 430
  − 75

3. 850
  − 59

4. 106
  − 58

5. 710
  − 43

6. 700
  − 43

7. 200
  − 24

8. 400
  − 89

9. 100
  − 65

10. 500
  − 37

11. 420
  − 152

12. 308
  − 219

13. 702
  − 636

14. 650
  − 385

15. 504
  − 247

16. 800
  − 283

17. 500
  − 128

18. 900
  − 354

19. 300
  − 179

20. 600
  − 561

21. 900
  − 567

22. 600
  − 189

23. 500
  − 238

24. 400
  − 357

25. 900
  − 711

26. 600
  − 27

27. 700
  − 412

28. 260
  − 193

29. 140
  − 96

30. 800
  − 341

31. 300
  − 274

32. 803
  − 538

33. 502
  − 44

34. 601
  − 3

★ 35. 4,000
  − 986

Solve.

36. A sofa cost $600.
Mr. Smith has $435.
How much more is needed?

37. Spent $700 for a freezer and a stove.
The stove cost $285.
How much for the freezer?

Blast Off

Subtracting amounts of money is the same as subtracting numbers.

Adele had $5.00.
She bought a model rocket for $3.65.
How much change did she get back?

$$\begin{array}{r} 500 \\ -365 \\ \hline 135 \end{array} \qquad \begin{array}{r} \$\,5.00 \\ -3.65 \\ \hline \$\,1.35 \end{array}$$

dollar sign ⌐

decimal point ⌐

Adele's change is $1.35.

A. Find $6.58 − $5.29. Complete.

WRITE

1. Rename tens and subtract ones.
   18 − 9 = ___?___

2. Subtract tens. 4 − 2 = ___?___

3. Complete the subtraction.

$$\begin{array}{r} {\scriptstyle 4\,18} \\ \$\,6.\cancel{5}\cancel{8} \\ -5.2\,9 \\ \hline \$\,1.2\,9 \end{array}$$

B. Subtract.

4. $\begin{array}{r} \$\,2.35 \\ -0.61 \\ \hline \end{array}$ 5. $\begin{array}{r} \$\,1.67 \\ -1.38 \\ \hline \end{array}$ 6. $\begin{array}{r} \$\,4.03 \\ -1.62 \\ \hline \end{array}$ 7. $\begin{array}{r} \$\,3.40 \\ -1.46 \\ \hline \end{array}$ 8. $\begin{array}{r} \$\,6.00 \\ -5.29 \\ \hline \end{array}$

_____ Practice

Subtract.

1. $\begin{array}{r} \$\,4.93 \\ -0.32 \\ \hline \end{array}$ 2. $\begin{array}{r} \$\,4.63 \\ -0.72 \\ \hline \end{array}$ 3. $\begin{array}{r} \$\,3.51 \\ -2.05 \\ \hline \end{array}$ 4. $\begin{array}{r} \$\,3.00 \\ -2.79 \\ \hline \end{array}$ 5. $\begin{array}{r} \$\,4.00 \\ -3.17 \\ \hline \end{array}$

Counting Change

You can find change by counting on.
Art supplies cost $4.69.
What is the change from $5.00?

Cost

$4.69

Change

Say: $4.70 $4.75 $5.00

The change is 31¢.

A. Paint cost $1.60. Gave $2.00.

Cost

$1.60

Change

Say: ___?___   ___?___   ___?___

1. Is the change correct?

2. What should the change be?

Practice

Is the change correct? What should the change be?

1. Cost: $1.88
    Gave: $2.00

2. Cost: $4.74
    Gave: $5.00

Estimating Differences

49 people at a bus station
22 people leave the station.
About how many people are left?

Round to the nearest ten, then subtract.

$$49 \longrightarrow 50$$
$$\underline{-\ 22} \longrightarrow \underline{-\ 20}$$
$$30$$

There are about 30 people left.

Estimate the differences to find **about** how many or how much.

A. Estimate the differences. Round to the nearest ten.

1.	**2.**	**3.**	**4.**	**5.**
75	57	69	31	27
$-\ 12$	$-\ 23$	$-\ 41$	$-\ 16$	$-\ 19$

B. Estimate $585 - 190$.
Round to the nearest hundred.

6. Round 585.

7. Round 190.

8. Subtract. $600 - 200 = \underline{\ ?\ }$

EXACT		ROUNDED
585	$\longrightarrow$	600
$-\ 190$	$\longrightarrow$	$-\ 200$

C. Estimate $\$3.98 - \$1.25$.
Round to the nearest dollar.

9. Round $3.98.

10. Round $1.25.

11. Subtract. $\$4.00 - \$1.00 = \underline{\ ?\ }$

EXACT		ROUNDED
$ 3.98	$\longrightarrow$	$ 4.00
$-\ 1.25$	$\longrightarrow$	$-\ 1.00$

D. Estimate the differences. Round to the nearest hundred or dollar.

12.	**13.**	**14.**	**15.**	**16.**
537	763	431	$ 7.32	$ 6.95
$-\ 217$	$-\ 442$	$-\ 176$	$-\ 4.98$	$-\ 4.10$

Estimate the differences. Round to the nearest ten.

1.	41 − 32	**2.**	62 − 19	**3.**	35 − 18	**4.**	77 − 31	**5.**	91 − 57

6.	86 − 42	**7.**	59 − 33	**8.**	68 − 27	**9.**	74 − 22	**10.**	83 − 16

Estimate the differences. Round to the nearest hundred or dollar.

11.	289 − 121	**12.**	679 − 268	**13.**	777 − 390	**14.**	940 − 215	**15.**	504 − 183

16.	942 − 303	**17.**	413 − 188	**18.**	882 − 427	**19.**	612 − 425	**20.**	394 − 270

21.	$ 3.68 − 1.79	**22.**	$ 8.05 − 4.84	**23.**	$ 9.18 − 4.36	**24.**	$ 5.80 − 2.92	**25.**	$ 4.76 − 3.23

26.	$ 6.30 − 2.99	**27.**	$ 5.13 − 1.20	**28.**	$ 2.84 − 1.11	**29.**	$ 7.72 − 2.65	**30.**	$ 9.37 − 6.62

Estimate the differences.

31.	$ 8.27 − 6.95	**32.**	540 − 133	**33.**	71 − 18	**34.**	489 − 190	**35.**	$ 9.06 − 2.31

36.	678 − 317	**37.**	87 − 26	**38.**	766 − 244	★ **39.**	989 − 107	★ **40.**	$ 9.77 − 4.19

Estimate to solve.

41. Eleanor had $8.75.
A bus ticket cost $4.13.
About how much was left?

42. A bus ticket cost $6.85.
Paul had $4.12.
About how much was needed?

Subtracting Thousands

Subtract 6,478 − 3,629.
Follow these steps.

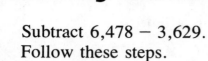

SUBTRACT ONES	SUBTRACT TENS	SUBTRACT HUNDREDS	SUBTRACT THOUSANDS
$\begin{array}{r} {}^{6}\,{}^{18}\\ 6,4\,7\,8 \\ -\,3,6\,2\,9 \\ \hline 9 \end{array}$	$\begin{array}{r} {}^{6}\,{}^{18}\\ 6,4\,7\,8 \\ -\,3,6\,2\,9 \\ \hline 4\,9 \end{array}$	$\begin{array}{r} {}^{5}\,{}^{14}\,{}^{6}\,{}^{18}\\ 6,4\,7\,8 \\ -\,3,6\,2\,9 \\ \hline 8\,4\,9 \end{array}$	$\begin{array}{r} {}^{5}\,{}^{14}\,{}^{6}\,{}^{18}\\ 6,4\,7\,8 \\ -\,3,6\,2\,9 \\ \hline 2,8\,4\,9 \end{array}$

A. Find 5,367 − 2,798. Complete.

1. Rename tens and subtract ones.
  17 − 8 = ___?___

2. Rename hundreds and subtract tens.
  15 − 9 = ___?___

3. Rename thousands and subtract hundreds.
  12 − 7 = ___?___

4. Complete. What is the difference?

WRITE

$\begin{array}{r} {}^{12}\,{}^{15}\\ {}^{4}\,\ {}^{2}\,{}^{3}\,{}^{17}\\ 5,3\,6\,7 \\ -\,2,7\,9\,8 \\ \hline 2,5\,6\,9 \end{array}$

B. Complete.

5. $\begin{array}{r} {}^{16}\\ {}^{5}\,{}^{6}\,{}^{12}\\ 4,6\,7\,2 \\ -\,2,9\,9\,6 \\ \hline 7\,6 \end{array}$
6. $\begin{array}{r} {}^{5}\,{}^{11}\\ 6,3\,6\,1 \\ -\,4,4\,8\,2 \\ \hline 9 \end{array}$
7. $\begin{array}{r} 9,4\,1\,0 \\ -\,5,6\,7\,3 \\ \hline \end{array}$
8. $\begin{array}{r} 2,5\,4\,7 \\ -\,1,8\,6\,9 \\ \hline \end{array}$
9. $\begin{array}{r} 5,1\,8\,4 \\ -\,2,6\,9\,7 \\ \hline \end{array}$

C. Subtract.

10. $\begin{array}{r} 3,5\,2\,7 \\ -\,1,3\,6\,8 \\ \hline \end{array}$
11. $\begin{array}{r} 9,1\,5\,6 \\ -\,3,6\,9\,0 \\ \hline \end{array}$
12. $\begin{array}{r} 6,6\,3\,2 \\ -\,4,8\,5\,7 \\ \hline \end{array}$
13. $\begin{array}{r} 3,7\,1\,5 \\ -\,1,7\,1\,9 \\ \hline \end{array}$
14. $\begin{array}{r} 7,2\,0\,3 \\ -\,6,4\,2\,7 \\ \hline \end{array}$

Subtract.

1. 5,281 − 1,046	**2.** 9,436 − 6,219	**3.** 7,560 − 2,258	**4.** 4,792 − 4,324	**5.** 6,374 − 1,207
6. 8,464 − 5,295	**7.** 3,845 − 2,186	**8.** 5,614 − 3,277	**9.** 7,384 − 4,576	**10.** 2,453 − 1,970
11. 8,456 − 3,985	**12.** 3,720 − 1,369	**13.** 6,742 − 5,938	**14.** 4,625 − 2,630	**15.** 8,043 − 4,617
16. 5,628 − 1,859	**17.** 9,204 − 5,847	**18.** 7,461 − 2,793	**19.** 2,102 − 1,375	**20.** 4,326 − 2,987
21. 6,234 − 2,375	**22.** 5,623 − 4,987	**23.** 7,004 − 5,538	**24.** 4,293 − 1,899	**25.** 8,312 − 3,784
26. 9,582 − 4,193	**27.** 4,141 − 1,182	**28.** 8,941 − 2,109	**29.** 5,334 − 4,769	**30.** 6,047 − 4,392

★ **31.** 47,623 − 22,846   ★ **32.** 33,874 − 21,218   ★ **33.** 29,403 − 13,388   ★ **34.** 27,426 − 16,388

Solve.

35. A new car cost $8,164.
A used car cost $5,782.
How much more for the new car?

36. A truck cost $9,125.
A car cost $6,448.
How much more for the truck?

Problem Solving
Real Estate Agents

Solve.

1. 6 houses sold in May
9 houses sold in June
How many sold in all?

2. Earned $420 last week
Earned $367 this week
How much more earned last
week than this week?

3. 5 houses for sale on North Street
7 houses for sale on South Street
How many in all?

4. 13 offices rented on the east side
9 offices rented on the west side
How many more rented on east side?

5. Real estate fee $400
Have $245
How much more needed?

Career

Subtract.

1. 53	**2.** 658	**3.** 291	**4.** 51	**5.** 835
(90) − 20	(90) − 304	(94) − 9	(94) − 35	(94) − 316

6. 648	**7.** 333	**8.** 726	**9.** 522	**10.** 441
(98) − 567	(98) − 93	(98) − 374	(104) − 46	(104) − 278

11. 978	**12.** 500	**13.** 804	**14.** $ 7.39	**15.** $ 9.01
(104) − 289	(106) − 276	(106) − 349	(108) − 5.87	(108) − 4.19

Estimate the differences. *(110)*

16. 783	**17.** 92	**18.** $ 3.69
− 114	− 33	− 1.10

Solve. *(102, 114)*

19. 8 bags of potting soil
2 bags of grass seed
How many more bags of
potting soil?

20. Spent $9 for seeds
Spent $7 for soil
How much spent in all?

Find Out!
Brainteaser

How many blocks in each?

1.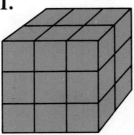

2.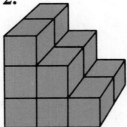

3.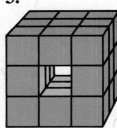

Subtract.

1. 49
(90) − 17

2. 936
(90) − 532

3. 351
(94) − 106

4. 85
(94) − 58

5. 271
(98) − 181

6. 834
(98) − 71

7. 567
(98) − 392

8. 635
(104) − 77

9. 752
(104) − 189

10. 314
(104) − 68

11. 703
(106) − 186

12. 400
(106) − 91

13. 600
(106) − 435

14. $ 8.00
(108) − 2.38

15. $ 4.83
(108) − 1.34

Estimate the differences. *(110)*

16. 78
− 21

17. 694
− 480

18. $ 7.41
− 5.18

Solve. *(102)*

19. 7 doctors
7 nurses
How many in all?

20. 12 people in the waiting room
7 people leave.
How many are left in the waiting room?

1.

	A 9
5	B 10
+ 4	C 12
	D 13

2.

	E 20
69	F 22
− 47	G 24
	H 26

3.

	A 25
23	B 27
+ 5	C 28
	D 30

4. 75 − 9 = ___?___

	E 50
	F 56
	G 60
	H 66

5.

	A 190
484	B 200
− 264	C 210
	D 220

6. 34 + 51 = ___?___

	E 84
	F 85
	G 86
	H 87

7.

	A 16
61	B 17
− 42	C 19
	D 20

8.

	E 111
459	F 112
− 348	G 113
	H 114

9. 9 − 4 = ___?___

	A 2
	B 3
	C 4
	D 5

10.

	E 105
375	F 115
− 250	G 125
	H 130

11. 93 − 56 = ___?___

	A 27
	B 37
	C 39
	D 49

12.

	E 56
25	F 64
+ 31	G 66
	H 70

At the Zoo

How many monkeys?

$3 + 3 = 6$ ⟵ Addition Sentence
$2 \times 3 = 6$ ⟵ Multiplication Sentence
↑

Read: Two times three equals six
There are 6 monkeys.

A. Look at the lions in the picture.

   1. How many lions in each cage?

   2. How many cages?

   3. Complete the addition sentence.
     $2 + 2 + 2 = \underline{\quad?\quad}$

   4. Complete the multiplication sentence.
     $3 \times 2 = \underline{\quad?\quad}$

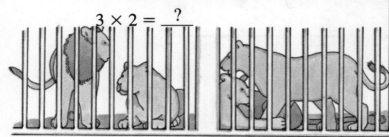

B. Complete.

   5. $2 + 2 + 2 + 2 = \underline{\quad?\quad}$ **6.** $3 + 3 + 3 = \underline{\quad?\quad}$ **7.** $5 + 5 = \underline{\quad?\quad}$
       $4 \times 2 = \underline{\quad?\quad}$ $3 \times 3 = \underline{\quad?\quad}$ $2 \times 5 = \underline{\quad?\quad}$

C. Write a multiplication sentence for each.

   8. $2 + 2 + 2 = 6$ **9.** $3 + 3 = 6$ **10.** $3 + 3 + 3 + 3 = 12$

MULTIPLICATION FACTS

Practice

Write a multiplication sentence for each.

1. $4 + 4 = 8$ **2.** $2 + 2 = 4$ **3.** $3 + 3 + 3 = 9$

4. $5 + 5 + 5 = 15$ **5.** $3 + 3 = 6$ **6.** $4 + 4 + 4 = 12$

7. $3 + 3 + 3 + 3 = 12$ **8.** $5 + 5 = 10$

9. $2 + 2 + 2 + 2 + 2 = 10$ **10.** $3 + 3 + 3 + 3 + 3 = 15$

★ Write an addition sentence for each.

11. $3 \times 5 = 15$ **12.** $4 \times 2 = 8$ **13.** $4 \times 4 = 16$

Factors and Products

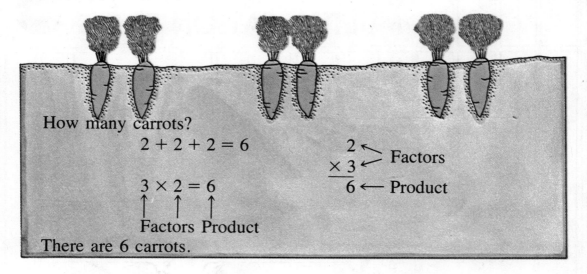

How many carrots?

$2 + 2 + 2 = 6$

$3 \times 2 = 6$

↑   ↑   ↑

Factors   Product

There are 6 carrots.

$$\begin{array}{r} 2 \\ \times 3 \\ \hline 6 \end{array}$$ ← Factors

← Product

A. Look at the picture.

1. How many ears of corn in each row?

2. How many rows of corn?

3. Complete. $5 \times 2 =$ ___?___

4. Name the factors.

5. What is the product?

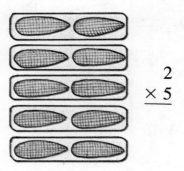

$$\begin{array}{r} 2 \\ \times 5 \\ \hline \end{array}$$

B. Find the products.

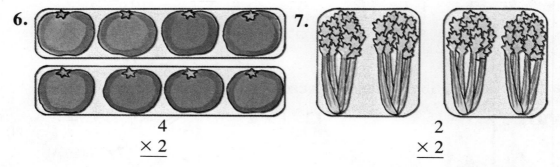

6. $$\begin{array}{r} 4 \\ \times 2 \\ \hline \end{array}$$

7. $$\begin{array}{r} 2 \\ \times 2 \\ \hline \end{array}$$

C. Multiply.

8.	**9.**	**10.**	**11.**	**12.**	**13.**
3 × 3	3 × 4	3 × 2	2 × 4	2 × 2	3 × 5

————————————————————————————————— Practice

Name the factors.

1. $5 \times 2 = 10$ **2.** $3 \times 2 = 6$ **3.** $4 \times 2 = 8$

Name the products.

4. $3 \times 2 = 6$ **5.** $4 \times 2 = 8$ **6.** $5 \times 2 = 10$

Find the products.

7.

2
× 2

8.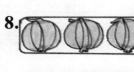
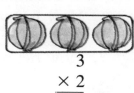

3
× 2

Multiply.

9.	**10.**	**11.**	**12.**	**13.**	**14.**
2 × 5	3 × 5	2 × 3	3 × 2	3 × 4	2 × 4

★ Draw a picture for each. Then solve.

15. $6 \times 2 = \underline{\ \ ?\ \ }$ **16.** $6 \times 3 = \underline{\ \ ?\ \ }$

More Factors and Products

How many snowballs?

$$5 \times 5 = 25 \qquad \begin{array}{r} 5 \\ \times\, 5 \\ \hline 25 \end{array}$$

There are 25 snowballs.

A. Find the products.

1.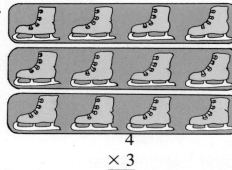

$$\begin{array}{r} 4 \\ \times\, 3 \\ \hline \end{array}$$

2.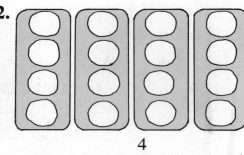

$$\begin{array}{r} 4 \\ \times\, 4 \\ \hline \end{array}$$

3.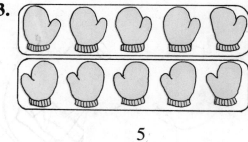

$$\begin{array}{r} 5 \\ \times\, 2 \\ \hline \end{array}$$

4.

$$\begin{array}{r} 5 \\ \times\, 3 \\ \hline \end{array}$$

B. Multiply.

5. $\begin{array}{r} 3 \\ \times\, 4 \\ \hline \end{array}$ 6. $\begin{array}{r} 5 \\ \times\, 4 \\ \hline \end{array}$ 7. $\begin{array}{r} 3 \\ \times\, 5 \\ \hline \end{array}$ 8. $\begin{array}{r} 4 \\ \times\, 5 \\ \hline \end{array}$ 9. $\begin{array}{r} 5 \\ \times\, 5 \\ \hline \end{array}$ 10. $\begin{array}{r} 4 \\ \times\, 4 \\ \hline \end{array}$

Multiply.

1. 4 $\times 2$	**2.** 2 $\times 3$	**3.** 2 $\times 5$	**4.** 4 $\times 5$	**5.** 5 $\times 3$
6. 5 $\times 2$	**7.** 4 $\times 3$	**8.** 2 $\times 2$	**9.** 2 $\times 4$	**10.** 4 $\times 4$
11. 5 $\times 5$	**12.** 3 $\times 4$	**13.** 3 $\times 3$	**14.** 5 $\times 4$	**15.** 3 $\times 5$

★ Name the missing factors.

16. __?__ × __?__ = 16   **17.** __?__ × __?__ = 15

Solve.

18. 4 people
Each person has 2 skis.
How many skis in all?
$4 \times 2 =$ __?__

19. 5 skiing teams
4 people on each team
How many people in all?
$5 \times 4 =$ __?__

Multiply. (120, 122)

1. 2 ×2	**2.** 3 ×4	**3.** 2 ×3	**4.** 3 ×5	**5.** 3 ×3	**6.** 2 ×4
7. 4 ×3	**8.** 5 ×4	**9.** 5 ×2	**10.** 5 ×5	**11.** 4 ×2	**12.** 4 ×4

Find Out! _____
Brainteaser

Choose the picture that matches the first picture.

Example

  b

a   b   c   d

The answer is c.

1.   c

a   b   c   d

2.   b

a   b   c   d

3.   b

a   b   c   d

4.   b

a   b   c   d

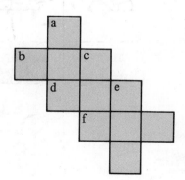

Subtract.

1. 87
    − 23

2. 564
    − 34

3. 849
    − 125

4. 453
    − 147

5. 221
    − 80

6. 748
    − 262

7. 72
    − 35

8. 938
    − 19

9. 865
    − 791

10. 354
    − 89

11. 636
    − 97

12. 555
    − 287

13. 462
    − 168

14. 300
    − 61

15. 801
    − 56

16. 700
    − 537

17. 940
    − 333

18. $ 5.79
    − 2.82

19. $ 8.34
    − 4.06

20. $ 4.61
    − 1.94

21. $ 5.00
    − 3.86

Estimate the differences.

22. 59
    − 31

23. 83
    − 17

24. 622
    − 403

25. 734
    − 279

26. 480
    − 194

Find Out!
Activity

Copy and complete the puzzle.

Across
a. 999 − 990

b. 392 − 177

d. 841 − 335

f. 309 − 49

Down
a. 974 − 59

b. 274 − 272

c. 791 − 289

e. 843 − 183

Problem-Solving Steps

You can use these steps
to solve problems.

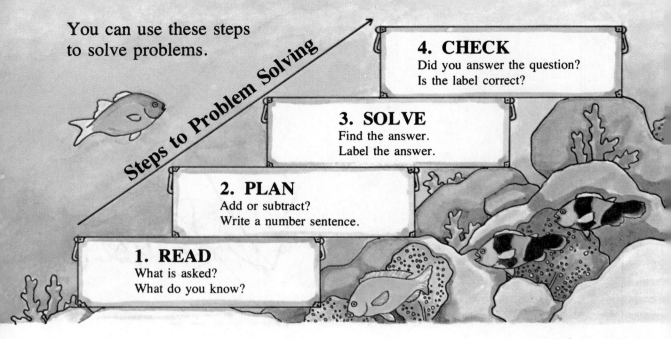

Steps to Problem Solving

4. CHECK
Did you answer the question?
Is the label correct?

3. SOLVE
Find the answer.
Label the answer.

2. PLAN
Add or subtract?
Write a number sentence.

1. READ
What is asked?
What do you know?

Use the four steps to solve.

A. There were 6 divers.
4 of them found gold.
How many did not find gold?

    1. Step 1.   **READ**   What is asked?
    2. Step 2.   **PLAN**   Write a number sentence.
    3. Step 3.   **SOLVE**   Find the answer and label it.
    4. Step 4.   **CHECK**   Did you answer the question?

B. A diver saw 2 starfish. Another diver saw 3 starfish.
How many starfish were seen in all?

    5. Step 1.   **READ**   What is asked?
    6. Step 2.   **PLAN**   Write a number sentence.
    7. Step 3.   **SOLVE**   Find the answer and label it.
    8. Step 4.   **CHECK**   Did you answer the question?

Use the four steps to solve.

1. Mr. Guerra found 12 old coins at the shipwreck.
Ms. Goldberg found 15 old coins.
How many coins did they find in all?

2. There were 27 pearls found on Monday.
There were 16 pearls found on Tuesday.
How many more pearls were found on Monday?

3. A diver saw 3 green butterfly fish.
Another diver saw 8 yellow butterfly fish.
How many fish in all?

4. There were 5 divers in a diving bell.
There were 6 divers in another diving bell.
How many divers in all?

Two as a Factor

How many sneakers?   2
6 × 2 = 12   × 6
                     ———
                      12

There are 12 sneakers.

A. Multiply.

1.   2   2   2   2   2   2   2   2
   × 2   × 3   × 4   × 5   × 6   × 7   × 8   × 9

B. Find the products.

2.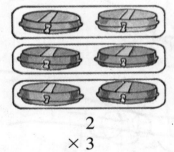

     2
   × 3

3.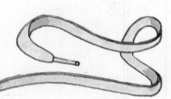

     3
   × 2

▶ Changing the order of the factors does not change
the product.

C. Multiply.

4.   2   5.   4   6.   2   7.   5   8.   2   9.   6
   × 4   × 2   × 5   × 2   × 6   × 2

10.   2   11.   7   12.   2   13.   8   14.   2   15.   9
   × 7   × 2   × 8   × 2   × 9   × 2

Multiply.

1. 7 × 2	**2.** 2 × 4	**3.** 5 × 2	**4.** 2 × 7	**5.** 6 × 2	**6.** 9 × 2
7. 2 × 5	**8.** 6 × 2	**9.** 8 × 2	**10.** 2 × 9	**11.** 2 × 8	**12.** 4 × 2
13. 2 × 3	**14.** 4 × 3	**15.** 3 × 2	**16.** 4 × 4	**17.** 5 × 3	**18.** 2 × 2
19. 3 × 3	**20.** 5 × 4	**21.** 3 × 4	**22.** 4 × 5	**23.** 3 × 5	**24.** 5 × 5

Solve.

25. 8 children
2 shoes each
How many shoes in all?

26. Bought 2 pairs of shoes
Each pair cost 9 dollars.
How much spent for shoes?

Zero and One as Factors

How many birds?

$0 + 0 + 0 = 0$ 0

$3 \times 0 = 0$ $\underline{\times\, 3}$

                        0

There are no birds.

How many cages?

$1 + 1 + 1 = 3$ 1

$3 \times 1 = 3$ $\underline{\times\, 3}$

                        3

There are 3 cages.

▶ When 0 is a factor the product is 0.

▶ When 1 is a factor the product is the other factor.

A. Multiply.

1.	2.	3.	4.	5.	6.
0	0	0	0	0	0
$\times\,0$	$\times\,1$	$\times\,2$	$\times\,3$	$\times\,4$	$\times\,5$

7.	8.	9.	10.	11.	12.
0	1	2	3	4	5
$\times\,0$	$\times\,0$	$\times\,0$	$\times\,0$	$\times\,0$	$\times\,0$

B. Multiply.

13.	14.	15.	16.	17.
1	1	1	1	1
$\times\,1$	$\times\,2$	$\times\,3$	$\times\,4$	$\times\,5$

18.	19.	20.	21.	22.
1	2	3	4	5
$\times\,1$	$\times\,1$	$\times\,1$	$\times\,1$	$\times\,1$

C. Multiply.

23. 2   **24.** 1   **25.** 5   **26.** 0   **27.** 1   **28.** 4
    $\times 0$ $\times 4$ $\times 1$ $\times 3$ $\times 2$ $\times 0$

Multiply.

1. 3   **2.** 2   **3.** 4   **4.** 0   **5.** 1   **6.** 5
   $\times 1$ $\times 0$ $\times 1$ $\times 3$ $\times 3$ $\times 1$

7. 0   **8.** 5   **9.** 1   **10.** 0   **11.** 1   **12.** 0
   $\times 0$ $\times 0$ $\times 1$ $\times 4$ $\times 2$ $\times 5$

13. 1   **14.** 1   **15.** 2   **16.** 0   **17.** 3   ★ **18.** 34
    $\times 4$ $\times 0$ $\times 1$ $\times 1$ $\times 0$ $\times\ \ 0$

Keeping Fit

Complete.

1.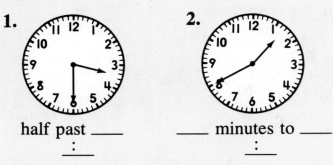

half past ____

____ : ____

2.

____ minutes to ____

____ : ____

How much is shown?

3.

4.

Three and Four as Factors

How many kittens?

$$4 \times 3 = 12$$

There are 12 kittens.

A. Count by 3's.

3, $\boxed{+3}$ 6, $\boxed{+3}$ 9, $\boxed{+3}$ 12, $\boxed{+3}$ 15, _?_, _?_, _?_, _?_

B. Multiply.

1.
$$\begin{array}{ccccccccc} 3 & 3 & 3 & 3 & 3 & 3 & 3 & 3 & 3 \\ \times 1 & \times 2 & \times 3 & \times 4 & \times 5 & \times 6 & \times 7 & \times 8 & \times 9 \end{array}$$

2.
$$\begin{array}{ccccccccc} 1 & 2 & 3 & 4 & 5 & 6 & 7 & 8 & 9 \\ \times 3 & \times 3 & \times 3 & \times 3 & \times 3 & \times 3 & \times 3 & \times 3 & \times 3 \end{array}$$

3. What is the pattern in the answers in 1. and 2.?

C. Count by 4's.

4, $\boxed{+4}$ 8, $\boxed{+4}$ 12, $\boxed{+4}$ 16, $\boxed{+4}$ 20, _?_, _?_, _?_, _?_

D. Multiply.

4.
$$\begin{array}{ccccccccc} 4 & 4 & 4 & 4 & 4 & 4 & 4 & 4 & 4 \\ \times 1 & \times 2 & \times 3 & \times 4 & \times 5 & \times 6 & \times 7 & \times 8 & \times 9 \end{array}$$

5.
$$\begin{array}{ccccccccc} 1 & 2 & 3 & 4 & 5 & 6 & 7 & 8 & 9 \\ \times 4 & \times 4 & \times 4 & \times 4 & \times 4 & \times 4 & \times 4 & \times 4 & \times 4 \end{array}$$

6. What is the pattern in the answers in 4. and 5.?

E. Multiply.

7.	8.	9.	10.	11.	12.
3 × 7	4 × 7	8 × 4	3 × 8	9 × 3	0 × 6

Practice

Multiply.

1.	2.	3.	4.	5.	6.
7 × 3	4 × 9	5 × 2	8 × 3	0 × 3	3 × 5

7.	8.	9.	10.	11.	12.
4 × 2	6 × 4	2 × 6	3 × 4	7 × 4	4 × 5

13.	14.	15.	16.	17.	18.
4 × 6	3 × 2	3 × 8	5 × 3	1 × 5	9 × 3

19.	20.	21.	22.	23.	24.
4 × 4	2 × 4	3 × 9	4 × 1	3 × 3	3 × 0

25.	26.	27.	28.	29.	30.
6 × 3	0 × 4	3 × 1	8 × 4	5 × 5	4 × 3

31.	32.	33.	34.	35.	36.
6 × 2	2 × 3	2 × 5	3 × 6	4 × 7	1 × 2

37.	38.	39.	40.	★ 41.
9 × 4	3 × 7	4 × 8	5 × 4	$1 \times 3 \times 6 = \underline{}$

Solve.

42. 4 cages of kittens
    5 in each cage
    How many kittens in all?

43. Bought 4 boxes of cat food
    8 cans in a box
    How many cans in all?

Multiplication Table

Here's how to find 3×4 in the table.

a. Find 3 on blue.

b. Find 4 on pink.

The product is where the yellow paths meet.

$$3 \times 4 = 12$$

×	0	1	2	3	4	5	6	7	8	9
0	0	0	0	0	0	0	0	0	0	0
1	0	1	2	3	4	5	6	7	8	9
2	0	2	4	6	8	10	12	14	16	18
3	0	3	6	9	12					
4	0	4	8							
5	0	5	10							
6	0	6	12							
7	0	7	14							
8	0	8	16							
9	0	9	18							

Multiply.

1. $\begin{array}{r} 3 \\ \times 5 \\ \hline \end{array}$	**2.** $\begin{array}{r} 3 \\ \times 6 \\ \hline \end{array}$	**3.** $\begin{array}{r} 3 \\ \times 7 \\ \hline \end{array}$	**4.** $\begin{array}{r} 3 \\ \times 8 \\ \hline \end{array}$	**5.** $\begin{array}{r} 3 \\ \times 9 \\ \hline \end{array}$	**6.** $\begin{array}{r} 4 \\ \times 3 \\ \hline \end{array}$
7. $\begin{array}{r} 5 \\ \times 3 \\ \hline \end{array}$	**8.** $\begin{array}{r} 6 \\ \times 3 \\ \hline \end{array}$	**9.** $\begin{array}{r} 7 \\ \times 3 \\ \hline \end{array}$	**10.** $\begin{array}{r} 8 \\ \times 3 \\ \hline \end{array}$	**11.** $\begin{array}{r} 9 \\ \times 3 \\ \hline \end{array}$	**12.** $\begin{array}{r} 4 \\ \times 4 \\ \hline \end{array}$
13. $\begin{array}{r} 4 \\ \times 5 \\ \hline \end{array}$	**14.** $\begin{array}{r} 4 \\ \times 6 \\ \hline \end{array}$	**15.** $\begin{array}{r} 4 \\ \times 7 \\ \hline \end{array}$	**16.** $\begin{array}{r} 4 \\ \times 8 \\ \hline \end{array}$	**17.** $\begin{array}{r} 4 \\ \times 9 \\ \hline \end{array}$	**18.** $\begin{array}{r} 5 \\ \times 4 \\ \hline \end{array}$
19. $\begin{array}{r} 6 \\ \times 4 \\ \hline \end{array}$	**20.** $\begin{array}{r} 0 \\ \times 4 \\ \hline \end{array}$	**21.** $\begin{array}{r} 7 \\ \times 4 \\ \hline \end{array}$	**22.** $\begin{array}{r} 8 \\ \times 4 \\ \hline \end{array}$	**23.** $\begin{array}{r} 3 \\ \times 0 \\ \hline \end{array}$	**24.** $\begin{array}{r} 9 \\ \times 4 \\ \hline \end{array}$

25. Make your own multiplication table. Fill in all the products for 3 and 4 as factors on your table.

Fairy Tale Fun

Some fairy tales use numbers.

A. Multiply each by 3.

1. The number of little pigs.

2. The number of dwarfs Snow White met.

3. The number of wishes Aladdin was granted.

4. The number of Cinderella's stepsisters.

5. The number of legs Charlotte has. (Charlotte is the spider in *Charlotte's Web*.)

6. The number of men in a tub.

B. Now multiply each of the above by 4.

Can you think of other fairy tale questions?

Five and Six as Factors

How many glasses of milk?

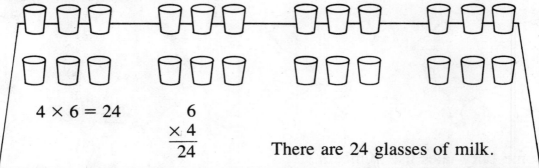

$4 \times 6 = 24$

$$\begin{array}{r} 6 \\ \times\ 4 \\ \hline 24 \end{array}$$

There are 24 glasses of milk.

A. Count by 5's.

5, 10, 15, 20, ___?___ , ___?___ , ___?___ , ___?___

B. Multiply.

1.
$$\begin{array}{cccccccccc}
5 & 5 & 5 & 5 & 5 & 5 & 5 & 5 & 5 \\
\times 1 & \times 2 & \times 3 & \times 4 & \times 5 & \times 6 & \times 7 & \times 8 & \times 9
\end{array}$$

2.
$$\begin{array}{cccccccccc}
1 & 2 & 3 & 4 & 5 & 6 & 7 & 8 & 9 \\
\times 5 & \times 5 & \times 5 & \times 5 & \times 5 & \times 5 & \times 5 & \times 5 & \times 5
\end{array}$$

3. What is the pattern in the answers in 1. and 2.?

C. Multiply.   [HINT: Think of counting by 6's.]

4.
$$\begin{array}{cccccccccc}
6 & 6 & 6 & 6 & 6 & 6 & 6 & 6 & 6 \\
\times 1 & \times 2 & \times 3 & \times 4 & \times 5 & \times 6 & \times 7 & \times 8 & \times 9
\end{array}$$

5.
$$\begin{array}{cccccccccc}
1 & 2 & 3 & 4 & 5 & 6 & 7 & 8 & 9 \\
\times 6 & \times 6 & \times 6 & \times 6 & \times 6 & \times 6 & \times 6 & \times 6 & \times 6
\end{array}$$

6. What is the pattern in the answers in 4. and 5.?

D. Multiply.

7. 9	**8.** 7	**9.** 5	**10.** 7	**11.** 0	**12.** 6
× 5	× 6	× 8	× 5	× 8	× 6

E. Take out your multiplication table. Fill in the facts for 5 and 6.

_____ Practice

Multiply.

1. 4	**2.** 6	**3.** 5	**4.** 4	**5.** 6	**6.** 5
× 5	× 1	× 2	× 6	× 7	× 1

7. 3	**8.** 6	**9.** 3	**10.** 5	**11.** 2	**12.** 5
× 6	× 8	× 5	× 6	× 6	× 7

13. 6	**14.** 9	**15.** 6	**16.** 5	**17.** 7	**18.** 8
× 6	× 5	× 5	× 3	× 5	× 5

19. 6	**20.** 6	**21.** 5	**22.** 7	**23.** 6	**24.** 5
× 9	× 3	× 5	× 6	× 4	× 9

25. 5	**26.** 5	**27.** 1	**28.** 5	**29.** 6	**30.** 0
× 4	× 8	× 6	× 2	× 2	× 5

★ **31.** $3 \times 2 \times 8 = $ _____?

★ **32.** $9 \times 5 \times 1 = $ _____?

★ **33.** $4 \times 2 \times 3 = $ _____?

★ **34.** $2 \times 3 \times 5 = $ _____?

Solve.

35. 8 cans of juice in a pack
Bought 5 packs
How many cans in all?

36. 4 sticks of butter in a pack
Bought 6 packs
How many sticks in all?

Seven and Eight as Factors

How many balloons?

$3 \times 7 = 21$ or

$$\begin{array}{r} 7 \\ \times\ 3 \\ \hline 21 \end{array}$$

There are 21 balloons.

A. Multiply.

1.
$$\begin{array}{r} 7 \\ \times\ 1 \end{array}\quad \begin{array}{r} 7 \\ \times\ 2 \end{array}\quad \begin{array}{r} 7 \\ \times\ 3 \end{array}\quad \begin{array}{r} 7 \\ \times\ 4 \end{array}\quad \begin{array}{r} 7 \\ \times\ 5 \end{array}\quad \begin{array}{r} 7 \\ \times\ 6 \end{array}\quad \begin{array}{r} 7 \\ \times\ 7 \end{array}\quad \begin{array}{r} 7 \\ \times\ 8 \end{array}\quad \begin{array}{r} 7 \\ \times\ 9 \end{array}$$

2.
$$\begin{array}{r} 1 \\ \times\ 7 \end{array}\quad \begin{array}{r} 2 \\ \times\ 7 \end{array}\quad \begin{array}{r} 3 \\ \times\ 7 \end{array}\quad \begin{array}{r} 4 \\ \times\ 7 \end{array}\quad \begin{array}{r} 5 \\ \times\ 7 \end{array}\quad \begin{array}{r} 6 \\ \times\ 7 \end{array}\quad \begin{array}{r} 7 \\ \times\ 7 \end{array}\quad \begin{array}{r} 8 \\ \times\ 7 \end{array}\quad \begin{array}{r} 9 \\ \times\ 7 \end{array}$$

3. What is the pattern in the answers in 1. and 2.?

B. Multiply.

4.
$$\begin{array}{r} 8 \\ \times\ 1 \end{array}\quad \begin{array}{r} 8 \\ \times\ 2 \end{array}\quad \begin{array}{r} 8 \\ \times\ 3 \end{array}\quad \begin{array}{r} 8 \\ \times\ 4 \end{array}\quad \begin{array}{r} 8 \\ \times\ 5 \end{array}\quad \begin{array}{r} 8 \\ \times\ 6 \end{array}\quad \begin{array}{r} 8 \\ \times\ 7 \end{array}\quad \begin{array}{r} 8 \\ \times\ 8 \end{array}\quad \begin{array}{r} 8 \\ \times\ 9 \end{array}$$

5.
$$\begin{array}{r} 1 \\ \times\ 8 \end{array}\quad \begin{array}{r} 2 \\ \times\ 8 \end{array}\quad \begin{array}{r} 3 \\ \times\ 8 \end{array}\quad \begin{array}{r} 4 \\ \times\ 8 \end{array}\quad \begin{array}{r} 5 \\ \times\ 8 \end{array}\quad \begin{array}{r} 6 \\ \times\ 8 \end{array}\quad \begin{array}{r} 7 \\ \times\ 8 \end{array}\quad \begin{array}{r} 8 \\ \times\ 8 \end{array}\quad \begin{array}{r} 9 \\ \times\ 8 \end{array}$$

6. What is the pattern in the answers in 4. and 5.?

C. Multiply.

7. $\begin{array}{r} 8 \\ \times\ 7 \end{array}$ **8.** $\begin{array}{r} 9 \\ \times\ 8 \end{array}$ **9.** $\begin{array}{r} 7 \\ \times\ 7 \end{array}$ **10.** $\begin{array}{r} 8 \\ \times\ 8 \end{array}$ **11.** $\begin{array}{r} 8 \\ \times\ 6 \end{array}$ **12.** $\begin{array}{r} 9 \\ \times\ 0 \end{array}$

D. Fill in all the facts for 7 and 8 as factors on your multiplication table.

Multiply.

1. 7
   × 1

2. 2
   × 7

3. 8
   × 4

4. 7
   × 6

5. 8
   × 2

6. 8
   × 9

7. 5
   × 7

8. 3
   × 8

9. 8
   × 1

10. 7
    × 3

11. 8
    × 8

12. 4
    × 7

13. 6
    × 8

14. 7
    × 8

15. 9
    × 8

16. 4
    × 8

17. 6
    × 6

18. 7
    × 7

19. 9
    × 7

20. 1
    × 8

21. 7
    × 5

22. 0
    × 8

23. 3
    × 7

24. 5
    × 6

25. 7
    × 2

26. 8
    × 3

27. 5
    × 8

28. 8
    × 7

29. 2
    × 8

30. 1
    × 7

31. 5
    × 0

32. 7
    × 9

33. 6
    × 7

34. 8
    × 6

35. 7
    × 4

36. 8
    × 5

★ 37. $4 \times 2 \times 7 = \underline{}$

★ 38. $3 \times 3 \times 8 = \underline{}$

Solve.

39. 8 party hats in each bag
    6 bags of hats
    How many hats in all?

40. 6 plastic whistles in each bag
    7 bags of whistles
    How many whistles in all?

Nine as a Factor

$3 \times 9 = 27$

There are 27 flowers.

A. Multiply.

1.
$$
\begin{array}{ccccccccc}
9 & 9 & 9 & 9 & 9 & 9 & 9 & 9 & 9 \\
\times 1 & \times 2 & \times 3 & \times 4 & \times 5 & \times 6 & \times 7 & \times 8 & \times 9 \\
\end{array}
$$

2.
$$
\begin{array}{ccccccccc}
1 & 2 & 3 & 4 & 5 & 6 & 7 & 8 & 9 \\
\times 9 & \times 9 & \times 9 & \times 9 & \times 9 & \times 9 & \times 9 & \times 9 & \times 9 \\
\end{array}
$$

3. What is the pattern in the answers in 1. and 2.?

B. Multiply.

4.
$$
\begin{array}{c}
9 \\
\times 7 \\
\end{array}
$$
5.
$$
\begin{array}{c}
6 \\
\times 9 \\
\end{array}
$$
6.
$$
\begin{array}{c}
0 \\
\times 9 \\
\end{array}
$$
7.
$$
\begin{array}{c}
9 \\
\times 9 \\
\end{array}
$$
8.
$$
\begin{array}{c}
9 \\
\times 8 \\
\end{array}
$$
9.
$$
\begin{array}{c}
4 \\
\times 9 \\
\end{array}
$$

C. Complete your multiplication table.

_____ Practice

Multiply.

1.
$$
\begin{array}{c}
9 \\
\times 5 \\
\end{array}
$$
2.
$$
\begin{array}{c}
8 \\
\times 6 \\
\end{array}
$$
3.
$$
\begin{array}{c}
8 \\
\times 7 \\
\end{array}
$$
4.
$$
\begin{array}{c}
9 \\
\times 9 \\
\end{array}
$$
5.
$$
\begin{array}{c}
5 \\
\times 8 \\
\end{array}
$$
6.
$$
\begin{array}{c}
8 \\
\times 9 \\
\end{array}
$$

7.
$$
\begin{array}{c}
0 \\
\times 7 \\
\end{array}
$$
8.
$$
\begin{array}{c}
8 \\
\times 8 \\
\end{array}
$$
9.
$$
\begin{array}{c}
9 \\
\times 6 \\
\end{array}
$$
10.
$$
\begin{array}{c}
7 \\
\times 6 \\
\end{array}
$$
11.
$$
\begin{array}{c}
9 \\
\times 1 \\
\end{array}
$$
12.
$$
\begin{array}{c}
7 \\
\times 9 \\
\end{array}
$$

Multiplication-Addition Property

$$2 \times (5 + 3) \quad = \quad (2 \times 5) \quad + (2 \times 3)$$

This is the multiplication-addition property.
It can help you remember facts.

A. Complete.

1.
$$3 \times 5$$
$$3 \times (2 + 3)$$
$$(3 \times 2) + (3 \times 3)$$
$$6 + \underline{\quad ? \quad}$$
$$\underline{\quad ? \quad}$$

2.
$$5 \times 9$$
$$5 \times (5 + 4)$$
$$(5 \times 5) + (5 \times 4)$$
$$25 + \underline{\quad ? \quad}$$
$$\underline{\quad ? \quad}$$

B. Complete.

3. $4 \times (4 + 4) = (4 \times 4) + (4 \times \square)$

4. $6 \times (5 + 4) = (6 \times 5) + (6 \times \square)$

5. $3 \times (4 + 3) = (3 \times 4) + (3 \times \square)$

6. $8 \times (3 + 2) = (8 \times 3) + (8 \times \square)$

7. $9 \times (7 + 2) = (9 \times 7) + (9 \times \square)$

8. $7 \times (1 + 3) = (7 \times 1) + (7 \times \square)$

9. $6 \times (5 + 2) = (6 \times 5) + (6 \times \square)$

Problem Solving

Look at the picture to solve these problems.

1. Pat bought a pencil case and a pencil. How much did he spend in all?

2. How much more does a notebook cost than a pen?

3. Carl bought a notebook and a pack of looseleaf paper. How much did he spend in all?

4. How much more do scissors cost than glue?

5. How much would a ruler and a book cover cost?

★ 6. Andre bought 2 pencils, 1 eraser, and 1 notebook. How much change should he get back from $1.00?

Multiply.

1. 2
(120) × 4

2. 3
(120) × 5

3. 5
(122) × 2

4. 4
(122) × 5

5. 2
(128) × 9

6. 2
(128) × 6

7. 4
(130) × 0

8. 1
(130) × 2

9. 4
(132) × 7

10. 3
(132) × 9

11. 5
(136) × 9

12. 6
(136) × 6

13. 7
(138) × 6

14. 8
(138) × 5

15. 9
(140) × 9

16. 8
(140) × 9

17. 7
(140) × 9

18. 9
(140) × 6

Solve. (126, 142)

19. Ben read 36 pages.
He read 48 pages later.
How many pages read in all?

20. A pack of paper costs $1.80.
How much for 2 packs?

Find Out!
Aid to Memory

Here's a way to check a product when 9 is a factor.

a. Add the digits in each product.

$$3 \times 9 = 27 \leftarrow 2 + 7 = \underline{\ ?\ }$$
$$4 \times 9 = 36 \leftarrow 3 + 6 = \underline{\ ?\ }$$
$$5 \times 9 = 45 \leftarrow 4 + 5 = \underline{\ ?\ }$$

b. What did you find?

Try these: $6 \times 9, 7 \times 9, 8 \times 9, 9 \times 9$

Multiply.

1.   3
(120) × 2

2.   2
(120) × 5

3.   4
(122) × 4

4.   5
(122) × 4

5.   2
(128) × 8

6.   9
(128) × 2

7.   0
(130) × 5

8.   4
(130) × 1

9.   3
(132) × 6

10. 4
(132) × 8

11. 5
(136) × 8

12. 6
(136) × 9

13. 7
(138) × 2

14. 8
(138) × 6

15. 9
(140) × 5

16. 9
(140) × 8

17. 9
(140) × 3

18. 9
(140) × 9

Solve. *(126, 142)*

19. A library had 183 books about sports.
It had 104 books about gardening.
How many more sports books?

20. The library spent $3.25 for newspapers.
It spent $4.50 for magazines.
How much was spent in all?

Find Out!
Brainteaser

Follow the steps to find my age.

(a) Find 3 times your own age.
(b) Add 27.
(c) Subtract 2 times your age.
(d) Add 23.
(e) Subtract your age. What is my age?

Basic Skills Check

1. How many 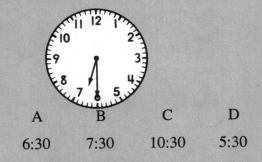 ?

A	B	C	D
10	11	12	14

---

2. Count by 2's. Which number is missing?

514   _?_   518   520   522

E	F	G	H
515	516	517	518

---

3. What time is it?

A	B	C	D
6:30	7:30	10:30	5:30

---

4. Which shows 6 tens and 5 ones?

E	F	G	H
605	6105	65	56

5. Compare.

63 ◯ 54

A	B	C	D
>	=	<	+

---

6. Which is a square?

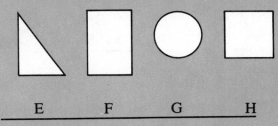

E	F	G	H

---

7. What time is it?

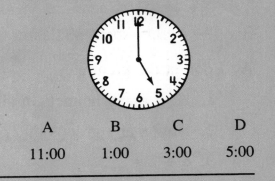

A	B	C	D
11:00	1:00	3:00	5:00

---

8. Which coin is a quarter?

E	F	G	H

At the Castle

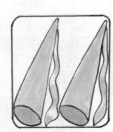

How many groups of 2 in 10?

$10 \div 2 = 5$ ← **Division Sentence**

Read: 10 divided by 2 is equal to 5

5 is called the **quotient.**

There are 5 groups.

A. Look at the picture.

1. How many helmets in all?

2. How many groups of 2?

3. $6 \div 2 = \underline{\quad ? \quad}$

4. What is the quotient?

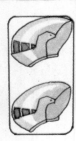

B. Look at the picture.

5. How many hats in all?

6. How many groups of 2?

7. Write the division sentence.

8. What is the quotient?

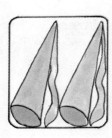
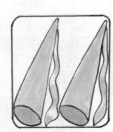

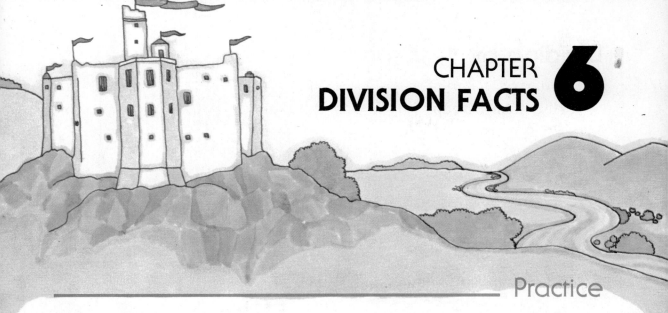

Practice

Find the quotients.

1.

$$6 \div 3 = \underline{\quad?\quad}$$

2.

$$8 \div 2 = \underline{\quad?\quad}$$

3.

$$4 \div 2 = \underline{\quad?\quad}$$

4.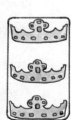

$$9 \div 3 = \underline{\quad?\quad}$$

Write a division sentence for each.

5.

6.

Dividing by 1, 2, and 3

How many groups of 3 in 9?

$$9 \div 3 = 3$$

There are 3 groups of 3.

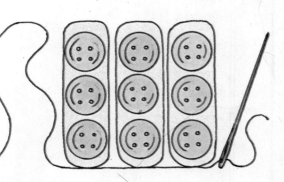

A. Look at the picture.

1. How many buttons in all?

2. How many groups of 1?

3. $5 \div 1 = \underline{\quad ? \quad}$

4. What is the quotient?

B. Complete.

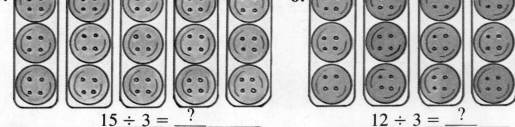

5. $15 \div 3 = \underline{\quad ? \quad}$

6. $12 \div 3 = \underline{\quad ? \quad}$

7. $3 \div 1 = \underline{\quad ? \quad}$

8. $8 \div 2 = \underline{\quad ? \quad}$

C. Divide.

9. $6 \div 2$

10. $4 \div 2$

11. $2 \div 1$

12. $6 \div 3$

Divide.

1. $2 \div 2$ **2.** $4 \div 1$ **3.** $10 \div 2$ **4.** $6 \div 3$

5. $1 \div 1$ **6.** $6 \div 2$ **7.** $3 \div 3$ **8.** $9 \div 3$

9. $8 \div 2$ **10.** $12 \div 3$ **11.** $2 \div 1$ **12.** $4 \div 2$

Solve.

13. 12 buttons in all
3 buttons on each card
How many cards?
$12 \div 3 = \underline{\ ?\ }$

14. 6 buttons in all
2 buttons on each card
How many cards?
$6 \div 2 = \underline{\ ?\ }$

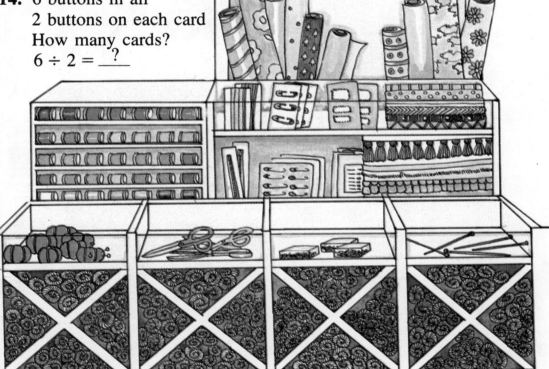

Dividing by 4 and 5

How many groups of 5 in 20?

$$20 \div 5 = 4$$

There are 4 groups.

A. Complete.

1.

$$10 \div 5 = \underline{\quad ? \quad}$$

2.

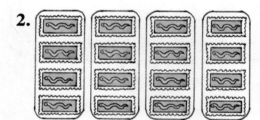

$$16 \div 4 = \underline{\quad ? \quad}$$

3.

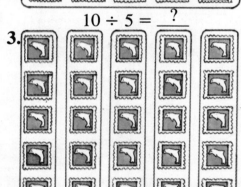

$$25 \div 5 = \underline{\quad ? \quad}$$

4.

$$12 \div 4 = \underline{\quad ? \quad}$$

B. Divide.

5. $15 \div 5$ **6.** $4 \div 4$ **7.** $5 \div 5$ **8.** $20 \div 4$

Divide.

1. $10 \div 5$ 2. $8 \div 2$ 3. $2 \div 1$ 4. $9 \div 3$

5. $4 \div 2$ 6. $5 \div 1$ 7. $3 \div 3$ 8. $16 \div 4$

9. $12 \div 4$ 10. $6 \div 2$ 11. $4 \div 4$ 12. $20 \div 5$

13. $1 \div 1$ 14. $8 \div 4$ 15. $15 \div 3$ 16. $2 \div 2$

17. $25 \div 5$ 18. $12 \div 3$ 19. $20 \div 4$ 20. $4 \div 1$

21. $6 \div 3$ 22. $10 \div 2$ 23. $3 \div 1$ 24. $5 \div 5$

Solve.

25. 15 stamps in all
3 stamps on each letter
How many letters?
$15 \div 3 = \underline{\quad?\quad}$

26. 8 stamps in all
2 stamps on each postcard
How many postcards?
$8 \div 2 = \underline{\quad?\quad}$

Keeping Fit

Multiply.

1. 2 ×0	**2.** 5 ×3	**3.** 1 ×1	**4.** 0 ×5	**5.** 4 ×2					

6. 3 ×4   **7.** 2 ×2   **8.** 3 ×5   **9.** 2 ×3   **10.** 3 ×1

11. 5 ×2   **12.** 0 ×1   **13.** 5 ×5   **14.** 4 ×0   **15.** 1 ×4   **16.** 3 ×3   **17.** 4 ×5

18. 5 ×8   **19.** 3 ×9   **20.** 8 ×2   **21.** 7 ×5   **22.** 2 ×6   **23.** 7 ×9   **24.** 6 ×4

25. 8 ×3   **26.** 9 ×8   **27.** 7 ×6   **28.** 2 ×7   **29.** 8 ×1   **30.** 6 ×9   **31.** 0 ×6

32. 7 ×7   **33.** 2 ×9   **34.** 7 ×8   **35.** 8 ×6   **36.** 9 ×3   **37.** 6 ×7   **38.** 2 ×8

39. 9 ×2   **40.** 1 ×6   **41.** 4 ×7   **42.** 7 ×0   **43.** 4 ×9   **44.** 8 ×8   **45.** 1 ×9

46. 3 ×6   **47.** 9 ×5   **48.** 3 ×8   **49.** 1 ×7   **50.** 9 ×9   **51.** 7 ×4   **52.** 6 ×1

53. 6 ×6   **54.** 9 ×0   **55.** 6 ×3   **56.** 4 ×8   **57.** 9 ×7   **58.** 4 ×6   **59.** 6 ×5

60. 5 ×7   **61.** 8 ×4   **62.** 0 ×8   **63.** 9 ×6   **64.** 7 ×2   **65.** 8 ×9   **66.** 3 ×7

67. 4 ×4   **68.** 1 ×2   **69.** 0 ×3   **70.** 1 ×5   **71.** 5 ×6   **72.** 9 ×1   **73.** 3 ×2

74. 7 ×3   **75.** 6 ×2   **76.** 9 ×4   **77.** 0 ×4   **78.** 2 ×5   **79.** 6 ×8   **80.** 4 ×1

Missing Factors

20 bananas
4 bunches
Same number in each bunch
How many in each bunch?
$4 \times \square = 20$
↑
missing factor

Think: $4 \times 5 = 20$, so the missing factor is 5.

A. Find the missing factor.
25 berries in all
5 berries on each bunch
How many bunches?
   1. $\square \times 5 = 25$

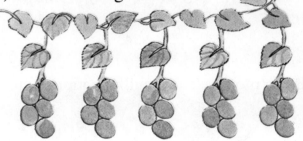

B. Find the missing factors.

    2. $1 \times \square = 3$ **3.** $\square \times 4 = 16$ **4.** $\square \times 5 = 10$

    5. $4 \times \square = 28$ **6.** $\square \times 9 = 27$ **7.** $3 \times \square = 12$

Practice

Find the missing factors.

    1. $\square \times 3 = 6$ **2.** $5 \times \square = 45$ **3.** $2 \times \square = 14$

    4. $4 \times \square = 0$ **5.** $2 \times \square = 18$ **6.** $\square \times 4 = 32$

Related Sentences

Here are four **related sentences** for this array.

$5 \times 3 = 15$ $15 \div 3 = 5$
$3 \times 5 = 15$ $15 \div 5 = 3$

A. Write a related division sentence for each.

1.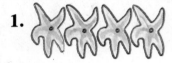

$2 \times 4 = 8$

2.

$2 \times 5 = 10$

3.

$2 \times 3 = 6$

B. Write a related multiplication sentence for each.

4.

$9 \div 3 = 3$

5.

$3 \div 1 = 3$

6.

$12 \div 4 = 3$

C. Solve. Use the related multiplication sentence to help you.

Example $10 \div 2 = \square$ ⟵— Think: $\square \times 2 = 10$
                                       $5 \times 2 = 10$, so $10 \div 2 = 5$

7. $20 \div 4 = \square$
     $\square \times 4 = 20$

8. $16 \div 4 = \square$
     $\square \times 4 = 16$

9. $4 \div 1 = \square$
     $\square \times 1 = 4$

Write a related division sentence for each.

1. $1 \times 5 = 5$ **2.** $3 \times 1 = 3$ **3.** $4 \times 3 = 12$

Write a related multiplication sentence for each.

4. $20 \div 4 = 5$ **5.** $6 \div 2 = 3$ **6.** $10 \div 5 = 2$

Solve.

7. $15 \div 5 = \square$
$\square \times 5 = 15$

8. $9 \div 3 = \square$
$\square \times 3 = 9$

9. $8 \div 4 = \square$
$\square \times 4 = 8$

10. $25 \div 5 = \square$
$\square \times 5 = 25$

11. $12 \div 4 = \square$
$\square \times 4 = 12$

12. $20 \div 5 = \square$
$\square \times 5 = 20$

Solve.

13. 20 seashells
4 seashells in each pail
How many pails?

14. 12 seashells
3 children share them.
How many seashells for
each child?

Divide. *(148, 150)*

1. $10 \div 2$ **2.** $3 \div 3$ **3.** $4 \div 2$ **4.** $12 \div 3$

5. $3 \div 1$ **6.** $15 \div 3$ **7.** $4 \div 1$ **8.** $6 \div 2$

9. $5 \div 5$ **10.** $16 \div 4$ **11.** $8 \div 4$ **12.** $25 \div 5$

13. $12 \div 4$ **14.** $10 \div 5$ **15.** $20 \div 4$ **16.** $20 \div 5$

17. Write a related division sentence for $3 \times 3 = 9$. *(154)*

18. Write a related multiplication sentence for $20 \div 5 = 4$. *(154)*

Solve. *(154)*

19. $8 \div 2 = \square$
    $\square \times 2 = 8$

20. $15 \div 5 = \square$
    $\square \times 5 = 15$

21. $9 \div 3 = \square$
    $\square \times 3 = 9$

Find Out! _ _ _ _ _ _ _ _ _ _ _ _ _ _ _ _ _ _
Calculator Activity

A. Play this addition game with a partner.

    1. Use the numbers 1, 2, and 3 in any order.
    2. Take turns adding on the same calculator.
The first player to reach 21 without going
over is the winner.

B. Play the game again using the numbers 1, 2, 3, 4, 5, and 6.
The first player to reach 40 without going over
is the winner.

Another Way to Divide

Find $6 \div 2$.

Think: How many 2's can be subtracted from 6?

Take 2.

Take 2 more.

Take 2 more.

$$\begin{array}{r} 6 \\ -2 \\ \hline 4 \\ -2 \\ \hline 2 \\ -2 \\ \hline 0 \end{array}$$

Three 2's can be subtracted from 6.
So, $6 \div 2 = 3$

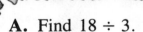

A. Find $18 \div 3$.

1. Think: how many 3's can be
   subtracted from 18?

2. $18 \div 3 = \underline{\quad ? \quad}$

Practice

Find the following. Use subtraction.

1. $16 \div 4$ **2.** $35 \div 5$ **3.** $36 \div 6$ **4.** $20 \div 4$ **5.** $18 \div 6$

6. $20 \div 5$ **7.** $10 \div 2$ **8.** $15 \div 3$ ★**9.** $44 \div 11$ ★**10.** $48 \div 12$

Problem Solving

6 robots on each spaceship
6 spaceships
How many robots in all?

Think:

1. What is asked? ⟶ How many in all?

2. Do you multiply or divide? ⟶ Multiply.

A. Complete.

63 children in a space school
9 classes in the school
Same number of children in each class
How many children in each class?

1. What is asked?

2. Do you multiply or divide?

B. Which operation would you use? Write × or ÷.

3. 30 moon rocks collected
6 space crews collected the same
number of moon rocks.
How many moon rocks did each crew collect?

Which operation would you use? Write × or ÷.

1. Space police visited 5 planets.
Made 4 stops on each planet
How many stops made in all?

2. 32 bottles of Jupiter juice
8 bottles in each pack
How many packs of juice in all?

3. 3 buses
9 people on each bus
How many people in all?

4. Planted 24 Venus plants
4 Venus plants in each row
How many rows of Venus plants?

5. 6 boxes of spacesuits
9 spacesuits in a box
How many spacesuits in all?

6. Ship control has 3 panels.
Each panel has 8 buttons.
How many buttons in all?

Working with 1, 2, and 3

Multiplication facts can help you find division facts.

factor × factor = product   quotient

$$6 \times 2 = 12 \quad \text{so,} \quad 12 \div 2 = 6$$

A. Find $14 \div 2$.

   1. Think: What number times 2 equals 14?
        $\square \times 2 = 14$

   2. So, $14 \div 2 = \underline{\quad?\quad}$

▶ To find a quotient, think of the related multiplication fact.

B. Solve.

   3. $18 \div 3 = \square$ **4.** $6 \div 1 = \square$ **5.** $18 \div 2 = \square$
   Think: $\square \times 3 = 18$ Think: $\square \times 1 = 6$ Think: $\square \times 2 = 18$

   6. $27 \div 3 = \square$ **7.** $16 \div 2 = \square$ **8.** $21 \div 3 = \square$
   Think: $\square \times 3 = 27$ Think: $\square \times 2 = 16$ Think: $\square \times 3 = 21$

C. Divide.   *Example* $8 \div 4 \longleftarrow$ $\boxed{\text{Think: } \square \times 4 = 8}$

   9. $24 \div 3$ **10.** $7 \div 1$ **11.** $12 \div 2$ **12.** $15 \div 3$

   13. $8 \div 1$ **14.** $10 \div 2$ **15.** $9 \div 1$ **16.** $8 \div 2$

Divide.

1. 8 ÷ 2   **2.** 15 ÷ 3   **3.** 9 ÷ 1   **4.** 12 ÷ 2

5. 9 ÷ 3   **6.** 3 ÷ 1   **7.** 18 ÷ 3   **8.** 4 ÷ 2

9. 5 ÷ 1   **10.** 8 ÷ 1   **11.** 10 ÷ 2   **12.** 7 ÷ 1

13. 27 ÷ 3   **14.** 1 ÷ 1   **15.** 18 ÷ 2   **16.** 3 ÷ 3

17. 12 ÷ 3   **18.** 14 ÷ 2   **19.** 4 ÷ 1   **20.** 2 ÷ 2

21. 6 ÷ 2   **22.** 24 ÷ 3   **23.** 2 ÷ 1   **24.** 6 ÷ 3

Solve.

25. 16 pieces of colored paper
2 children share the paper.
How many pieces of paper
for each child?

26. 21 crayons
3 children
Same number for each child
How many crayons for each child?

Working with 4, 5, and 6

12 plants
2 shelves
How many plants on each?

There are two ways to write
12 divided by 2.
12 ÷ 2   or   2)12

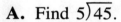

There are 6 plants on each shelf.

A. Find 5)45.

1. Think: ☐ × 5 = 45
   What is the missing factor?

2. What is the quotient?

B. Solve.

3. 6)24
   Think: ☐ × 6 = 24

4. 5)35
   Think: ☐ × 5 = 35

5. 6)36
   Think: ☐ × 6 = 36

6. 4)36
   Think: ☐ × 4 = 36

7. 4)32
   Think: ☐ × 4 = 32

8. 6)54
   Think: ☐ × 6 = 54

C. Divide. *Example* 6)48 ← Think: 6 × 8 = 48, so 6)48

9. 4)28

10. 5)30

11. 4)20

12. 6)18

13. 5)25

14. 6)42

15. 4)16

16. 5)40

17. 4)24

18. 6)30

Divide.

1. $3\overline{)24}$ 2. $6\overline{)18}$ 3. $4\overline{)24}$ 4. $5\overline{)35}$ 5. $6\overline{)30}$

6. $4\overline{)8}$ 7. $5\overline{)30}$ 8. $6\overline{)12}$ 9. $2\overline{)14}$ 10. $4\overline{)4}$

11. $5\overline{)45}$ 12. $5\overline{)10}$ 13. $3\overline{)21}$ 14. $4\overline{)16}$ 15. $5\overline{)25}$

16. $2\overline{)10}$ 17. $3\overline{)15}$ 18. $2\overline{)8}$ 19. $5\overline{)20}$ 20. $6\overline{)6}$

21. $2\overline{)4}$ 22. $5\overline{)5}$ 23. $3\overline{)27}$ 24. $6\overline{)36}$ 25. $2\overline{)12}$

26. $4\overline{)20}$ 27. $2\overline{)6}$ 28. $2\overline{)16}$ 29. $4\overline{)12}$ 30. $3\overline{)18}$

31. $6\overline{)48}$ 32. $2\overline{)2}$ 33. $5\overline{)40}$ 34. $4\overline{)28}$ 35. $5\overline{)15}$

36. $3\overline{)12}$ 37. $2\overline{)18}$ 38. $4\overline{)32}$ 39. $6\overline{)42}$ 40. $6\overline{)54}$

Solve.

41. 36 flowers
    4 vases
    Same number of flowers
    in each vase
    How many flowers in each vase?

42. 24 tomato plants
    6 in each box
    How many boxes of tomato plants?

Working with 7, 8, and 9

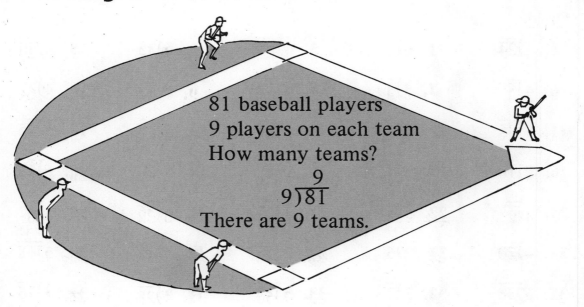

81 baseball players
9 players on each team
How many teams?
$$9\overline{)81}$$
$$\phantom{9\overline{)}}9$$
There are 9 teams.

A. Solve.

1. $9\overline{)72}$
Think: $\square \times 9 = 72$

2. $8\overline{)64}$
Think: $\square \times 8 = 64$

3. $8\overline{)56}$
Think: $\square \times 8 = 56$

4. $7\overline{)63}$
Think: $\square \times 7 = 63$

5. $8\overline{)72}$
Think: $\square \times 8 = 72$

6. $9\overline{)54}$
Think: $\square \times 9 = 54$

B. Divide. *Example* $7\overline{)63}$ ← Think: $9 \times 7 = 63$, so $7\overline{)63}^{\,9}$

7. $7\overline{)56}$ **8.** $8\overline{)64}$ **9.** $9\overline{)63}$ **10.** $8\overline{)48}$ **11.** $9\overline{)45}$

12. $8\overline{)72}$ **13.** $7\overline{)49}$ **14.** $8\overline{)56}$ **15.** $7\overline{)63}$ **16.** $9\overline{)72}$

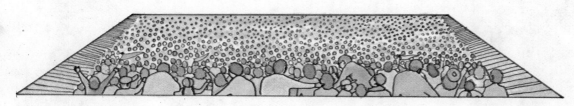

Divide.

1. $5\overline{)45}$
2. $8\overline{)72}$
3. $7\overline{)28}$
4. $9\overline{)54}$
5. $6\overline{)24}$

6. $9\overline{)27}$
7. $5\overline{)35}$
8. $3\overline{)21}$
9. $2\overline{)14}$
10. $8\overline{)64}$

11. $6\overline{)36}$
12. $2\overline{)16}$
13. $8\overline{)40}$
14. $6\overline{)48}$
15. $7\overline{)7}$

16. $7\overline{)63}$
17. $1\overline{)9}$
18. $9\overline{)72}$
19. $5\overline{)40}$
20. $8\overline{)24}$

21. $4\overline{)24}$
22. $7\overline{)42}$
23. $9\overline{)18}$
24. $8\overline{)32}$
25. $1\overline{)8}$

26. $6\overline{)54}$
27. $9\overline{)36}$
28. $8\overline{)16}$
29. $7\overline{)14}$
30. $7\overline{)21}$

31. $8\overline{)8}$
32. $3\overline{)24}$
33. $7\overline{)56}$
34. $4\overline{)28}$
35. $3\overline{)18}$

36. $8\overline{)48}$
37. $2\overline{)18}$
38. $9\overline{)9}$
39. $9\overline{)63}$
40. $6\overline{)30}$

41. $4\overline{)32}$
42. $7\overline{)49}$
43. $3\overline{)27}$
44. $1\overline{)6}$
45. $4\overline{)36}$

46. $5\overline{)30}$
47. $9\overline{)81}$
48. $8\overline{)56}$
49. $6\overline{)42}$
50. $7\overline{)35}$

Solve.

51. 8 frankfurters
    Each child ate 2.
    How many children?

52. 45 peanuts
    9 people share them.
    How many peanuts
    For each person?

Using a Multiplication Table

You can use a multiplication table to find quotients.

Example Find $42 \div 7$

a. Find 7 on blue.

b. Find 42 in the yellow path.

c. Go up to find the quotient.

$$42 \div 7 = 6$$

×	0	1	2	3	4	5	6	7	8	9
0	0	0	0	0	0	0	0	0	0	0
1	0	1	2	3	4	5	6	7	8	9
2	0	2	4	6	8	10	12	14	16	18
3	0	3	6	9	12	15	18	21	24	27
4	0	4	8	12	16	20	24	28	32	36
5	0	5	10	15	20	25	30	35	40	45
6	0	6	12	18	24	30	36	42	48	54
7	0	7	14	21	28	35	42	49	56	63
8	0	8	16	24	32	40	48	56	64	72
9	0	9	18	27	36	45	54	63	72	81

Practice

Divide. Use the table to check.

1. $2\overline{)10}$ **2.** $1\overline{)1}$ **3.** $6\overline{)18}$ **4.** $7\overline{)14}$ **5.** $7\overline{)63}$

6. $5\overline{)45}$ **7.** $4\overline{)20}$ **8.** $7\overline{)56}$ **9.** $9\overline{)81}$ **10.** $2\overline{)16}$

11. $8\overline{)48}$ **12.** $5\overline{)25}$ **13.** $4\overline{)36}$ **14.** $6\overline{)42}$ **15.** $5\overline{)40}$

16. $4\overline{)32}$ **17.** $7\overline{)49}$ **18.** $9\overline{)72}$ **19.** $4\overline{)16}$ **20.** $7\overline{)35}$

21. $9\overline{)45}$ **22.** $2\overline{)12}$ **23.** $9\overline{)9}$ **24.** $6\overline{)36}$ **25.** $4\overline{)28}$

26. $7\overline{)28}$ **27.** $5\overline{)35}$ **28.** $3\overline{)15}$ **29.** $9\overline{)63}$ **30.** $9\overline{)18}$

31. $9\overline{)54}$ **32.** $4\overline{)12}$ **33.** $9\overline{)27}$ **34.** $6\overline{)48}$ **35.** $8\overline{)16}$

36. $7\overline{)7}$ **37.** $8\overline{)72}$ **38.** $2\overline{)18}$ **39.** $6\overline{)54}$ **40.** $8\overline{)64}$

Keeping Fit

Add.

1. 14 + 3	**2.** 37 + 12	**3.** 401 + 37			

4. 37 + 46	**5.** 239 + 45	**6.** 462 + 119			

7. 386 + 293	**8.** 432 + 87	**9.** 467 + 144	**10.** 678 + 149	**11.** 486 + 35

12. 36 29 + 31	**13.** 425 187 + 293	**14.** $ 4.98 + 1.16	**15.** $ 6.26 + 2.94	**16.** $ 1.14 2.67 + 3.36

Subtract.

17. 36 − 5	**18.** 312 − 101	**19.** 85 − 27	**20.** 337 − 19	**21.** 682 − 19

22. 687 − 93	**23.** 246 − 185	**24.** 741 − 47	**25.** 154 − 68	**26.** 925 − 387

27. 306 − 128	**28.** 208 − 199	**29.** 400 − 87	**30.** $ 5.00 − 1.87	**31.** $ 6.73 − 4.94

Find Out!
Aid to Memory

1. To find $4\overline{)36}$, Think: $4 \times 4 = 16$.
$16 < 36$ so the answer is more than 4.
Now try $6\overline{)30}$. Think: $6 \times 6 = 36$.
$36 > 30$ so the answer is less than 6.

Tell if the answer is more or less than the divisor.

2. $5\overline{)40}$ **3.** $7\overline{)35}$ **4.** $8\overline{)72}$ **5.** $6\overline{)48}$ **6.** $7\overline{)56}$

Problem Solving • The Watch Repairer

Solve.

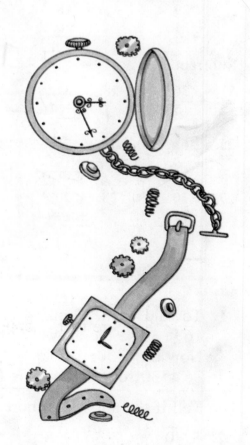

1. 2 hours to fix one watch
Fixed 9 watches
How many hours in all?

2. Ordered 24 watch springs
6 springs in a box
How many boxes in all?

3. 6 boxes of watch batteries
Each box cost $9
What was the total cost?

4. 20 watch bands
4 bands in each box
How many boxes in all?

5. Tray holds 5 watches
Have 25 watches
How many trays are needed?

1. Write the related division sentence for $5 \times 5 = 25$. *(154)*

2. Write a related multiplication sentence for $18 \div 3 = 6$. *(154)*

Solve. *(154)*

3. $16 \div 4 = \square$
   $\square \times 4 = 16$

4. $15 \div 3 = \square$
   $\square \times 3 = 15$

Divide.

5. $2\overline{)6}$ *(148)*   **6.** $3\overline{)3}$ *(148)*   **7.** $3\overline{)24}$ *(148)*   **8.** $4\overline{)12}$ *(150)*   **9.** $5\overline{)15}$ *(150)*

10. $4\overline{)20}$ *(150)*   **11.** $2\overline{)14}$ *(160)*   **12.** $3\overline{)18}$ *(160)*   **13.** $4\overline{)8}$ *(162)*   **14.** $6\overline{)48}$ *(162)*

15. $5\overline{)45}$ *(162)*   **16.** $4\overline{)32}$ *(162)*   **17.** $8\overline{)56}$ *(164)*   **18.** $9\overline{)63}$ *(164)*   **19.** $8\overline{)64}$ *(164)*

Which operation would you use? Write $\times$ or $\div$. *(158)*

20. 8 pencils in each box
   4 boxes
   How many pencils?

---------------------------------- **Find Out!**
Brainteaser

Choose the figure that is opposite the one shown.

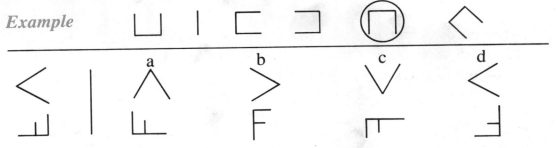

Example

1. Write a related division sentence for $8 \times 2 = 16$. *(154)*

2. Write the related multiplication sentence for $49 \div 7 = 7$. *(154)*

Solve. *(154)*

3. $56 \div 7 = \square$
$\square \times 7 = 56$

4. $15 \div 5 = \square$
$\square \times 5 = 15$

Divide.

5. $3\overline{)9}$
(148)

6. $1\overline{)4}$
(148)

7. $2\overline{)10}$
(148)

8. $3\overline{)12}$
(150)

9. $4\overline{)8}$
(150)

10. $5\overline{)5}$
(150)

11. $2\overline{)18}$
(160)

12. $3\overline{)24}$
(160)

13. $2\overline{)12}$
(160)

14. $5\overline{)35}$
(162)

15. $6\overline{)36}$
(162)

16. $4\overline{)24}$
(162)

17. $9\overline{)81}$
(164)

18. $8\overline{)72}$
(164)

19. $7\overline{)63}$
(164)

Which operation would you use? Write $\times$ or $\div$. *(158)*

20. 18 sandwiches
2 sandwiches in each bag
How many bags are needed?

Basic Skills Check

1. Diane wakes up at 7:00 each morning. She washes her face. She brushes her hair. Then she gets dressed. What is the next thing Diane does?

A Goes to bed   B Eats breakfast

C Eats dinner   D Gets out of bed

2. How many months are there in one year?

A 6   B 10

C 12   D 13

3. How many kilograms is the melon?

A 1   B 2

C 3   D 4

4. How many inches long is the crayon?

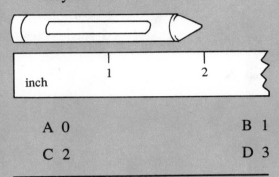

A 0   B 1

C 2   D 3

5. Jessica had 91¢. She bought carrots for 69¢. How much money was left?

A 22¢   B 40¢

C 42¢   D 61¢

6. Jackie received 40¢ from her father on Saturday. Wednesday, her mother gave her 55¢. How much money does she have now?

A 15¢   B 20¢

C 95¢   D 99¢

Ways to Measure

one palm

one span

one cubit

1. How many steps wide is your classroom?

2. Is everyone's step the same?

3. Would you use a step to measure your desk top?

4. What could you use?

5. Compare your hand span with your neighbor's.

6. How many hand spans wide is your desk?

Practice

1. Measure the length of your teacher's desk using your hand span.

2. Measure the length of your classroom with your feet.
[HINT: measure using heel-to-toe.]

3. Draw an outline on a piece of paper of your hand span, hand, and foot. Make marks as shown below.
Compare them with your neighbor's.

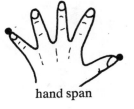

hand span

hand

foot

Centimeters

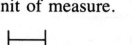

A centimeter (cm) is
a unit of measure.

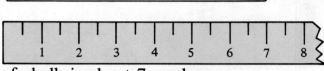

|—————|

1 cm   The piece of chalk is about 7 cm long.

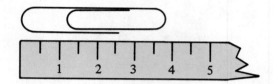

A. Is the length of the clip
closer to 3 cm or 4 cm?

B. Measure to the nearest centimeter.

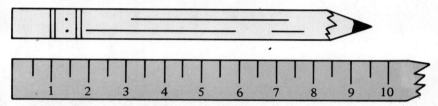

▶ If the length is halfway, use the larger number.

C. Measure to the nearest centimeter.

1.

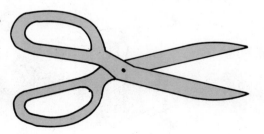

2.

3.

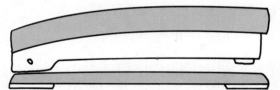

4.

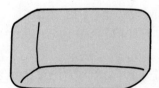

D. Draw a line 3 cm long. Here's how.

    5. Mark one dot on your paper.

    6. Place the end of the ruler under the dot.

    7. Place another dot at the 3-cm mark.

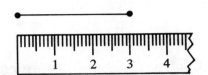

    8. Connect the dots.

E. Draw lines with these lengths.

    9. 6 cm   **10.** 8 cm   **11.** 4 cm   **12.** 9 cm   **13.** 10 cm

Practice

Measure to the nearest centimeter.

1.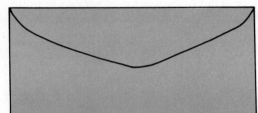

2.

3.

4.

Draw lines with these lengths.

    5. 2 cm   **6.** 11 cm   **7.** 3 cm   **8.** 5 cm   **9.** 15 cm

Meter and Centimeter

A. Make your own meter stick

    1. Mark 10 centimeters on the edge of your paper.

    2. Cut out the 10-centimeter strip.

    3. Make another strip of the same size.
        Label each centimeter from 11 to 20.

    4. Make 8 more strips. Label each centimeter
        from 21 to 100.

    5. Paste the strips end to end like this.

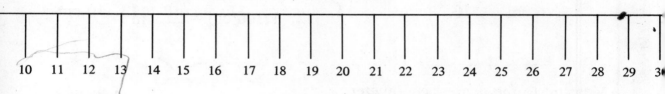

    6. How many centimeters long is your meter stick?

       ▶ 100 centimeters (cm) = 1 meter (m)

B. Complete.

    7. 3 m = 1 m + 1 m + 1 m
          = 100 cm + 100 cm + 100 cm or __?__ cm

    8. 6 m = __?__ cm

C. Complete.

    9. 400 cm = 100 cm + 100 cm + 100 cm + 100 cm
            = 1 m + 1 m + 1 m + 1 m or __?__ m

    10. 500 cm = __?__ m

Complete.

1. 100 cm = __?__ m
2. 4 m = __?__ cm
3. 700 cm = __?__ m
4. 8 m = __?__ cm
5. 5 m = __?__ cm
6. 300 cm = __?__ m
7. 600 cm = __?__ m
8. 9 m = __?__ cm
9. 200 cm = __?__ m
10. 7 m = __?__ cm
11. 10 m = __?__ cm
★ 12. 1,100 cm = __?__ m

Find Out!
Activity

Use your meter stick to go on a metric hunt.

1. Find something that is about 3 meters long.
2. Find something that is about 20 cm high.
3. Find two things that are about 50 cm long.

Chapter 7   177

Liter and Milliliter

Liquids are measured in liters and milliliters.

▶ 1 liter (L) = 1,000 milliliters (mL)

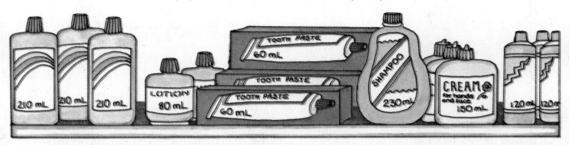

A. Complete.

1. 2 L = 1 L + 1 L
   = 1,000 mL + 1,000 mL or __?__ mL

2. 4 L = __?__ mL

B. Complete.

3. 3,000 mL = 1,000 mL + 1,000 mL + 1,000 mL
   = 1 L + 1 L + 1 L or __?__ L

4. 5,000 mL = __?__ L

Practice

Complete.

1. 6,000 mL = __?__ L

2. 4,000 mL = __?__ L

3. 7 L = __?__ mL

4. 8,000 mL = __?__ L

5. 9 L = __?__ mL

6. 3 L = __?__ mL

★ 7. 12,000 mL = __?__ L

★ 8. 13 L = __?__ mL

Grams and Kilograms

These things are measured in grams and kilograms.

▶ 1 kilogram (kg) = 1,000 grams (g)

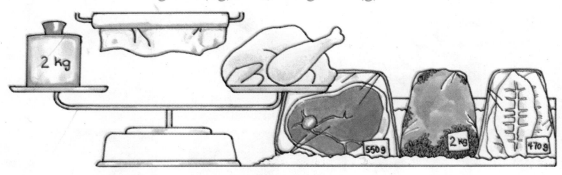

A. Complete.

   1. 3 kg = 1 kg + 1 kg + 1 kg
        = 1,000 g + 1,000 g + 1,000 g or __?__ g

   2. 4 kg = __?__ g

B. Complete.

   3. 2,000 g = 1,000 g + 1,000 g
         = 1 kg + 1 kg or __?__ kg

   4. 6,000 g = __?__ kg

Practice

Complete.

   1. 5 kg = __?__ g   **2.** 9 kg = __?__ g

   3. 8,000 g = __?__ kg   **4.** 7,000 g = __?__ kg

 ★**5.** 12 kg = __?__ g   ★**6.** 10,000 g = __?__ kg

Choosing a Unit

Use a small unit to measure small amounts.

Centimeter

Milliliter

Gram

Use a large unit to measure large amounts.

Meter

Liter

Kilogram

A. Would you use centimeters or meters to measure each?

1. A house

2. A classroom

3. A flagpole

4. A dollar bill

B. Would you use milliliters or liters to measure each?

5. A small can of soup

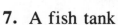

6. A large jug of apple juice

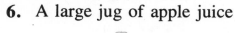

7. A fish tank

8. A glass of milk

C. Would you use grams or kilograms to measure each?

9. A dog

10. An apple

11. A sofa

12. A watermelon slice

★ **D.** Complete. Use meter, liter, or kilogram.

13. Pat made a __?__ of ice tea.

14. Ricardo bought a __?__ of bananas.

Temperature

Temperature is measured in degrees.
Each space on the thermometer is 2 degrees.
This thermometer shows 24 degrees Celsius.
Write this as 24°C.

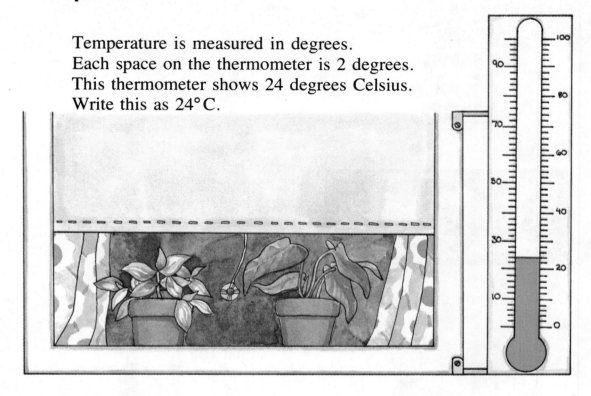

Look at the temperatures shown.

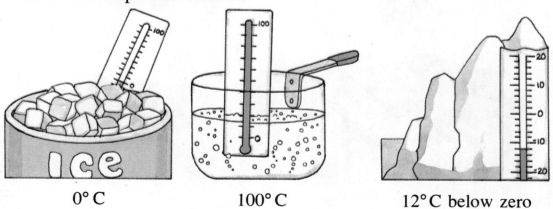

| 0°C | 100°C | 12°C below zero |

▶ Water freezes at 0°C.
▶ Water boils at 100°C.
▶ When a temperature is lower than 0°C, it is below zero.

A. What temperatures are shown?

1.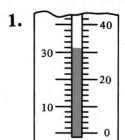

2.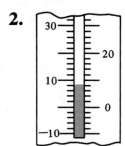

3.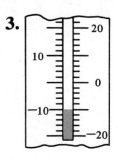

What temperatures are shown?

1.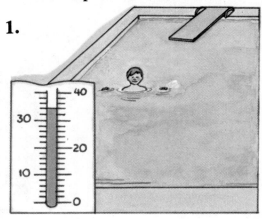

2.

3.

4.

Measure to the nearest centimeter. (174)

1.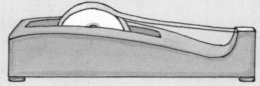

2.

Complete.

3. 400 cm = __?__ m

(176)

4. 9 m = __?__ cm

(176)

5. 8 L = __?__ mL

(178)

6. 3,000 mL = __?__ L

(178)

7. 1 kg = __?__ g

(179)

8. 7 kg = __?__ g

(179)

What temperatures are shown? (182)

9.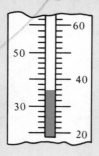

10.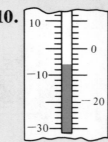

11.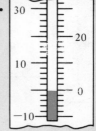

Find Out!
Brainteaser

4		3	=	12
2		2	=	4
=		=		=
2		1	=	3

Copy this puzzle.
Put + , − , ×, or ÷ in the
blanks to make true
sentences going across
and down.

Divide.

1. $1\overline{)8}$ **2.** $2\overline{)18}$ **3.** $2\overline{)14}$ **4.** $3\overline{)6}$

5. $2\overline{)2}$ **6.** $1\overline{)5}$ **7.** $3\overline{)18}$ **8.** $3\overline{)24}$

9. $2\overline{)16}$ **10.** $1\overline{)7}$ **11.** $2\overline{)8}$ **12.** $3\overline{)12}$ **13.** $2\overline{)10}$ **14.** $3\overline{)27}$

15. $5\overline{)30}$ **16.** $6\overline{)6}$ **17.** $4\overline{)28}$ **18.** $5\overline{)20}$ **19.** $5\overline{)25}$ **20.** $4\overline{)24}$

21. $6\overline{)54}$ **22.** $4\overline{)32}$ **23.** $5\overline{)45}$ **24.** $6\overline{)48}$ **25.** $5\overline{)5}$ **26.** $6\overline{)24}$

27. $4\overline{)4}$ **28.** $6\overline{)42}$ **29.** $5\overline{)40}$ **30.** $4\overline{)8}$ **31.** $6\overline{)18}$ **32.** $5\overline{)10}$

33. $4\overline{)36}$ **34.** $5\overline{)35}$ **35.** $6\overline{)30}$ **36.** $4\overline{)12}$ **37.** $6\overline{)36}$ **38.** $4\overline{)20}$

39. $7\overline{)35}$ **40.** $8\overline{)24}$ **41.** $8\overline{)48}$ **42.** $9\overline{)36}$ **43.** $9\overline{)27}$ **44.** $9\overline{)54}$

45. $8\overline{)32}$ **46.** $7\overline{)7}$ **47.** $9\overline{)72}$ **48.** $7\overline{)63}$ **49.** $7\overline{)28}$ **50.** $7\overline{)49}$

51. $8\overline{)64}$ **52.** $9\overline{)45}$ **53.** $7\overline{)14}$ **54** $9\overline{)9}$ **55.** $8\overline{)8}$ **56.** $8\overline{)56}$

57. $7\overline{)21}$ **58.** $9\overline{)81}$ **59.** $7\overline{)56}$ **60.** $8\overline{)40}$ **61.** $7\overline{)42}$ **62.** $9\overline{)18}$

What times are shown?

63.

____ o'clock

___ : ___

64.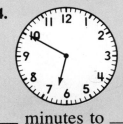

___ minutes to ___

___ : ___

65.

___ minutes after ___

___ : ___

Problem Solving

101 people went to Chicago by bus. 180 people went by train. 315 people went by plane. How many people went to Chicago?

Solve: $101 + 180 + 315 = 596$
596 people went to Chicago.

Is the answer reasonable? Estimate to check.

		Estimate
101	$\longrightarrow$	100
180	$\longrightarrow$	200
+ 315	$\longrightarrow$	+ 300
		600

600 is close to 596.
The answer is reasonable.

A. Complete.

23 bus tickets to Chicago were sold last month. 66 tickets were sold this month. How many tickets were sold in all?

Solve
$$\begin{array}{r} 23 \\ + 66 \\ \hline 89 \end{array}$$
last month
this month
tickets

1. Estimate the sum.

2. Is the estimated sum close to 89?

3. Is the answer reasonable?

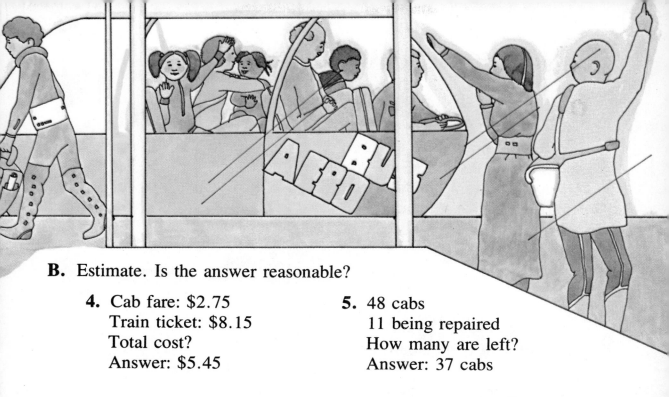

B. Estimate. Is the answer reasonable?

4. Cab fare: $2.75
Train ticket: $8.15
Total cost?
Answer: $5.45

5. 48 cabs
11 being repaired
How many are left?
Answer: 37 cabs

_____ Practice

Estimate. Is the answer reasonable?

1. 323 passengers
186 women
How many men?
Answer: 137 men

2. 91 tickets in all
Sold 36
How many are left?
Answer: 51 tickets left

3. 186 seats
115 people seated
How many empty seats?
Answer: 91 empty seats

4. Bus ticket: $9.10
Lunch: $4.75
Total cost?
Answer: $13.85

5. 141 suitcases
98 tote bags
How many more suitcases?
Answer: 43 suitcases

6. 24 buses left at 4:00.
49 buses left at 6:00.
How many buses left in all?
Answer: 93 buses

Time to the Minute

There are 60 minutes in an hour.
Each mark on the clock is 1 minute.
The clock shows 41 minutes after 3
or 3:41.

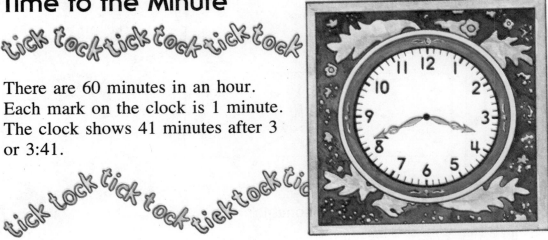

A. Look at the clock.

    1. Where is the hour hand?

    2. Where is the minute hand?

    3. What is the time? 1:____

B. Look at the clock.

    4. How many minutes after the hour?

    5. What is the time? ____

C. What time is shown? Use the __:__ form.

    6. 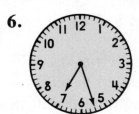   **7.** 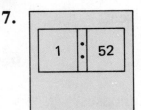   **8.**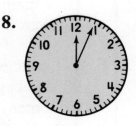

What time is shown? Use the __:__ form.

1.

2.

3.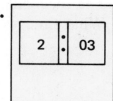

4.

5.

6.

7.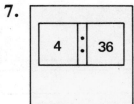

8.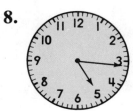

9.

10.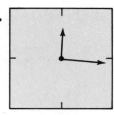

11.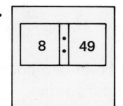

12.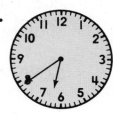

★**13.**

★**14.**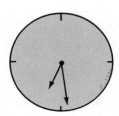

★**15.**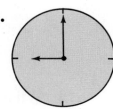

Catch You Later

Mr. Armstrong brought his car for a tune-up at 3:05.
The mechanic said it would take two hours.
What time will Mr. Armstrong's car be ready?

The car will be ready at 5:05.

A. Look at the clock.

1. What is the time?

2. What time will it be in one hour?
   [HINT: add one hour to the
   time shown.]

B. Look at the clock.

3. What is the time?

4. What time was it one hour ago?
   [HINT: subtract one hour from
   the time shown.]

What time will it be in two hours?

1.

2.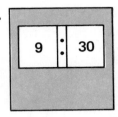

3.

What time will it be in three hours?

4.

5.

6.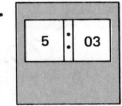

What time was it two hours ago?

7.

8.

9.

What time will it be in three hours?

★**10.**

★**11.**

Solve.

12. Ms. Valdez began washing her car at 12:30. She finished one hour later. What time was that?

Minutes Later and Earlier

Inez awoke at 7:05. She left the house 40 minutes later.
What time was that?

Inez left the house at 7:45.

A. Look at the clock.

   1. What is the time?

   2. What time will it be in 20 minutes?

   3. What time was it 20 minutes ago?

B. What time will it be in a half hour?

   4.   **5.**   **6.**

C. What time was it 15 minutes ago?

   7.   **8.**   **9.**

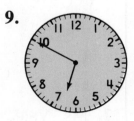

What time will it be in 20 minutes?

1.  **2.**  **3.**

What time will it be in 35 minutes?

4.

| 11 | : | 05 |

5.  **6.**

What time was it 30 minutes ago?

7.  **8.**  **9.**

| 6 | : | 53 |

What time will it be in 1 hour and 10 minutes?

★ **10.**    ★ **11.**

Solve.

12. Dino leaves school at 3:00. It takes him 25 minutes to walk home. What time does he get home?

Customary Measurement

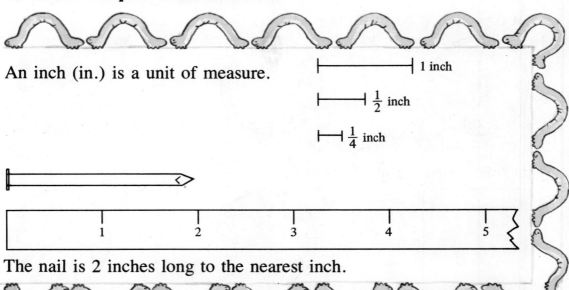

An inch (in.) is a unit of measure.

	1 inch
	$\frac{1}{2}$ inch
	$\frac{1}{4}$ inch

The nail is 2 inches long to the nearest inch.

A. Some rulers are marked in half inches.

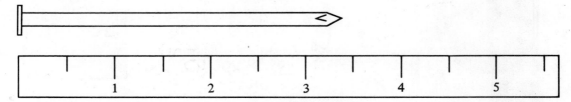

1. What is the length to the nearest $\frac{1}{2}$ in.?

Some rulers are marked in quarter inches.

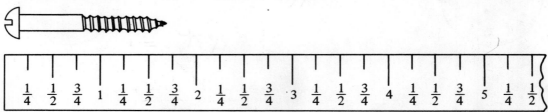

This screw is $1\frac{3}{4}$ in. to the nearest $\frac{1}{4}$ inch.

Measure to the nearest inch.

2.

3.

4.

5.

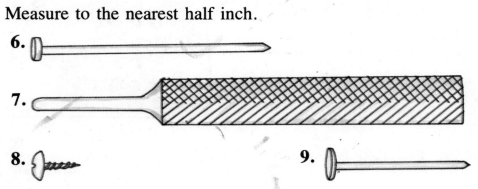

Measure to the nearest half inch.

6.

7.

8.   **9.**

Measure to the nearest quarter inch.

10.   **11.**

12.

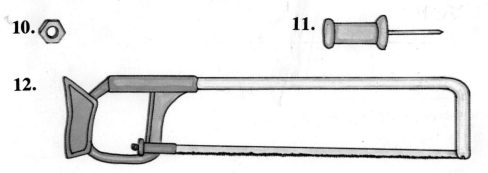

Inches, Feet, and Yards

You can also measure in inches, feet, and yards.

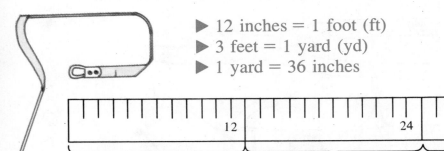

▶ 12 inches = 1 foot (ft)
▶ 3 feet = 1 yard (yd)
▶ 1 yard = 36 inches

12	24	36
1 foot	1 foot	1 foot

A. Complete.

1. 2 ft = 1 ft + 1 ft
= 12 in. + 12 in. or __?__ in.

2. 2 yd = 1 yd + 1 yd
= 3 ft + 3 ft or __?__ ft

3. 2 yd = 1 yd + 1 yd
= 36 in. + 36 in. or __?__ in.

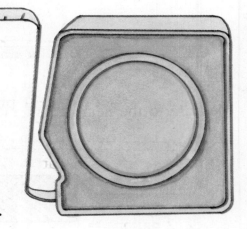

Practice

Complete.

1. 1 ft = __?__ in.   2. 3 ft = __?__ in.

3. 3 yd = __?__ ft   4. 3 yd = __?__ in.

Solve.

5. A sidewalk is 4 yards wide.
How many feet is that?

Cups, Pints, Quarts, and Gallons

You can measure liquids in cups, pints, quarts, and gallons.

2 cups = 1 pint   2 pints = 1 quart   4 quarts = 1 gallon

A. Complete.

1. 2 pints = 1 pint + 1 pint
= 2 cups + 2 cups or __?__ cups

2. 2 quarts = 1 quart + 1 quart
= 2 pints + 2 pints or __?__ pints

3. 2 gallons = 1 gallon + 1 gallon
= 4 quarts + 4 quarts or __?__ quarts

_____ Practice

Complete.

1. 3 pints = __?__ cups

2. 4 pints = __?__ cups

3. 4 quarts = __?__ pints

4. 3 quarts = __?__ pints

5. 3 gallons = __?__ quarts

6. 4 gallons = __?__ quarts

Pounds and Ounces

The scale shows that the book weighs 3 pounds.

A. Look at the scale.

    1. How many spaces are between
        0 and 1 pound on the scale?
        We call each of these marks
        ounce marks.

    2. How many ounces are in 1
        pound?

        ▶ 16 ounces (oz) = 1 pound (lb)

B. Complete.

    3. 2 lb = 1 lb + 1 lb
            = 16 oz + 16 oz or __?__ oz

_____ Practice

Complete.

  1. 3 lb = __?__ oz   **2.** 4 lb = __?__ oz

★ **3.** 6 lb = __?__ oz   ★ **4.** 5 lb = __?__ oz

Temperature

This thermometer shows 76 degrees Fahrenheit.
Write this as 76°F.

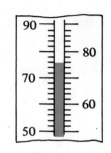

A. What temperatures are shown?

1.

2.

What temperatures are shown?

1.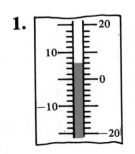

2.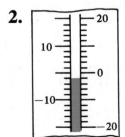

3.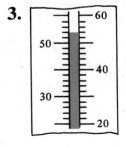

4.

Problem Solving

Solve.

1. Juan left school at 3:00. He has one hour to get to softball practice. What time is the softball practice? [HINT: add one hour]

2. Mary has a dental appointment at 5:00. She gets out of school 2 hours earlier. What time does she get out of school?

3. Mark has a piano lesson at 10:15 on Saturday morning. His lesson lasts 40 minutes. What time will he finish his piano lesson?

4. Chris arrives at the bus stop at 9:15. He waits 10 minutes for the bus. What time does the bus arrive?

★ 5. Benita has basketball practice at 4:30. She must leave by 6:15 to get home in time for dinner. How much time does she have to play basketball?

Measure to the nearest centimeter. *(174)*

1.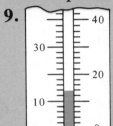

2.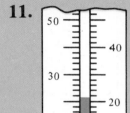

Complete.

3. 800 cm = __?__ m   **4.** 7 m = __?__ cm   **5.** 1 L = __?__ mL
(176)   *(176)*   *(178)*

6. 3,000 mL = __?__ L   **7.** 3 kg = __?__ g   **8.** 2,000 g = __?__ kg
(178)   *(179)*   *(179)*

What temperatures are shown? *(182)*

9.

10.

11.

Look at the clock.

12. What is the time? *(188)*

13. What time will it be in one hour? *(190)*

14. What time was it 10 minutes ago? *(192)*

Is the answer reasonable? *(186)*

15. 13 bluejays
37 wrens
How many birds in all?
Answer: 40 birds

16. 71 sparrows
38 crows
How many more sparrows?
Answer: 33 sparrows

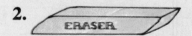

Measure to the nearest centimenter. *(174)*

1.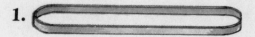

2.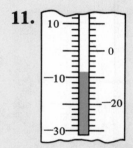

Complete.

3. 4 m = ___?___ cm   **4.** 900 cm = ___?___ m   **5.** 2,000 mL = ___?___ L
(176)   *(176)*   *(178)*

6. 4 L = ___?___ mL   **7.** 1 kg = ___?___ g   **8.** 3,000 g = ___?___ kg
(178)   *(179)*   *(179)*

What temperatures are shown? *(182)*

9.    **10.** 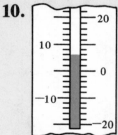   **11.**

Look at the clock.

12. What is the time? *(188)*

13. What time was it an hour ago? *(190)*

14. What time was it 15 minutes ago? *(192)*

Is the answer reasonable? *(186)*

15. Picked 26 daisies
Picked 34 roses
How many flowers in all?
Answer: 60 flowers

16. 28 violets
17 lilies
How many more violets?
Answer: 11 violets

Basic Skills Check

1.

$$\begin{array}{r} 50 \\ + 46 \\ \hline \end{array}$$

A 90

B 96

C 100

D 106

2. $4 + 3 + 5 =$ ___?___

E 9

F 12

G 15

H 18

3.

$$\begin{array}{r} 21 \\ + 69 \\ \hline \end{array}$$

A 80

B 90

C 98

D 99

4. $15 - 8 =$ ___?___

E 4

F 5

G 6

H 7

5.

$$\begin{array}{r} 56 \\ - 32 \\ \hline \end{array}$$

A 21

B 22

C 24

D 26

6. $16 + 2 =$ ___?___

E 6

F 10

G 14

H 18

7. $82 - 10 =$ ___?___

A 52

B 62

C 72

D 92

8.

$$\begin{array}{r} 9 \\ 2 \\ + 4 \\ \hline \end{array}$$

E 15

F 17

G 21

H 23

9.

$$\begin{array}{r} 59 \\ + 7 \\ \hline \end{array}$$

A 52

B 66

C 67

D 70

10.

$$\begin{array}{r} 47 \\ - 37 \\ \hline \end{array}$$

E 1

F 7

G 10

H 14

11. $36 + 55 =$ ___?___

A 91

B 92

C 93

D 94

12.

$$\begin{array}{r} 312 \\ + 236 \\ \hline \end{array}$$

E 124

F 242

G 524

H 548

Multiples of 10

Look for patterns.

10	10	10	10	10
×1	×2	×3	×4	×5
10	20	30	40	50

▶ A number that ends in a zero is a **multiple** of 10.

A. Which are multiples of 10? Write yes or no.

1. 40   **2.** 70   **3.** 170   **4.** 39   **5.** 90   **6.** 115

B. Complete.

7. $2 \times 2 = \underline{\ ?\ }$, $2 \times 20 = \underline{\ ?\ }$

8. $4 \times 2 = \underline{\ ?\ }$, $4 \times 20 = \underline{\ ?\ }$

9. $5 \times 2 = \underline{\ ?\ }$, $5 \times 20 = \underline{\ ?\ }$

C. Multiply.

10. 10	**11.** 10	**12.** 10	**13.** 20	**14.** 30
×9	×6	×7	×4	×3

Practice

Which are multiples of 10? Write yes or no.

1. 110   **2.** 30   **3.** 47   **4.** 126   **5.** 50   **6.** 300

Multiply.

7. 10
  × 4

8. 10
  × 2

9. 10
  × 8

10. 30
   × 2

11. 20
   × 10

★ **12.** 40
     × 40

RACE TIME

Multiply.

1. 3
 9

2. 5
 9

3. 3
 0

4. 3
 5

5. 4
 8

6. 2
 4

7. 1
 3

8. 0
 8

9. 2
 7

10. 6
 1

11. 8
 8

12. 6
 5

13. 3
 7

14. 6
 8

15. 8
 7

16. 6
 6

17. 9
 4

18. 8
 5

19. 6
 0

20. 7
 8

21. 1
 2

22. 5
 1

23. 8
 9

24. 2
 8

25. 3
 4

26. 5
 5

27. 6
 7

28. 0
 1

29. 4
 7

30. 2
 0

31. 3
 6

32. 7
 9

33. 2
 3

34. 5
 2

35. 1
 7

36. 5
 7

37. 1
 9

38. 2
 6

39. 4
 5

40. 6
 9

41. 7
 0

42. 9
 5

43. 1
 4

44. 2
 2

45. 9
 2

46. 0
 4

47. 9
 9

48. 8
 3

49. 5
 8

50. 0
 5

51. 3
 3

52. 1
 8

53. 4
 4

54. 7
 2

55. 8
 6

56. 8
 4

57. 9
 6

58. 4
 9

59. 5
 6

60. 7
 7

61. 9
 0

62. 6
 2

63. 7
 3

64. 1
 1

65. 4
 6

66. 0
 0

67. 2
 5

68. 7
 6

69. 3
 8

70. 7
 4

Multiplying Three Numbers

Dina ran 2 days each week. She ran
morning and evening. She did this for 3 weeks.
How many times did she run in all?

$$2 \times (2 \times 3) \qquad\qquad (2 \times 2) \times 3$$
$$2 \times 6 \qquad\qquad\qquad 4 \times 3$$
$$12 \qquad\qquad\qquad 12$$

Dina ran 12 times in all.

▶ Changing the grouping does not change the product.

A. Complete.

   1. $(2 \times 2) \times 4 = \underline{\ ?\ }$
       $2 \times (2 \times 4) = \underline{\ ?\ }$

   2. $(5 \times 2) \times 2 = \underline{\ ?\ }$
       $5 \times (2 \times 2) = \underline{\ ?\ }$

_____ Practice

Complete.

   1. $(3 \times 2) \times 4 = \underline{\ ?\ }$
       $3 \times (2 \times 4) = \underline{\ ?\ }$

   2. $(3 \times 3) \times 2 = \underline{\ ?\ }$
       $3 \times (3 \times 2) = \underline{\ ?\ }$

   3. $(3 \times 2) \times 5 = \underline{\ ?\ }$
       $3 \times (2 \times 5) = \underline{\ ?\ }$

   4. $2 \times (4 \times 2) = \underline{\ ?\ }$
       $(2 \times 4) \times 2 = \underline{\ ?\ }$

★ **5.** $(3 \times 5) \times 4 = 3 \times (5 \times \underline{\ ?\ })$

★ **6.** $25 \times (14 \times 4) = (\underline{\ ?\ } \times 14) \times 4$

No Renaming

Multiply.

```
                ┌──────── THINK ────────┐        ┌─ WRITE ─┐
              MULTIPLY ONES      MULTIPLY TENS
              ┌─Tens─┬─Ones─┐    ┌─Tens─┬─Ones─┐
   43            4 │  3         4 │  3              43
  × 2         ×    │  2       ×   │  2             × 2
  ───            ──┴──6         8 │  6              ──
                                                    86
```

A. Find 3 × 31. Complete.

   WRITE

  1. Multiply ones.
     3 × 1 = _____?_____

```
   3 1
  × 3
  ───
    3
```

  2. Multiply tens.
     3 × 3 tens = ___?___ tens

```
   3 1
  × 3
  ───
  9 3
```

  3. What is the product?

B. Complete.

4.	**5.**	**6.**	**7.**	**8.**	**9.**
22	26	11	61	32	42
× 2	× 1	× 5	× 2	× 3	× 4
4	6	5			

C. Multiply.

10.	**11.**	**12.**	**13.**	**14.**	**15.**
34	23	10	21	45	21
× 2	× 3	× 7	× 4	× 1	× 5

16.	**17.**	**18.**	**19.**	**20.**	**21.**
21	11	47	22	23	10
× 3	× 8	× 1	× 4	× 2	× 6

Multiply.

1. 13
   × 2

2. 11
   × 4

3. 23
   × 3

4. 42
   × 2

5. 10
   × 8

6. 34
   × 2

7. 40
   × 1

8. 21
   × 5

9. 12
   × 3

10. 31
    × 2

11. 30
    × 4

12. 81
    × 2

13. 44
    × 2

14. 62
    × 4

15. 30
    × 5

16. 32
    × 2

17. 31
    × 6

18. 40
    × 2

19. 21
    × 3

20. 43
    × 3

21. 35
    × 1

22. 72
    × 4

23. 82
    × 3

24. 20
    × 3

25. 63
    × 2

26. 21
    × 9

27. 40
    × 3

28. 60
    × 2

29. 32
    × 4

30. 52
    × 4

31. 72
    × 3

32. 20
    × 7

33. 51
    × 5

34. 24
    × 2

35. 42
    × 3

36. 70
    × 4

37. 67
    × 1

38. 51
    × 3

39. 23
    × 2

40. 50
    × 6

41. 74
    × 2

42. 62
    × 3

43. 31
    × 4

44. 31
    × 7

45. 52
    × 3

46. 20
    × 4

47. 84
    × 2

48. 41
    × 3

Solve.

★49. $24 \times \square = 48$

★50. $14 \times \square = 28$

★51. $13 \times \square = 39$

Solve.

52. 42 people in each car
    4 cars in a train
    How many people in all?

53. 20 rows of seats
    6 seats in each row
    How many seats in all?

Renaming Ones

Multiply.

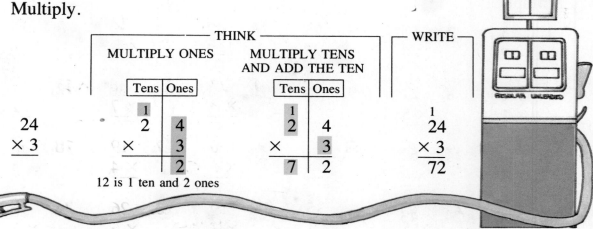

THINK

MULTIPLY ONES

Tens	Ones
1	
2	4
×	3
	2

12 is 1 ten and 2 ones

MULTIPLY TENS
AND ADD THE TEN

Tens	Ones
1	
2	4
×	3
7	2

WRITE

```
  1
 24
× 3
 72
```

24
× 3

A. Find 2 × 68. Complete.

WRITE

1. Multiply ones.
2 × 8 = ___?___

```
  1
 68
× 2
  6
```

2. How is 16 written?

3. Multiply tens.
2 × 6 tens = ___?___ tens
Add, 12 tens + 1 ten = ___?___ tens

```
  1
 68
× 2
136
```

4. What is the product?

B. Complete.

5.   2
   15
  × 5
  ___
    5

6.   1
   23
  × 4
  ___
    2

7.   2
   13
  × 7
  ___
    1

8.   26
  × 3
  ___

9.   24
  × 6
  ___

10.   45
  × 2
  ___

C. Multiply.

11.   48
  × 2

12.   14
  × 3

13.   34
  × 5

14.   43
  × 6

15.   24
  × 4

16.   27
  × 2

Multiply.

1. 16
    × 2

2. 13
    × 5

3. 38
    × 2

4. 14
    × 4

5. 28
    × 3

6. 12
    × 7

7. 25
    × 5

8. 14
    × 7

9. 28
    × 4

10. 27
     × 3

11. 26
     × 7

12. 47
     × 2

13. 35
     × 2

14. 53
     × 4

15. 18
     × 5

16. 66
     × 6

17. 19
     × 4

18. 75
     × 3

19. 54
     × 3

20. 15
     × 5

21. 35
     × 4

22. 19
     × 3

23. 26
     × 6

24. 57
     × 2

25. 77
     × 2

26. 29
     × 4

27. 22
     × 9

28. 58
     × 5

29. 36
     × 2

30. 39
     × 3

31. 31
     × 6

32. 46
     × 2

33. 82
     × 7

34. 43
     × 2

35. 44
     × 8

36. 19
     × 2

37. 40
     × 5

38. 33
     × 3

39. 61
     × 7

40. 77
     × 4

41. 42
     × 2

42. 16
     × 4

★ Complete.

43.   52
     × □
     ─────
      260

44.   17
     × □
     ─────
      102

45.   12
     × □
     ─────
       60

46.   25
     × □
     ─────
       75

47.   43
     × □
     ─────
      301

48. 2□
     × 2
     ─────
      56

Solve.

49. 26 cars
    5 people in each car
    How many people in all?

50. 22 people on each plane
    6 planes
    How many people in all?

Multiply.

1. 10	**2.** 10	**3.** 30	**4.** 10	**5.** 23	**6.** 34
(204) × 7	(204) × 12	(204) × 2	(204) × 4	(208) × 3	(208) × 2
7. 20	**8.** 41	**9.** 15	**10.** 27	**11.** 14	**12.** 49
(208) × 4	(208) × 2	(210) × 3	(210) × 4	(210) × 6	(210) × 2

Find Out! ━ ━ ━ ━ ━ ━ ━ ━ ━ ━ ━ ━ ━ ━ ━ ━ ━
Brainteaser

Arrange each from smallest to largest.

Example:

 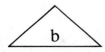

The answer is c, a, b.

1.

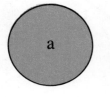 

2.

3.

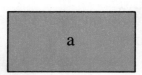 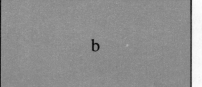

Keeping Fit

Measure to the nearest centimeter.

1.

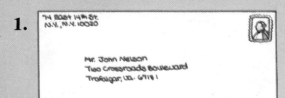

2.

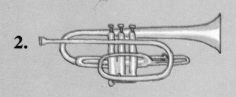

Complete.

3. 10 m = __?__ cm

4. 900 cm = __?__ m

5. 2 L = __?__ mL

6. 2,000 mL = __?__ L

7. 9 kg = __?__ g

8. 4,000 g = __?__ kg

What time is shown? Use the __:__ form.

9.

10.

11.

What time will it be in 2 hours? Use the __:__ form.

12.

10 : 00

13.

14.

Problem Solving

8 dancers in a set
16 sets of dancers
How many dancers
at the square dance?

What is asked? ⟶ How many dancers in all?
What do you know? ⟶ 8 dancers in a set, 16 sets of dancers
Do you multiply or divide? ⟶ Multiply.

This number sentence fits the story.

$$8 \quad \times \quad 16 \quad = \quad \underline{\ ?\ }$$

dancers   sets of dancers   dancers in all

A. 72 people at the dance
8 people in each set
How many sets of dancers?

1. What is asked?

2. What do you know?

3. Do you multiply or divide?

4. Which number sentence fits the story?

$72 \times 8 = \underline{\ ?\ }$ $72 \div 9 = \underline{\ ?\ }$ $72 \div 8 = \underline{\ ?\ }$

B. Which number sentence fits the story?

    5. 16 people eating corn
        Each person eats 2 ears of corn.
        How many ears of corn are eaten?

        $8 \times 2 = $ _?_ $16 \times 2 = $ _?_ $16 \div 2 = $ _?_

Practice

Which number sentence fits the story?

1. 81 straw hats
   9 hats in each pile
   How many piles of straw hats?

   $81 \div 9 = $ _?_ $9 \times 9 = $ _?_ $81 \times 9 = $ _?_

2. Mr. Packer calls the dances.
   Calls 4 dances in an hour
   How many dances called in 3 hours?

   $4 \div 3 = $ _?_ $12 \div 4 = $ _?_ $4 \times 3 = $ _?_

3. 64 glasses of apple cider
   2 glasses for each person
   How many people drink apple cider?

   $64 \times 2 = $ _?_ $64 \div 2 = $ _?_ $32 \times 2 = $ _?_

4. 4 banjos
   5 strings on each banjo
   How many strings in all?

   $4 \times 5 = $ _?_ $20 \div 5 = $ _?_ $20 \times 5 = $ _?_

Multiples of 100

Look for patterns.

$$\begin{array}{r} 100 \\ \times 1 \\ \hline 100 \end{array} \quad \begin{array}{r} 100 \\ \times 2 \\ \hline 200 \end{array} \quad \begin{array}{r} 100 \\ \times 3 \\ \hline 300 \end{array} \quad \begin{array}{r} 100 \\ \times 4 \\ \hline 400 \end{array} \quad \begin{array}{r} 100 \\ \times 5 \\ \hline 500 \end{array} \quad \begin{array}{r} 100 \\ \times 6 \\ \hline 600 \end{array}$$

▶ A number that ends in 2 zeros is a **multiple** of 100

A. Which are multiples of 100? Write yes or no.

    1. 800   **2.** 920   **3.** 700   **4.** 1,300   **5.** 4,020

B. Complete.

  6. $2 \times 2 = $ _?_ , $2 \times 20 = $ _?_ , $2 \times 200 = $ _?_

  7. $3 \times 2 = $ _?_ , $3 \times 20 = $ _?_ , $3 \times 200 = $ _?_

  8. $6 \times 3 = $ _?_ , $6 \times 30 = $ _?_ , $6 \times 300 = $ _?_

  9. $4 \times 7 = $ _?_ , $4 \times 70 = $ _?_ , $4 \times 700 = $ _?_

 10. $9 \times 3 = $ _?_ , $9 \times 30 = $ _?_ , $9 \times 300 = $ _?_

C. Multiply.

11. $\begin{array}{r} 100 \\ \times 6 \\ \hline \end{array}$	**12.** $\begin{array}{r} 300 \\ \times 3 \\ \hline \end{array}$	**13.** $\begin{array}{r} 700 \\ \times 2 \\ \hline \end{array}$	**14.** $\begin{array}{r} 900 \\ \times 7 \\ \hline \end{array}$	**15.** $\begin{array}{r} 100 \\ \times 8 \\ \hline \end{array}$
16. $\begin{array}{r} 400 \\ \times 3 \\ \hline \end{array}$	**17.** $\begin{array}{r} 800 \\ \times 6 \\ \hline \end{array}$	**18.** $\begin{array}{r} 100 \\ \times 7 \\ \hline \end{array}$	**19.** $\begin{array}{r} 500 \\ \times 3 \\ \hline \end{array}$	**20.** $\begin{array}{r} 400 \\ \times 4 \\ \hline \end{array}$

Which are multiples of 100? Write yes or no.

1. 320   **2.** 1,000   **3.** 600   **4.** 316   **5.** 200

Multiply.

6. 200
× 4

7. 500
× 5

8. 400
× 2

9. 600
× 3

10. 200
× 6

11. 500
× 7

12. 800
× 2

13. 100
× 9

14. 900
× 7

15. 600
× 9

16. 600
× 8

17. 900
× 9

18. 400
× 7

19. 500
× 4

20. 800
× 9

21. 200
× 5

22. 400
× 9

23. 300
× 7

24. 600
× 6

25. 300
× 2

26. 100
× 8

27. 300
× 4

28. 900
× 2

★ **29.** 2,000
× 2

★ **30.** 2,400
× 2

Solve.

31. 500 dollars in each pack
9 packs
How many dollars in all?

32. 50 dimes in each roll
6 rolls of dimes
How many dimes in all?

Chapter 8   **217**

Multiplying Hundreds

Multiply 2 × 314.

Follow these steps.

MULTIPLY ONES	MULTIPLY TENS	MULTIPLY HUNDREDS
3 1 4	3 1 4	3 1 4
× 2	× 2	× 2
8	2 8	6 2 8

A. Find 3 × 802. Complete.

WRITE

1. Multiply ones.
   3 × 2 = __?__

   8 0 2
   × 3
   6

2. Multiply tens.
   3 × 0 tens = __?__ tens

   8 0 2
   × 3
   0 6

3. Multiply hundreds.
   3 × 8 hundreds = __?__ hundreds

   8 0 2
   × 3

4. What is the product?

   2,4 0 6

B. Complete.

5. 210	6. 532	7. 323	8. 204	9. 231
× 4	× 2	× 3	× 2	× 3
40	4			

C. Multiply.

10. 110	11. 312	12. 322	13. 412	14. 201
× 5	× 3	× 4	× 2	× 8

Multiply.

1. 123
  × 3

2. 323
  × 2

3. 221
  × 4

4. 302
  × 3

5. 201
  × 4

6. 103
  × 3

7. 204
  × 2

8. 430
  × 2

9. 120
  × 3

10. 211
  × 4

11. 101
  × 6

12. 303
  × 3

13. 321
  × 3

14. 430
  × 1

15. 203
  × 3

16. 402
  × 2

17. 121
  × 2

18. 230
  × 3

19. 222
  × 4

20. 303
  × 2

21. 213
  × 3

22. 110
  × 6

23. 144
  × 2

24. 111
  × 7

25. 104
  × 2

26. 231
  × 3

27. 134
  × 2

28. 101
  × 9

29. 222
  × 2

30. 212
  × 3

31. 222
  × 3

32. 333
  × 3

33. 203
  × 2

★ **34.** 1,012
  × 3

★ **35.** 2,312
  × 3

Solve.

36. 103 beams on each truck
2 trucks
How many beams in all?

37. 110 bales of hay on each truck
4 trucks
How many bales of hay in all?

Renaming Ones in Multiplication

Multiply 4 × 219.

Follow these steps.

MULTIPLY ONES	MULTIPLY TENS THEN ADD THE TENS	MULTIPLY HUNDREDS
³ 2 1 9 × 4 —— 6	³ 2 1 9 × 4 —— 7 6	³ 2 1 9 × 4 —— 8 7 6

36 is 3 tens and 6 ones

A. Find 3 × 426. Complete.

WRITE

1. Multiply ones.
   3 × 6 = ___?___

   1
   4 2 6
   × 3
   ——
   8

2. How is 18 written?

3. Multiply tens.
   3 × 2 tens = ___?___ tens
   Add, 6 tens + 1 ten = ___?___ tens

   1
   4 2 6
   × 3
   ——
   7 8

4. Complete the example.

B. Complete.

5. ²
    218
    × 3
    ——
    4

6. ¹
    103
    × 5
    ——
    5

7. 546
   × 2
   ——

8. 315
   × 4
   ——

9. 347
   × 2
   ——

C. Multiply.

10. 516
    × 3
    ——

11. 439
    × 2
    ——

12. 607
    × 5
    ——

13. 112
    × 8
    ——

14. 423
    × 4
    ——

Multiply.

1. 347 × 2	**2.** 329 × 3	**3.** 116 × 6	**4.** 218 × 4	**5.** 118 × 5
6. 836 × 2	**7.** 908 × 7	**8.** 539 × 2	**9.** 806 × 9	**10.** 723 × 4
11. 316 × 3	**12.** 414 × 6	**13.** 726 × 3	**14.** 224 × 4	**15.** 316 × 5
16. 639 × 2	**17.** 412 × 8	**18.** 319 × 4	**19.** 225 × 3	**20.** 947 × 2
21. 205 × 7	**22.** 914 × 5	**23.** 707 × 4	**24.** 419 × 3	**25.** 503 × 5
26. 118 × 4	**27.** 645 × 2	**28.** 528 × 3	**29.** 436 × 2	**30.** 307 × 6
31. 540 × 2	**32.** 224 × 3	**33.** 314 × 7	**34.** 812 × 4	**35.** 714 × 2
36. 429 × 3	**37.** 514 × 4	**38.** 413 × 6	★ **39.** 1,416 × 2	★ **40.** 1,109 × 8

Solve.

41. 138 cars through a tollgate
2 dollars for each car
How many dollars in all?

42. 927 people pay tolls each day.
How many people pay tolls in 3 days?

Renaming Tens in Multiplication

Multiply 2 × 384.

Follow these steps.

MULTIPLY ONES	MULTIPLY TENS	MULTIPLY HUNDREDS THEN ADD THE HUNDREDS
38**4** × **2** **8**	¹384 × 2 68	¹384 × 2 **7**68

A. Find 3 × 273. Complete.

    1. Multiply tens.
        3 × 7 tens = __?__ tens

    2. How is 21 tens written?

    3. Multiply hundreds.
        3 × 2 hundreds = __?__ hundreds
        Add, 6 hundreds + 2 hundreds = __?__ hundreds

    4. What is the product?

WRITE

²273
 × 3
 19

²273
 × 3
 819

B. Complete.

5. ¹242 × 4 68	6. ²351 × 5 55	7. 673 × 2 6	8. 260 × 3	9. 241 × 7

C. Multiply.

10. 250 × 3	11. 151 × 6	12. 492 × 3	13. 854 × 2	14. 394 × 2

Multiply.

1. 293
   × 3

2. 241
   × 4

3. 354
   × 2

4. 161
   × 6

5. 281
   × 3

6. 361
   × 5

7. 472
   × 4

8. 353
   × 3

9. 764
   × 2

10. 370
    × 8

11. 463
    × 2

12. 321
    × 7

13. 742
    × 3

14. 740
    × 4

15. 581
    × 3

16. 341
    × 5

17. 650
    × 7

18. 271
    × 4

19. 573
    × 2

20. 371
    × 6

21. 141
    × 8

22. 662
    × 4

23. 794
    × 2

24. 182
    × 3

25. 130
    × 5

26. 532
    × 4

27. 452
    × 3

28. 550
    × 2

29. 360
    × 5

30. 431
    × 9

31. 873
    × 2

32. 332
    × 4

33. 761
    × 6

34. 960
    × 3

35. 452
    × 3

36. 301
    × 5

37. 791
    × 4

38. 132
    × 4

★ 39. 1,342
    × 3

★ 40. 2,431
    × 7

Solve.

41. 263 people on each plane
    3 planes to San Francisco
    How many people going
    to San Francisco?

42. 248 people on each plane
    2 planes to Dallas
    How many people going
    to Dallas?

Renaming Twice

Multiply 3×257.

Follow these steps.

MULTIPLY ONES	MULTIPLY TENS THEN ADD THE TENS	MULTIPLY HUNDREDS THEN ADD THE HUNDREDS
$\begin{array}{r} \overset{2}{2\,5\,7} \\ \times\ 3 \\ \hline 1 \end{array}$	$\begin{array}{r} \overset{1\ 2}{2\,5\,7} \\ \times\ 3 \\ \hline 7\,1 \end{array}$	$\begin{array}{r} \overset{1\ 2}{2\,5\,7} \\ \times\ 3 \\ \hline 7\,7\,1 \end{array}$

A. Find 4×398. Complete.

WRITE

1. Multiply ones.
   $4 \times 8 = \underline{}$

   $\begin{array}{r} \overset{3}{3\,9\,8} \\ \times\ 4 \\ \hline 2 \end{array}$

2. How is 32 written?

3. Multiply tens.
   4×9 tens $= \underline{}$ tens
   Add, 36 tens $+$ 3 tens $= \underline{}$ tens

   $\begin{array}{r} \overset{3\ 3}{3\,9\,8} \\ \times\ 4 \\ \hline 9\,2 \end{array}$

4. Complete the example.

B. Complete.

5. $\begin{array}{r} \overset{1\,1}{234} \\ \times\ 3 \\ \hline 02 \end{array}$

6. $\begin{array}{r} \overset{1}{578} \\ \times\ 2 \\ \hline 56 \end{array}$

7. $\begin{array}{r} \overset{1}{172} \\ \times\ 5 \\ \hline 0 \end{array}$

8. $\begin{array}{r} 336 \\ \times\ 4 \\ \hline \end{array}$

9. $\begin{array}{r} 119 \\ \times\ 8 \\ \hline \end{array}$

C. Multiply.

10. $\begin{array}{r} 254 \\ \times\ 5 \end{array}$

11. $\begin{array}{r} 429 \\ \times\ 4 \end{array}$

12. $\begin{array}{r} 367 \\ \times\ 2 \end{array}$

13. $\begin{array}{r} 218 \\ \times\ 6 \end{array}$

14. $\begin{array}{r} 156 \\ \times\ 3 \end{array}$

Multiply.

1. 274
× 3

2. 777
× 7

3. 475
× 6

4. 369
× 5

5. 389
× 2

6. 278
× 6

7. 249
× 5

8. 186
× 7

9. 269
× 4

10. 539
× 3

11. 133
× 4

12. 365
× 8

13. 566
× 2

14. 487
× 5

15. 174
× 7

16. 936
× 9

17. 328
× 7

18. 416
× 8

19. 675
× 5

20. 279
× 2

21. 329
× 4

22. 159
× 2

23. 456
× 2

24. 149
× 5

25. 267
× 3

26. 352
× 7

27. 552
× 8

28. 372
× 5

29. 555
× 6

30. 266
× 9

31. 334
× 4

32. 427
× 5

33. 305
× 7

34. 616
× 7

35. 732
× 8

36. 291
× 3

37. 187
× 7

38. 132
× 9

★ **39.** 2,621
× 6

★ **40.** 4,206
× 5

Solve.

41. 206 crates on each barge
8 barges
How many crates in all?

42. 267 people on each ferry
4 ferries
How many people in all?

Problem Solving
Bus Drivers

Solve.

1. There were 23 people at each bus stop.
The bus driver made 3 stops.
How many people in all?

2. There were 54 people on the bus.
There were 6 people in each row of seats.
How many rows of seats were there?

3. Mr. Alvarez drives a bus 8 hours each day.
How many hours does he drive in 5 days?

4. The bus made 8 stops in an hour.
How many stops were made in 8 hours?

5. On Monday, 72 transfer tickets were sold.
There were 9 bus drivers selling transfer tickets.
Each bus driver sold the same number. How many
tickets did each driver sell?

Multiply.

1. 10 *(204)* $\times 11$

2. 20 *(204)* $\times 3$

3. 12 *(208)* $\times 3$

4. 22 *(208)* $\times 4$

5. 17 *(210)* $\times 5$

6. 28 *(210)* $\times 3$

7. 500 *(216)* $\times 5$

8. 100 *(216)* $\times 6$

9. 402 *(218)* $\times 2$

10. 211 *(218)* $\times 6$

11. 214 *(220)* $\times 5$

12. 307 *(220)* $\times 2$

13. 252 *(222)* $\times 4$

14. 120 *(222)* $\times 8$

15. 161 *(222)* $\times 6$

16. 132 *(224)* $\times 7$

17. 225 *(224)* $\times 4$

18. 153 *(224)* $\times 8$

Which number sentence fits the story? *(214)*

19. 48 minutes to practice
8 songs to practice
How many minutes for each song?
$48 \div 8 =$ ___?___ $48 \times 8 =$ ___?___ $8 \times 6 =$ ___?___

20. 6 rows of drummers
36 drummers in each row
How many drummers in all?
$36 \div 6 =$ ___?___ $6 \times 6 =$ ___?___ $36 \times 6 =$ ___?___

Find Out!
Calculator Activity

Complete.

$9 \times 8 \times 7 \times 6 \times 5 \times 4 \times 3 \times 2 \times 1 \times 0 =$ ___?___

Multiply.

1. 40	**2.** 30	**3.** 32	**4.** 11	**5.** 18
(204) × 9	*(204)* × 3	*(208)* × 2	*(208)* × 7	*(210)* × 4

6. 25	**7.** 100	**8.** 400	**9.** 340	**10.** 201
(210) × 6	*(216)* × 24	*(216)* × 8	*(218)* × 2	*(218)* × 7

11. 217	**12.** 415	**13.** 181	**14.** 394	**15.** 231
(220) × 4	*(220)* × 3	*(222)* × 5	*(222)* × 2	*(222)* × 9

16. 126	**17.** 329	**18.** 117
(224) × 5	*(224)* × 4	*(224)* × 6

Which number sentence fits the story? *(214)*

19. 32 players in a band
4 players at each music stand
How many music stands needed?

$32 \times 4 = $ ___?___ $8 \times 4 = $ ___?___ $32 \div 4 = $ ___?___

20. 72 records on each shelf
9 shelves
How many records in all?

$72 \div 9 = $ ___?___ $72 \times 9 = $ ___?___ $8 \times 9 = $ ___?___

1. Find the fourth duck.

A   B   C   D

---

2. What is another name for 31?

A Three ones   C One-thirty

B Thirty-one   D Thirty

---

3. Which is a rectangle?

A   B   C   D

---

4. What time is it?

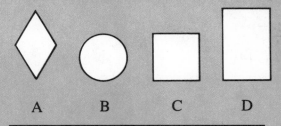

A	B	C	D
7:01	7:05	7:10	7:12

---

5. What time is it?

A	B	C	D
4:09	4:45	9:20	9:45

---

6. Count by 5's. What number is missing?

775   780   785   790   _____

A	B	C	D
791	792	794	795

---

7. How much in all?

A	B	C	D
20¢	30¢	37¢	40¢

---

8. What is another way to write 50 + 4?

E	F	G	H
45	54	405	504

Using Subtraction

A. There are 12 apples on a tree.
4 hungry horses are under the tree.

Each horse eats one apple.

Each horse eats another apple.

Each horse eats another apple.

$$\begin{array}{r} 12 \\ -\ 4 \\ \hline 8 \\ -\ 4 \\ \hline 4 \\ -\ 4 \\ \hline 0 \end{array}$$

1. How many apples did each horse eat?
[HINT: How many 4's were subtracted?]

CHAPTER
DIVISION 9

B. Mrs. Jones picked 54 apples. She sells them in boxes. She puts 6 apples in each box. How many boxes will she need?

She is sure she will need at least 5 boxes. $5 \times 6 = 30$. Subtract 5 sixes or 30.

$$
\begin{array}{r}
54 \\
-\ 30 \\
\hline
24
\end{array}
$$

She has 24 apples left. How many sixes in 24? $4 \times 6 = 24$. Subtract 4 sixes.

$$
\begin{array}{r}
-\ 24 \\
\hline
0
\end{array}
$$

2. How many boxes did she need?
[HINT: How many 6's in 54?]

C. Complete.

3. How many 4's in 36?

$$
\begin{array}{r}
36 \\
-\ 12 \quad \text{(3 fours)} \\
\hline
24 \\
-\ 12 \quad \text{(3 fours)} \\
\hline
12 \\
-\ 12 \quad \text{(3 fours)} \\
\hline
0
\end{array}
$$

4. How many 4's in 48?

$$
\begin{array}{r}
48 \\
-\ 40 \quad \text{(10 fours)} \\
\hline
8 \\
-\ 8 \quad \text{(2 fours)} \\
\hline
0
\end{array}
$$

RACE TIME

Divide.

1. $4\overline{)4}$ **2.** $3\overline{)9}$ **3.** $3\overline{)6}$ **4.** $4\overline{)8}$ **5.** $2\overline{)10}$

6. $3\overline{)15}$ **7.** $3\overline{)18}$ **8.** $4\overline{)12}$ **9.** $4\overline{)24}$ **10.** $4\overline{)16}$

11. $5\overline{)30}$ **12.** $2\overline{)14}$ **13.** $2\overline{)12}$ **14.** $4\overline{)20}$ **15.** $3\overline{)21}$

16. $4\overline{)28}$ **17.** $5\overline{)25}$ **18.** $5\overline{)35}$ **19.** $6\overline{)42}$ **20.** $2\overline{)16}$

21. $6\overline{)36}$ **22.** $3\overline{)24}$ **23.** $2\overline{)8}$ **24.** $8\overline{)48}$ **25.** $8\overline{)56}$

26. $7\overline{)49}$ **27.** $8\overline{)40}$ **28.** $2\overline{)18}$ **29.** $9\overline{)36}$ **30.** $9\overline{)45}$

31. $9\overline{)54}$ **32.** $9\overline{)63}$ **33.** $8\overline{)64}$ **34.** $3\overline{)27}$ **35.** $9\overline{)81}$

36. $9\overline{)72}$ **37.** $9\overline{)9}$ **38.** $5\overline{)45}$ **39.** $9\overline{)18}$ **40.** $6\overline{)54}$

41. $7\overline{)63}$ **42.** $8\overline{)16}$ **43.** $5\overline{)40}$ **44.** $8\overline{)24}$ **45.** $9\overline{)27}$

46. $4\overline{)36}$ **47.** $8\overline{)72}$ **48.** $6\overline{)48}$ **49.** $7\overline{)56}$ **50.** $7\overline{)14}$

51. $8\overline{)32}$ **52.** $7\overline{)21}$ **53.** $6\overline{)18}$ **54.** $7\overline{)35}$ **55.** $6\overline{)30}$

56. $7\overline{)42}$ **57.** $6\overline{)24}$ **48.** $7\overline{)28}$ **59.** $5\overline{)15}$ **60.** $3\overline{)12}$

61. $8\overline{)8}$ **62.** $6\overline{)12}$ **63.** $7\overline{)7}$ **64.** $5\overline{)20}$ **65.** $6\overline{)6}$

66. $5\overline{)10}$ **67.** $5\overline{)5}$ **68.** $4\overline{)32}$ **69.** $2\overline{)6}$ **70.** $3\overline{)3}$

Patterns in Division

You can use patterns in division.

$$2 \times 3 = 6 \qquad 6 \div 3 = 2 \qquad 3\overline{)6}^{\,2}$$

$$20 \times 3 = 60 \qquad 60 \div 3 = 20 \qquad 3\overline{)60}^{\,20}$$

$$200 \times 3 = 600 \qquad 600 \div 3 = 200 \qquad 3\overline{)600}^{\,200}$$

A. Divide. Look for a pattern.

1. $4 \times 2 = \underline{\;?\;}, \qquad 8 \div 2 = \underline{\;?\;}, \qquad 2\overline{)8}$

2. $40 \times 2 = \underline{\;?\;}, \qquad 80 \div 2 = \underline{\;?\;}, \qquad 2\overline{)80}$

3. $400 \times 2 = \underline{\;?\;}, \; 800 \div 2 = \underline{\;?\;}, \qquad 2\overline{)800}$

B. Divide.

4. $2\overline{)60}$ 5. $6\overline{)60}$ 6. $5\overline{)500}$ 7. $4\overline{)320}$ 8. $8\overline{)720}$

Practice

Divide.

1. $3\overline{)60}$ 2. $8\overline{)80}$ 3. $7\overline{)70}$ 4. $5\overline{)50}$ 5. $4\overline{)80}$

6. $8\overline{)800}$ 7. $9\overline{)900}$ 8. $7\overline{)700}$ 9. $3\overline{)600}$ 10. $3\overline{)900}$

11. $3\overline{)120}$ 12. $5\overline{)200}$ 13. $3\overline{)210}$ 14. $6\overline{)480}$ 15. $4\overline{)200}$

16. $6\overline{)420}$ 17. $4\overline{)360}$ 18. $9\overline{)810}$ 19. $5\overline{)350}$ 20. $4\overline{)240}$

21. $8\overline{)640}$ 22. $7\overline{)210}$ 23. $4\overline{)120}$ 24. $7\overline{)490}$ 25. $6\overline{)360}$

A Ghostly Game

SECRET

Your partner goes ahead 3.

Go back 3 spaces.

Skip your next turn.

Go ahead 2 spaces.

START

Go back to start.

Take another turn.

Skip your next turn.

Your partner goes ahead 2.

Go ahead 2 spaces.

Take another turn.

Go back to the GHOST.

FINISH

YOU WIN

Division with Remainders

Use the 3 steps to find $3\overline{)7}$.

Step 1:   Estimate

How many 3's in 7 ?

$3\overline{)7}$

Think: $1 \times 3 = 3$
         $2 \times 3 = 6$
         $3 \times 3 = 9$

6 is the largest product less then 7. Write 2.

Step 2:   Multiply

$2 \times 3 = 6$

$$\begin{array}{r} 2 \\ 3\overline{)7} \\ 6 \end{array}$$

Step 3:   Subtract

$7 - 6 = 1$

$$\begin{array}{r} 2\,r\,1 \\ 3\overline{)7} \\ -6 \\ \hline 1 \end{array}$$

The divisor is 3.
The quotient is 2.
The remainder is 1.

▶ The remainder must always be less than the divisor.

A. Find $5\overline{)32}$. Complete.

1. **Estimate:**   How many 5's in 32 ?
   Think: $5 \times 5 = 25$
            $6 \times 5 = 30$
            $7 \times 5 = 35$

   Which is the best estimate?
   Write 6 in the ones place.

   $$\begin{array}{r} 6 \\ 5\overline{)32} \end{array}$$

2. **Multiply:** $6 \times 5 = $ ___?___

3. **Subtract:** $32 - 30 = $ ___?___

4. What is the quotient?

5. What is the remainder?

$$\begin{array}{r} 6\,r\,2 \\ 5\overline{)32} \\ -30 \\ \hline 2 \end{array}$$

B. Divide.

6. $2\overline{)7}$ 7. $3\overline{)8}$ 8. $6\overline{)32}$ 9. $3\overline{)19}$ 10. $7\overline{)50}$

C. Correct the remainders that are too large.

Example

$$\begin{array}{r} 7\,r\,9 \\ 7\overline{)58} \\ -49 \\ \hline 9 \end{array}$$
← Remainder is too large. Try 8.
$$\begin{array}{r} 8\,r\,2 \\ 7\overline{)58} \\ -56 \\ \hline 2 \end{array}$$

11. $\overset{5\,r\,7}{6\overline{)37}}$　**12.** $\overset{9\,r\,2}{4\overline{)38}}$　**13.** $\overset{7\,r\,1}{8\overline{)57}}$　**14.** $\overset{6\,r\,8}{5\overline{)38}}$　**15.** $\overset{8\,r\,3}{9\overline{)75}}$

Practice

Divide.

1. $7\overline{)15}$　**2.** $4\overline{)26}$　**3.** $6\overline{)39}$　**4.** $5\overline{)19}$　**5.** $6\overline{)41}$

6. $7\overline{)69}$　**7.** $5\overline{)31}$　**8.** $9\overline{)20}$　**9.** $4\overline{)35}$　**10.** $6\overline{)34}$

11. $7\overline{)61}$　**12.** $8\overline{)78}$　**13.** $4\overline{)17}$　**14.** $8\overline{)50}$　**15.** $5\overline{)33}$

16. $7\overline{)53}$　**17.** $8\overline{)61}$　**18.** $9\overline{)78}$　**19.** $2\overline{)13}$　**20.** $3\overline{)29}$

21. $4\overline{)30}$　**22.** $5\overline{)47}$　**23.** $6\overline{)50}$　**24.** $7\overline{)33}$　**25.** $8\overline{)70}$

26. $9\overline{)89}$　**27.** $9\overline{)56}$　**28.** $8\overline{)74}$　**29.** $5\overline{)36}$　**30.** $6\overline{)49}$

31. $6\overline{)37}$　**32.** $4\overline{)27}$　**33.** $7\overline{)44}$　**34.** $2\overline{)19}$　**35.** $6\overline{)56}$

36. $5\overline{)46}$　**37.** $6\overline{)39}$　**38.** $7\overline{)54}$　**39.** $9\overline{)83}$　**40.** $3\overline{)26}$

Solve.

41. 68 apples
8 apples in each bag
How many bags of apples?
How many apples left over?

Dividing Tens and Ones

Find $3\overline{)69}$.   Estimate: How many 3's in 6 ?
Think: $2 \times 3 = 6$
Write the 2 in the tens place.

$$
\begin{array}{r}
2 \\
3\overline{)69} \\
-6\downarrow \\
\hline
09
\end{array}
$$

Multiply: $2 \times 3 = 6$

Subtract: $6 - 6 = 0$
Bring down the 9.

$$
\begin{array}{r}
2 \\
3\overline{)69} \\
6 \\
\hline
9
\end{array}
$$

Repeat the steps.
Estimate: How many 3's in 9 ?
Think: $3 \times 3 = 9$
Write 3 in the ones place.

$$
\begin{array}{r}
23 \\
3\overline{)69} \\
6 \\
\hline
9 \\
-9 \\
\hline
0
\end{array}
$$

Multiply: $3 \times 3 = 9$
Subtract: $9 - 9 = 0$
The quotient is 23.

Check

$$
\begin{array}{r}
23 \leftarrow \text{quotient} \\
\times\, 3 \leftarrow \text{divisor} \\
\hline
69
\end{array}
$$

A. Find $2\overline{)56}$. Complete.

1. **Estimate:** How many 2's in 5 ? $2\overline{)56}$
   Think: $\underline{?} \times 2$ is about 5.

2. **Multiply** and **subtract.**
   Bring down the 6. Repeat the steps.
   What is the quotient?

$$
\begin{array}{r}
2 \\
2\overline{)56} \\
-4\downarrow \\
\hline
16
\end{array}
$$

3. **Check.**

B. Divide and check.

    4. $3\overline{)39}$ **5.** $5\overline{)55}$ **6.** $3\overline{)57}$ **7.** $4\overline{)92}$ **8.** $6\overline{)72}$

Divide and check.

1. 2$)\overline{48}$ **2.** 3$)\overline{63}$ **3.** 4$)\overline{48}$ **4.** 4$)\overline{84}$ **5.** 3$)\overline{69}$

6. 3$)\overline{57}$ **7.** 3$)\overline{96}$ **8.** 2$)\overline{48}$ **9.** 7$)\overline{77}$ **10.** 4$)\overline{88}$

11. 4$)\overline{56}$ **12.** 3$)\overline{75}$ **13.** 2$)\overline{34}$ **14.** 5$)\overline{65}$ **15.** 6$)\overline{78}$

16. 4$)\overline{52}$ **17.** 2$)\overline{36}$ **18.** 5$)\overline{75}$ **19.** 6$)\overline{72}$ **20.** 8$)\overline{96}$

21. 2$)\overline{66}$ **22.** 3$)\overline{96}$ **23.** 7$)\overline{84}$ **24.** 2$)\overline{64}$ **25.** 5$)\overline{85}$

26. 3$)\overline{99}$ **27.** 6$)\overline{84}$ **28.** 2$)\overline{44}$ **29.** 6$)\overline{96}$ **30.** 2$)\overline{98}$

31. 5$)\overline{55}$ **32.** 3$)\overline{39}$ **33.** 4$)\overline{72}$ **34.** 7$)\overline{84}$ **35.** 2$)\overline{46}$

36. 3$)\overline{84}$ **37.** 8$)\overline{96}$ **38.** 5$)\overline{75}$ **39.** 2$)\overline{84}$ **40.** 3$)\overline{36}$

41. 4$)\overline{76}$ **42.** 9$)\overline{99}$ **43.** 3$)\overline{51}$ **44.** 6$)\overline{84}$ **45.** 5$)\overline{65}$

Solve.

★ **46.** $\Box \div 3 = 17$ ★ **47.** $\Box \div 5 = 19$

48. There are 90 girls in Mrs. Lim's gym class.
There are 6 girls on each basketball team.
How many basketball teams in the class?

49. A basketball game is 48 minutes long.
There are 4 periods in the game.
How many minutes in each period?

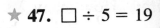

Dividing Tens and Ones with Remainders

Follow these steps to find $3\overline{)80}$.

$3\overline{)80}$

Estimate: How many **3's** in **8**?
Think: $\underline{} \times 3$ is about 8.
Try 2 in the tens place.

$$\begin{array}{r} 2 \\ 3\overline{)80} \\ -6\downarrow \\ \hline 20 \end{array}$$

Multiply: $2 \times 3 = 6$
Subtract: $8 - 6 = 2$
Bring down the 0.

$$\begin{array}{r} 2 \\ 3\overline{)80} \\ 6 \\ \hline 20 \end{array}$$

Repeat the steps.
Estimate: How many **3's** in **20**?
Think: $\underline{} \times 3$ is about 20.
Try 6 in the ones place.

$$\begin{array}{r} 26r2 \\ 3\overline{)80} \\ 6 \\ \hline 20 \\ -18 \\ \hline 2 \end{array}$$

Multiply: $3 \times 6 = 18$
Subtract: $20 - 18 = 2$
The quotient is 26.
The remainder is 2.

Check:
$$\begin{array}{r} 26 \\ \times 3 \\ \hline 78 \\ +2 \\ \hline 80 \end{array}$$

A. Complete.

1. $\begin{array}{r} 32 \\ 3\overline{)97} \\ -9\downarrow \\ \hline 7 \end{array}$
2. $\begin{array}{r} 19 \\ 4\overline{)77} \\ -4\downarrow \\ \hline 37 \end{array}$
3. $\begin{array}{r} 1 \\ 6\overline{)87} \\ -6\downarrow \\ \hline 27 \end{array}$
4. $\begin{array}{r} 1 \\ 5\overline{)56} \\ -5\downarrow \\ \hline 6 \end{array}$
5. $8\overline{)89}$

B. Divide.

6. $4\overline{)49}$ 7. $3\overline{)98}$ 8. $5\overline{)72}$ 9. $3\overline{)91}$ 10. $4\overline{)75}$

Practice

Divide.

1. $3\overline{)64}$ 2. $2\overline{)47}$ 3. $4\overline{)45}$ 4. $5\overline{)57}$ 5. $3\overline{)89}$

6. $2\overline{)29}$ 7. $4\overline{)86}$ 8. $5\overline{)52}$ 9. $9\overline{)94}$ 10. $4\overline{)82}$

11. $4\overline{)87}$ 12. $3\overline{)65}$ 13. $2\overline{)87}$ 14. $7\overline{)76}$ 15. $5\overline{)59}$

16. $3\overline{)77}$ 17. $4\overline{)69}$ 18. $6\overline{)80}$ 19. $4\overline{)70}$ 20. $3\overline{)67}$

21. $4\overline{)93}$ 22. $5\overline{)77}$ 23. $3\overline{)85}$ 24. $2\overline{)37}$ 25. $6\overline{)87}$

26. $7\overline{)85}$ 27. $5\overline{)88}$ 28. $3\overline{)53}$ 29. $3\overline{)49}$ 30. $4\overline{)79}$

31. $5\overline{)72}$ 32. $3\overline{)77}$ 33. $3\overline{)55}$ 34. $4\overline{)93}$ 35. $5\overline{)61}$

36. $8\overline{)97}$ 37. $4\overline{)63}$ 38. $7\overline{)86}$ 39. $2\overline{)79}$ 40. $6\overline{)82}$

★ Solve.

41. $83 \div \square = 13\,r\,5$ 42. $98 \div \square = 32\,r\,2$

Solve.

43. 77 yogurt bars
    6 bars in each box
    How many boxes?
    How many bars left over?

44. 88 strawberries
    9 children share them
    How many for each child?
    How many strawberries left over?

Divide.

1. 5)50
(233)
    2. 3)600
(233)
    3. 2)40
(233)
    4. 6)240
(233)
    5. 6)36
(232)

6. 8)32
(232)
    7. 7)63
(232)
    8. 4)36
(232)
    9. 8)28
(236)
    10. 2)15
(236)

11. 6)55
(236)
    12. 7)18
(236)
    13. 3)36
(238)
    14. 2)34
(238)
    15. 5)55
(238)

16. 6)96
(238)
    17. 5)77
(240)
    18. 4)93
(240)
    19. 8)90
(240)
    20. 2)45
(240)

Find Out!

Calculator Activities

A. Play this game with a partner.

Try to guess the answers to these problems.
Check your guess on the calculator. The one
with the closest guess wins the game.

   1. 3)33   **2.** 3)87   **3.** 4)68   **4.** 2)74   **5.** 4)96

B. Complete this magic square so that the sum in
each direction is 15.

8		4
	5	
6	7	

Keeping Fit

Multiply.

1. 20
    × 3

2. 10
    × 7

3. 22
    × 3

4. 14
    × 2

5. 42
    × 2

6. 34
    × 2

7. 39
    × 2

8. 15
    × 4

9. 36
    × 2

10. 47
    × 2

11. 36
    × 8

12. 200
    × 4

13. 300
    × 3

14. 400
    × 2

15. 123
    × 2

16. 211
    × 4

17. 314
    × 2

18. 103
    × 4

19. 315
    × 2

20. 216
    × 4

21. 108
    × 4

22. 360
    × 5

23. 273
    × 3

24. 471
    × 2

25. 130
    × 6

26. 121
    × 8

27. 378
    × 2

28. 273
    × 6

29. 265
    × 3

30. 416
    × 8

31. 365
    × 8

What time is shown? Use the ____:____ form.

32.

33.

34.

35.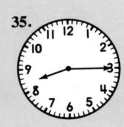

36.

37.

Problem Solving

It cost Mrs. Washington $3.00 to enter the fair. It cost $2.25 for her children to enter. How much did she pay in all?

What is asked? ⟶ How much in all?

What do you know? ⟶ $3.00 for herself
$2.25 for children

Which operation? ⟶ Add

This number sentence fits the story.

$3.00 + $2.25 = $5.25

Mrs. Washington   Children   Total Cost

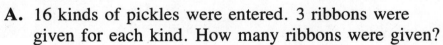

A. 16 kinds of pickles were entered. 3 ribbons were given for each kind. How many ribbons were given?

  1. What is asked?

  2. What do you know?

  3. Which operation?

  4. Which number sentence fits the story?

$$16 - 3 = \underline{\ ?\ } \qquad 16 \times 3 = \underline{\ ?\ } \qquad 16 \div 3 = \underline{\ ?\ }$$

B. Which number sentence fits the story?

  5. One building has 156 pigs. There are 2 pigs in each pen. How many pens are there?

$$156 \div 2 = \underline{\ ?\ } \qquad 156 - 2 = \underline{\ ?\ } \qquad 156 + 2 = \underline{\ ?\ }$$

Practice

Which number sentence fits the story?

1. There are 96 people sitting at the picnic tables. 6 people are at each table. How many tables are there?

$96 + 6 = $ __?__ $96 \div 6 = $ __?__ $96 \times 6 = $ __?__

2. There were 16 adults on line for the Ferris wheel. There were 24 children on line. How many people were on line?

$16 + 24 = $ __?__ $24 \times 16 = $ __?__ $24 - 16 = $ __?__

3. 116 people were watching the band. 32 people were standing. How many people were sitting?

$116 \times 32 = $ __?__ $116 + 32 = $ __?__ $116 - 32 = $ __?__

4. 18 kinds of cows were entered. 6 ribbons were given for each kind. How many ribbons were given?

$18 \div 6 = $ __?__ $6 \times 18 = $ __?__ $18 - 6 = $ __?__

Checking Division

A flow chart is a list of steps.
This flow chart shows how to check a quotient.

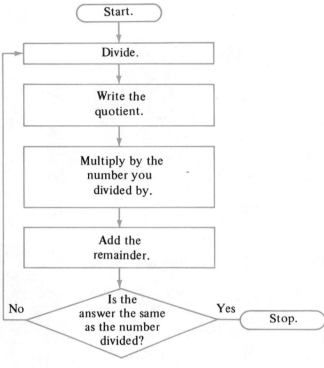

A. Look at the flow chart.

    1. What should you do after you write the quotient?

    2. What should you do if the answer does not check?

B. Divide and check.

    3. 2)̄9   **4.** 4)̄7   **5.** 2)̄13   **6.** 3)̄28   **7.** 2)̄19

    8. 3)̄98   **9.** 6)̄82   **10.** 2)̄54   **11.** 4)̄97   **12.** 3)̄97

Divide and check.

1. 8)36 **2.** 3)19 **3.** 5)49 **4.** 7)51 **5.** 4)37

6. 6)55 **7.** 3)14 **8.** 8)63 **9.** 9)83 **10.** 2)17

11. 4)22 **12.** 9)74 **13.** 2)15 **14.** 6)19 **15.** 5)23

16. 3)17 **17.** 4)27 **18.** 3)25 **19.** 7)26 **20.** 9)33

21. 6)98 **22.** 4)83 **23.** 2)95 **24.** 5)76 **25.** 3)83

26. 4)89 **27.** 7)93 **28.** 3)91 **29.** 2)85 **30.** 7)75

31. 3)47 **32.** 3)98 **33.** 8)97 **34.** 4)79 **35.** 2)79

36. 2)53 **37.** 6)95 **38.** 4)91 **39.** 3)77 **40.** 2)93

41. 3)49 **42.** 5)99 **43.** 6)89 **44.** 3)82 **45.** 3)95

Dividing Hundreds, Tens, and Ones

Find $4\overline{)504}$.

Estimate: How many 4's in 5?
Think: $\underline{\quad?\quad} \times 4$ is about 5.
Try 1 in the hundreds place.

$$
\begin{array}{r}
1 \\
4\overline{)504} \\
-4\downarrow \\
\hline
10
\end{array}
$$

Multiply: $1 \times 4 = 4$

Subtract: $5 - 4 = 1$
Bring down the 0.

$$
\begin{array}{r}
1 \\
4\overline{)504} \\
4 \\
\hline
10
\end{array}
$$

Repeat the steps.
Estimate: How many 4's in 10?
Think: $\underline{\quad?\quad} \times 4$ is about 10.
Try 2 in the tens place.

$$
\begin{array}{r}
126 \\
4\overline{)504} \\
4 \\
\hline
10 \\
-\ 8\downarrow \\
\hline
24 \\
-24 \\
\hline
0
\end{array}
$$

Multiply and **subtract.**
Bring down the 4.
Repeat the steps to complete.
The quotient is 126.

Check.

$$
\begin{array}{r}
126 \\
\times\ 4 \\
\hline
504
\end{array}
$$

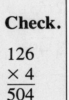

A. Complete.

1. $2\overline{)486}$ with 2 above and -4 below

2. $3\overline{)507}$ with 1 above and -3 below

3. $3\overline{)393}$ with 1 above

4. $4\overline{)484}$

B. Divide.

5. $2\overline{)862}$

6. $3\overline{)369}$

7. $4\overline{)608}$

8. $3\overline{)741}$

Divide.

1. 2)482   2. 4)884   3. 3)393   4. 4)488   5. 5)555

6. 3)339   7. 4)848   8. 2)842   9. 6)666   10. 2)882

11. 4)408   12. 7)777   13. 3)999   14. 2)884   15. 4)888

16. 3)525   17. 4)912   18. 5)685   19. 2)908   20. 3)861

21. 7)917   22. 3)831   23. 2)568   24. 7)903   25. 4)568

26. 3)504   27. 3)522   28. 8)904   29. 3)816   30. 2)768

31. 5)975   32. 2)658   33. 3)732   34. 4)656   35. 7)805

36. 6)702   37. 2)708   38. 4)512   39. 2)586   40. 5)795

41. 5)605   42. 3)402   43. 2)778   44. 7)973   45. 4)856

★46. 2)2,486   ★47. 4)8,448   ★48. 5)5,605

Solve.

49. 575 baseball cards in all
    5 packs of cards
    How many cards in each pack?

50. 976 marbles
    8 groups of marbles
    Same number in each group
    How many marbles in each group?

Larger Numbers with Remainders

Find $6\overline{)731}$.

Estimate: How many 6's in 7?
Try 1 in the hundreds place.

$$
\begin{array}{r}
1 \\
6\overline{)731} \\
-6\downarrow \\
\hline
13
\end{array}
$$

Multiply: $1 \times 6 = 6$
Subtract: $7 - 6 = 1$
Bring down the 3.

$$
\begin{array}{r}
12 \\
6\overline{)731} \\
6 \\
\hline
13
\end{array}
$$

Repeat the steps.
Estimate: How many 6's in 13?
Think: $\underline{?} \times 6$ is about 13.
Try 2 in the tens place.

$$
\begin{array}{r}
121\text{r}5 \\
6\overline{)731} \\
6 \\
\hline
13 \\
-12\downarrow \\
\hline
11 \\
-6 \\
\hline
5
\end{array}
$$

Multiply and **subtract.**
Bring down the 1.

Estimate, multiply, and **subtract**
to complete.
The quotient is 121.
The remainder is 5.

Check: $121 \times 6 = 726.$ $726 + 5 = 731$

A. Complete.

1. $\begin{array}{r} 32 \\ 2\overline{)645} \\ -6 \\ \hline 4 \end{array}$

2. $\begin{array}{r} 1 \\ 4\overline{)705} \\ -4 \\ \hline 30 \end{array}$

3. $\begin{array}{r} 1 \\ 6\overline{)854} \\ -6 \\ \hline 25 \end{array}$

4. $3\overline{)695}$

B. Divide.

5. $4\overline{)489}$

6. $2\overline{)689}$

7. $3\overline{)967}$

8. $3\overline{)703}$

Divide.

1. 6)677 **2.** 8)894 **3.** 3)986 **4.** 4)863 **5.** 2)833

6. 4)861 **7.** 7)781 **8.** 3)643 **9.** 5)573 **10.** 3)643

11. 2)447 **12.** 5)579 **13.** 4)849 **14.** 4)803 **15.** 6)611

16. 2)773 **17.** 3)877 **18.** 4)817 **19.** 6)743 **20.** 3)724

21. 3)737 **22.** 2)937 **23.** 3)791 **24.** 4)523 **25.** 4)674

26. 6)932 **27.** 4)934 **28.** 7)946 **29.** 3)764 **30.** 2)537

31. 3)854 **32.** 4)925 **33.** 3)704 **34.** 3)746 **35.** 8)926

36. 5)628 **37.** 6)734 **38.** 5)907 **39.** 3)709 **40.** 3)526

★ **41.** 3)3,964   ★ **42.** 3)3,743   ★ **43.** 5)5,432

Solve.

44. There are 828 books.
There are 6 books in each carton.
How many cartons are there?
How many books are left over?

45. There are 223 library books to sort.
There are 2 librarians. How many books
for each librarian to sort? How many are left?

Quotients Less than 100

Find $5\overline{)155}$.

Estimate: How many 5's in 1?
How many 5's in 15?

$5\overline{)155}$ Write the 3 in the tens place.

$$\begin{array}{r} 3 \\ 5\overline{)155} \\ -15\downarrow \\ \hline 5 \end{array}$$

Multiply: $3 \times 5 = 15$
Subtract: $15 - 15 = 0$
Bring down the 5.

$$\begin{array}{r} 3 \\ 5\overline{)155} \\ 15 \\ \hline 5 \end{array}$$

Repeat the steps.
Estimate: How many 5's in 5?
Write the 1 in the ones place.

$$\begin{array}{r} 31 \\ 5\overline{)155} \\ 15 \\ \hline 5 \\ -5 \\ \hline 0 \end{array}$$

Multiply and **subtract.**
The quotient is 31.

Check: $31 \times 5 = 155$

A. Find $3\overline{)222}$. Complete.

1. **Estimate:** How many 3's in 2? $3\overline{)222}$

   How many 3's in 22? $3\overline{)222}$

2. $22 \div 3$ is about ___?___ because
   $7 \times 3 = 21$.

3. Complete the division.

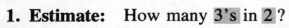

B. Divide.

4. $3\overline{)216}$ 5. $5\overline{)405}$ 6. $3\overline{)198}$ 7. $4\overline{)272}$

Divide.

1. $6\overline{)486}$ 2. $4\overline{)288}$ 3. $4\overline{)168}$ 4. $6\overline{)426}$ 5. $5\overline{)355}$

6. $4\overline{)368}$ 7. $7\overline{)567}$ 8. $3\overline{)276}$ 9. $5\overline{)455}$ 10. $6\overline{)366}$

11. $7\overline{)287}$ 12. $9\overline{)819}$ 13. $8\overline{)240}$ 14. $4\overline{)368}$ 15. $3\overline{)249}$

16. $6\overline{)186}$ 17. $5\overline{)305}$ 18. $7\overline{)427}$ 19. $8\overline{)648}$ 20. $3\overline{)213}$

21. $5\overline{)430}$ 22. $6\overline{)522}$ 23. $2\overline{)150}$ 24. $3\overline{)117}$ 25. $8\overline{)336}$

26. $5\overline{)265}$ 27. $3\overline{)195}$ 28. $4\overline{)136}$ 29. $9\overline{)378}$ 30. $7\overline{)602}$

31. $4\overline{)108}$ 32. $7\overline{)574}$ 33. $5\overline{)415}$ 34. $3\overline{)258}$ 35. $8\overline{)184}$

36. $6\overline{)144}$ 37. $4\overline{)340}$ 38. $9\overline{)315}$ 39. $7\overline{)154}$ 40. $6\overline{)216}$

Solve.

★ 41. $\square \div 3 = 69$ ★ 42. $\square \div 6 = 53$ ★ 43. $\square \div 4 = 76$

Solve.

44. There were 224 students at a class picnic. They went in 4 buses. Each bus had the same number of students. How many students went in each bus?

Two-Digit Quotients with Remainders

Find $7\overline{)428}$.

$7\overline{)428}$

Estimate: How many 7's in 4?
How many 7's in 42?
Write the 6 in the tens place.

$\begin{array}{r} 6 \\ 7\overline{)428} \\ -42 \\ \hline 8 \end{array}$

Multiply: $6 \times 7 = 42$
Subtract: $42 - 42 = 0$
Bring down the 8.

$\begin{array}{r} 6 \\ 7\overline{)428} \\ 42 \\ \hline 8 \end{array}$

Estimate: How many 7's in 8?
Think: $\underline{} \times 7$ is about 8.
Try 1 in the ones place.

$\begin{array}{r} 6\,1\,r\,1 \\ 7\overline{)428} \\ 42 \\ \hline 8 \\ -7 \\ \hline 1 \end{array}$

Multiply and **subtract.**
The quotient is 61.
The remainder is 1.

Check: $61 \times 7 = 427.\ 427 + 1 = 428$

A. Find $4\overline{)129}$. Complete.

   1. Estimate: How many 4's in 1? $4\overline{)129}$
How many 4's in 12? $\begin{array}{r} 3 \\ 4\overline{)129} \end{array}$

   2. Multiply: $3 \times 4 = \underline{}$

   3. Complete the division.

B. Divide.

   4. $5\overline{)457}$ **5.** $3\overline{)277}$ **6.** $5\overline{)343}$ **7.** $6\overline{)401}$

Divide.

1. $4\overline{)207}$ **2.** $6\overline{)549}$ **3.** $7\overline{)289}$ **4.** $3\overline{)274}$ **5.** $4\overline{)127}$

6. $7\overline{)498}$ **7.** $5\overline{)457}$ **8.** $6\overline{)368}$ **9.** $4\overline{)167}$ **10.** $5\overline{)158}$

11. $7\overline{)216}$ **12.** $4\overline{)326}$ **13.** $6\overline{)428}$ **14.** $5\overline{)309}$ **15.** $7\overline{)569}$

16. $3\overline{)143}$ **17.** $3\overline{)208}$ **18.** $5\overline{)461}$ **19.** $8\overline{)754}$ **20.** $3\overline{)208}$

21. $8\overline{)619}$ **22.** $6\overline{)404}$ **23.** $4\overline{)374}$ **24.** $6\overline{)553}$ **25.** $3\overline{)226}$

26. $2\overline{)139}$ **27.** $8\overline{)585}$ **28.** $9\overline{)401}$ **29.** $4\overline{)270}$ **30.** $3\overline{)193}$

31. $2\overline{)153}$ **32.** $4\overline{)307}$ **33.** $2\overline{)131}$ **34.** $4\overline{)343}$ **35.** $9\overline{)758}$

36. $4\overline{)386}$ **37.** $2\overline{)187}$ **38.** $5\overline{)468}$ **39.** $3\overline{)202}$ **40.** $5\overline{)393}$

41. $7\overline{)299}$ **42.** $7\overline{)300}$ **43.** $6\overline{)387}$ **44.** $8\overline{)607}$ **45.** $9\overline{)740}$

Solve.

★ **46.** $590 \div \square = 98\,r\,2$ ★ **47.** $444 \div \square = 55\,r\,4.$

Solve.

48. 452 baseball cards
7 children share them.
How many cards for each child?
How many cards left over?

49. 635 baseball yearbooks
Packaged 8 to a box
How many boxes?
How many yearbooks left over?

Problem Solving

Solve.

1. There were 5 players on the Tigers team. Each player scored 5 points by half time. What was the score? [HINT: $5 \times 5 = \underline{\ ?\ }$]

2. 96 people attended a game. There were 8 people in each row. How many rows of people were there?

3. 12 liters of apple juice were sold at half time. One liter made 4 glasses of juice. How many glasses of juice were sold?

4. The Lions scored 55 points. Each of 5 players scored an equal number of points. How many points did each player score?

5. One side of the gym holds 171 people. There are 9 rows of seats. How many people can fit in each row?

Divide.

1. $5\overline{)50}$ **2.** $5\overline{)500}$ **3.** $7\overline{)49}$ **4.** $9\overline{)63}$ **5.** $7\overline{)9}$
(233)   *(233)*   *(232)*   *(232)*   *(236)*

6. $8\overline{)70}$ **7.** $3\overline{)39}$ **8.** $7\overline{)84}$ **9.** $7\overline{)79}$ **10.** $8\overline{)94}$
(236)   *(238)*   *(238)*   *(240)*   *(240)*

11. $4\overline{)484}$ **12.** $2\overline{)724}$ **13.** $5\overline{)587}$ **14.** $5\overline{)609}$ **15.** $4\overline{)328}$
(248)   *(248)*   *(250)*   *(250)*   *(252)*

16. $3\overline{)228}$ **17.** $5\overline{)307}$ **18.** $9\overline{)865}$
(252)   *(254)*   *(254)*

Which number sentence fits the story? *(244)*

19. In one month Ben walks 68 blocks. How many blocks does he walk in 4 months.

$68 \times 4 = \underline{\ ?\ }$ $68 - 4 = \underline{\ ?\ }$ $68 \div 4 = \underline{\ ?\ }$

Solve. *(256)*

20. A small parking lot holds 75 cars. There are 5 rows of cars. How many cars are in each row?

Find Out!

Brainteasers

Solve these riddles.

1. How many apples can you put in an empty bag?

2. Carla had 8 apples. She ate all but 2. How many did she have left?

Divide.

1. $7\overline{)700}$ **2.** $7\overline{)70}$ **3.** $8\overline{)56}$ **4.** $9\overline{)81}$ **5.** $6\overline{)13}$
(233)   *(233)*   *(232)*   *(232)*   *(236)*

6. $6\overline{)44}$ **7.** $4\overline{)76}$ **8.** $6\overline{)66}$ **9.** $4\overline{)86}$ **10.** $3\overline{)82}$
(236)   *(238)*   *(238)*   *(240)*   *(240)*

11. $2\overline{)446}$ **12.** $3\overline{)411}$ **13.** $7\overline{)851}$ **14.** $6\overline{)803}$ **15.** $8\overline{)760}$
(248)   *(248)*   *(250)*   *(250)*   *(252)*

16. $6\overline{)366}$ **17.** $4\overline{)300}$ **18.** $4\overline{)306}$
(252)   *(254)*   *(254)*

Which number sentence fits the story? *(244)*

19. There are 333 different plants at the nursery. There are 9 plants on each table. How many tables are there?

$333 \times 9 = \underline{\quad?\quad}$ $333 \div 9 = \underline{\quad?\quad}$ $333 + 9 = \underline{\quad?\quad}$

Solve. *(256)*

20. There are 5 rose bushes in bloom. Each bush has 22 roses. How many roses have bloomed?

Basic Skills Check

1.

$$\begin{array}{r} 36 \\ + 48 \\ \hline \end{array}$$

  A 64
  B 74
  C 84
  D 86

2.

$$\begin{array}{r} 25 \\ + 35 \\ \hline \end{array}$$

  E 60
  F 61
  G 65
  H 70

3.

$60 - 37 =$

  A 17
  B 19
  C 21
  D 23

4.

$$\begin{array}{r} 7 \\ 1 \\ + 4 \\ \hline \end{array}$$

  E 10
  F 0
  G 7
  H 12

5.

$468 + 531 =$

  A 937
  B 939
  C 997
  D 999

6.

$$\begin{array}{r} 879 \\ - 516 \\ \hline \end{array}$$

  E 361
  F 362
  G 363
  H 364

7.

$77 - 48 =$

  A 21
  B 29
  C 31
  D 39

8.

$$\begin{array}{r} 451 \\ + 418 \\ \hline \end{array}$$

  E 869
  F 871
  G 873
  H 875

9.

$6 + 2 + 6 =$

  A 12
  B 14
  C 16
  D 18

10.

$$\begin{array}{r} 33 \\ - 26 \\ \hline \end{array}$$

  E 6
  F 7
  G 9
  H 10

11.

$59 + 29 =$

  A 78
  B 88
  C 98
  D 99

12.

$417 + 341 =$

  E 738
  F 756
  G 758
  H 759

Fraction Fun

We see **fractions** all around us.

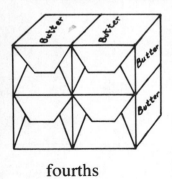
fourths

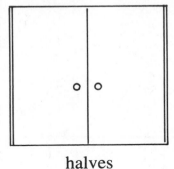
halves

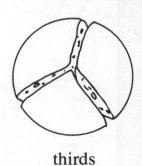
thirds

Here are some other fractions we see.

quarters

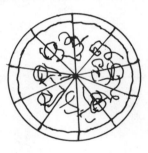
tenths

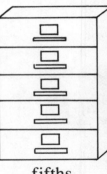
fifths

Sale

$1.89

Eileen,
Meet me
in a half
hour.
Janice

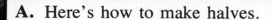

CHAPTER
FRACTIONS 10

A. Here's how to make halves.

    1. Take a sheet of paper.
       Fold it so the corners meet.

    2. Press it flat. Open it out.

    3. How many equal parts do
       you see?

    4. Color one half of the paper.

B. Here's how to make fourths.

    5. Take a sheet of paper.

    6. Fold it in half.

    7. Fold it in half again.

    8. Press it flat. Open it out.

    9. How many equal parts
       do you see?

    10. Color each fourth a
       different color.

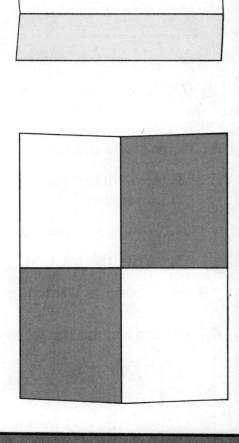

Fractions

Jeff, Zandra, and Elaine want to share a stick of cheese.
How much cheese will they each get?

Each one gets one third.
We write this as $\frac{1}{3}$.

A. Look at the picture.

1. How many equal parts
   are shown?

2. How many parts are shaded?

3. Write the fraction. $\frac{?}{4}$

▶ A fraction is written as $\frac{2}{4}$ $\frac{\text{number of parts shaded (numerator)}}{\text{number of parts in all (denominator)}}$

B. Write fractions for the shaded parts.

4.

5.

6.

Write fractions for the shaded parts.

1.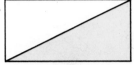

2.

3.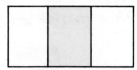

4.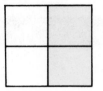

5.

6.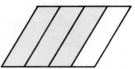

7.

8.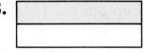

9.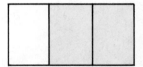

10.

★**11.**

★**12.**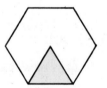

Find Out!
Brainteaser

Find the pattern. Complete.

1. $\frac{1}{2}, \frac{1}{3}, \frac{1}{4}, \frac{1}{5}, \underline{}, \underline{}, \underline{}$

2. $\frac{1}{2}, \frac{2}{4}, \frac{3}{6}, \frac{4}{8}, \underline{}, \underline{}, \underline{}$

3. $\frac{1}{2}, \frac{2}{2}, \frac{3}{2}, \frac{4}{2}, \underline{}, \underline{}, \underline{}$

Parts of a Set

Fractions also tell about parts of a group.
What part of the group is red flowers?

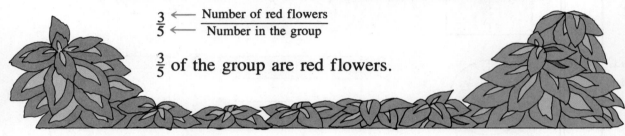

$\dfrac{3}{5}$ ← Number of red flowers / Number in the group

$\dfrac{3}{5}$ of the group are red flowers.

A. Look at the picture.

1. How many flowers in all?

2. How many flowers are yellow?

3. Write the fraction for the number of yellow flowers shown.

B. Look at the picture.

4. How many roses in all?

5. How many are red?

6. Write the fraction for the number of red roses.

C. Write a fraction for the shaded part of each group.

7.

8.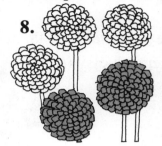

9.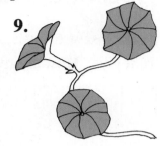

_____ Practice

Write a fraction for the shaded part of each group.

1.

2.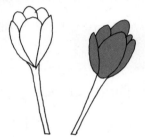

3.

4.

5.

6.

7.

8.

9.

Fractional Parts

Nancy saw 6 birds. She saw that $\frac{1}{2}$ of them were
bluejays. How many were bluejays?

To find $\frac{1}{2}$ of 6, think $6 \div 2 = \underline{\quad?\quad}$

Nancy saw 3 bluejays.

A. Look at the picture to find $\frac{1}{4}$ of 8.

    1. How many birds in all?

    2. Complete.

        $\frac{1}{4}$ of $8 = \underline{\quad?\quad}$

        [HINT: $8 \div 4 = \underline{\quad?\quad}$]

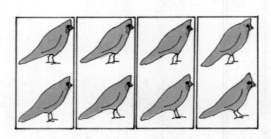

B. Complete.

    3.

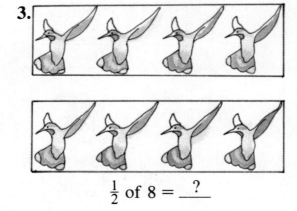

$\frac{1}{2}$ of $8 = \underline{\quad?\quad}$

    4.

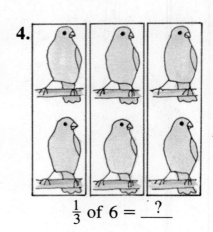

$\frac{1}{3}$ of $6 = \underline{\quad?\quad}$

Practice

Complete.

1.
$\frac{1}{2}$ of 4 = ___?___

2.
$\frac{1}{3}$ of 9 = ___?___

3.
$\frac{1}{4}$ of 12 = ___?___

4.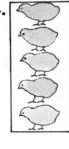
$\frac{1}{3}$ of 15 = ___?___

5.
$\frac{1}{5}$ of 10 = ___?___

6.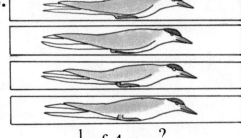
$\frac{1}{4}$ of 4 = ___?___

Solve.

7. 3 birds
$\frac{1}{3}$ flew away
How many flew away?

★**8.** 5 blackbirds
$\frac{1}{5}$ flew away
How many stay?

Equal Fractions

Look at the figures.

$\frac{1}{2}$ is yellow. $\frac{3}{6}$ is yellow.

$\frac{1}{2}$ is the same as $\frac{3}{6}$.

$\frac{1}{2}$ and $\frac{3}{6}$ are **equal fractions.**

A. Find another name for $\frac{1}{3}$.

1. What part of A is shaded?

2. What part of B is shaded?

3. Complete. $\frac{1}{3} = \frac{?}{6}$

B. Complete.

4.

$\frac{1}{2} = \frac{?}{4}$

5.

$\frac{2}{3} = \frac{?}{6}$

Complete.

1.

$$\frac{1}{4} = \frac{?}{8}$$

2.

$$\frac{3}{4} = \frac{?}{8}$$

3.

$$\frac{2}{5} = \frac{?}{10}$$

4.

$$\frac{2}{3} = \frac{?}{6}$$

5.

$$\frac{2}{4} = \frac{4}{?}$$

6.

$$\frac{1}{5} = \frac{2}{?}$$

★ **7.**

$$\frac{1}{?} = \frac{?}{6}$$

★ **8.**

$$\frac{2}{?} = \frac{1}{?}$$

Write a fraction for the shaded parts. *(262)*

1.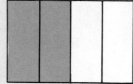

2.

3.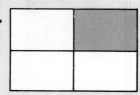

Write a fraction for the shaded part of each group. *(264)*

4.

5.

6.

Complete. *(266)*

7.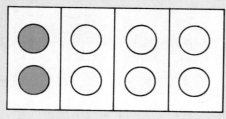

$\frac{1}{4}$ of 8 = ___?___

8.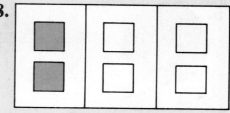

$\frac{1}{3}$ of 6 = ___?___

Complete. *(268)*

9.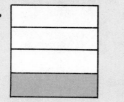

$\frac{1}{4} = \frac{?}{8}$

10.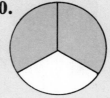

$\frac{2}{3} = \frac{4}{?}$

Keeping Fit

Divide.

1. 2)62   **2.** 4)56   **3.** 3)66

4. 3)68   **5.** 6)85   **6.** 4)47

7. 4)848   **8.** 3)360   **9.** 4)768

10. 8)864   **11.** 4)436   **12.** 7)455   **13.** 9)828   **14.** 6)540

15. 7)308   **16.** 3)470   **17.** 5)783   **18.** 8)964   **19.** 4)750

20. 7)374   **21.** 6)430   **22.** 8)521   **23.** 4)273   **24.** 4)341

25. 7)853   **26.** 4)625   **27.** 8)905   **28.** 4)934   **29.** 7)946

30. 3)746   **31.** 2)537   **32.** 3)854   **33.** 4)523   **34.** 4)674

What time is shown? Use the ⎯:⎯ form.

35.

36.
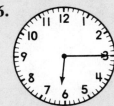

37.

38.

39.

40.

41.

42.
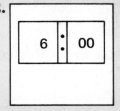

6 : 00

43.
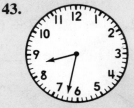

Problem Solving

Sometimes it takes two steps to solve a problem.

Dale bought 3 books of tickets for rides. Each book had 5 tickets. He used 8 tickets. How many tickets are left?

What is asked? ——————→ How many are left?

What do you know? ——→ 3 books of tickets
                        5 tickets in each book
                        8 tickets were used

Which operation? ——————→ **Step 1:** $3 \times 5 = 15$ tickets in all.

                        Step 2: $15 - 8 = 7$ tickets left.

Dale has 7 tickets left.

Solve.

The roller coaster had 15 riders. When it stopped 8 people got off. 6 more people got on. How many people were on the roller coaster?

1. Step 1: $15 - 8 = $ ___?___

2. Step 2: $7 + 6 = $ ___?___

3. There were ___?___ people on the roller coaster.

Solve.

Gabriel won 12 prizes. He gave away 7 of them. Then he won 3 more prizes. How many prizes does he have now?

1. Step 1: $12 - 7 = \underline{}$

2. Step 2: $5 + 3 = \underline{}$

3. Gabriel had $\underline{}$ prizes.

Denise knocked down 4 pins. 3 of the pins were worth 3 points each. One pin was worth 5 points. What was her score?

4. Step 1: $3 \times 3 = \underline{}$

5. Step 2: $9 + 5 = \underline{}$

6. Denise scored $\underline{}$ points.

Earl had 10 tickets. He used $\frac{1}{2}$ of them. Then Betty gave him 6 more tickets. How many tickets does he have now?

7. Step 1: $\frac{1}{2}$ of 10 [HINT: $10 \div 2 = \underline{}$]

8. Step 2: $5 + 6 = \underline{}$

9. Earl has $\underline{}$ tickets.

At the dart booth Mrs. Rivera broke 8 balloons. 7 balloons were worth 5 points. 1 balloon was worth 10 points. What was her score?

10. Step 1: $7 \times 5 = \underline{}$

11. Step 2: $35 + 10 = \underline{}$

12. Mrs. Rivera scored $\underline{}$ points.

Decimals

1 dime = 10¢   10 dimes = $1.00

1 dime is one tenth of a dollar.
You can write one tenth as 0.1.
0.1 is a decimal.

└── Remember to write a zero here.

A. Look at the picture.

    1. How many dimes are shown?

    2. 2 dimes is __?__ tenths
       of a dollar.

    3. Write the decimal.

B. Write a decimal for each.

    4.

    5.

Write a decimal for each.

1.

2.

3.

4.

5.

★ 6.

Comparing Fractions

Which is greater, $\frac{1}{2}$ or $\frac{1}{3}$?

$\frac{1}{2}$ is greater than $\frac{1}{3}$

Write this as $\frac{1}{2} > \frac{1}{3}$.

A. Look at the pictures.

1. What fraction is shown in W?

2. What fraction is shown in X?

3. Which is greater?

W   X

4. Compare. [Replace ≡ with > or <.]
   $\frac{1}{3} \equiv \frac{1}{5}$ and $\frac{1}{5} \equiv \frac{1}{3}$

B. Look at the pictures.

5. What fraction is shown in Y?

Y

6. What fraction is shown in Z?

Z

7. Which is greater?

8. Compare. $\frac{2}{3} \equiv \frac{4}{9}$ and $\frac{4}{9} \equiv \frac{2}{3}$

C. Compare. Use > or < to replace ≡ .

9.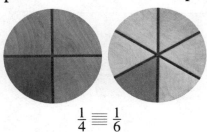

$$\frac{1}{4} \equiv \frac{1}{6}$$

10.

$$\frac{1}{3} \equiv \frac{2}{4}$$

Compare. Use > or < to replace ≡ .

1.

$$\frac{2}{3} \equiv \frac{1}{3}$$

2.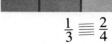

$$\frac{4}{8} \equiv \frac{6}{8}$$

3.

$$\frac{1}{6} \equiv \frac{1}{8}$$

4.

$$\frac{1}{5} \equiv \frac{1}{4}$$

5.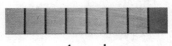

$$\frac{4}{12} \equiv \frac{3}{6}$$

6.

$$\frac{2}{3} \equiv \frac{2}{5}$$

★ **7.** $\frac{2}{8} \equiv \frac{2}{4}$ ★ **8.** $\frac{3}{8} \equiv \frac{3}{4}$ ★ **9.** $\frac{6}{9} \equiv \frac{1}{3}$ ★ **10.** $\frac{1}{5} \equiv \frac{1}{12}$

Problem Solving • Cooks

Solve.

1. 6 eggs
   $\frac{1}{3}$ are brown eggs.
   How many are brown?
   [HINT: Think: $6 \div 3 = \underline{\quad ? \quad}$]

2. 10 tomatoes
   $\frac{1}{2}$ are sliced.
   How many are sliced?

3. 8 slices of bread
   $\frac{1}{2}$ are toasted.
   How many slices are toasted?

4. 5 chickens
   $\frac{1}{5}$ are cooked.
   How many are cooked?

5. 12 apples
   $\frac{1}{6}$ are green.
   How many are green?

Career

Write fractions for the shaded parts. (262, 264)

1.

2.

3.

4.

Complete. (266, 268)

5.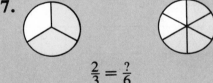

$\frac{1}{2}$ of 6 = _____?_____

6.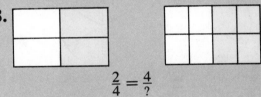

$\frac{1}{3}$ of 6 = _____?_____

7.

$\frac{2}{3} = \frac{?}{6}$

8.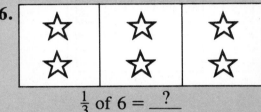

$\frac{2}{4} = \frac{4}{?}$

Compare. (276)

9.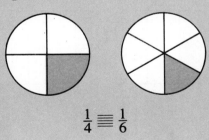

$\frac{1}{4} \equiv \frac{1}{6}$

10.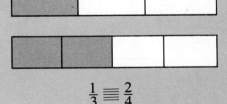

$\frac{1}{3} \equiv \frac{2}{4}$

Solve. (272, 278)

11. 30 people on a bus.
8 got off when it stopped.
3 more people got on.
How many people on the
bus?

12. 8 flowers
$\frac{1}{2}$ are yellow
How many flowers are
yellow?

Write fractions for the shaded parts. (262, 264)

1. 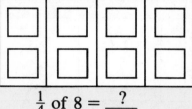 **2.** **3.** **4.**

Complete. (266, 268)

5.

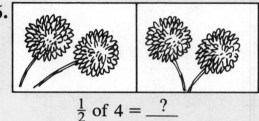

$\frac{1}{4}$ of 8 = ___?___

6.

$\frac{1}{2}$ of 4 = ___?___

7.

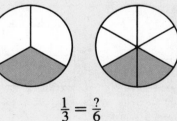

$\frac{1}{3} = \frac{?}{6}$

8.

$\frac{2}{5} = \frac{4}{?}$

Compare. (276)

9.

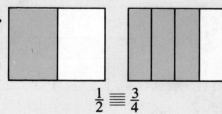

$\frac{1}{2} \equiv \frac{3}{4}$

10.

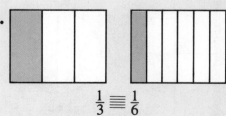

$\frac{1}{3} \equiv \frac{1}{6}$

Solve. (272, 278)

11. 12 people in the dentist's office. 3 people leave the office. 4 people arrive. How many people now in the office?

12. 12 apples
$\frac{1}{3}$ are green
How many green apples?

Basic Skills Check

1. What time is it?

A 11:05   B 11:25

C 11:50   D 5:55

2. Which figure does not show halves?

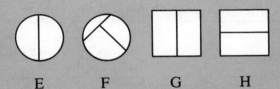

E   F   G   H

3. Count by 10's. What number is missing?

950   960   970   ____   990

A 790   B 976

C 978   D 980

4. Which is a triangle?

E   F   G   H

5. Which figure shows that it is divided into fourths?

A   B   C   D

6. What time is it?

E 12:15   F 12:30

G 12:45   H 1:00

7. Compare.

37 ○ 88

A <   B >

C =   D +

8. How much in all?

E 70¢   F 71¢

G 81¢   H 90¢

Lines and Line Segments

▶ The shortest path between two points is called a line segment.

▶ A line goes on forever in two directions.

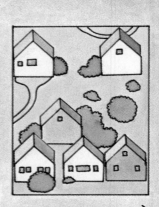

line

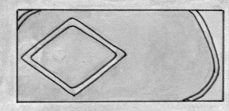
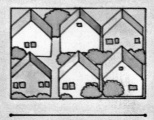

line segment

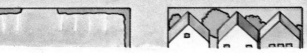

A. Follow these steps to make a line segment.

1. Mark 2 points on your paper.

2. Write *A* above one point.

3. Write *B* above the other point.

4. Use your ruler to connect the points.

B. Follow these steps to make a line.

5. Mark 2 points on your paper.

6. Label the points C and D.

7. Draw a line segment through C and D like this.

8. Put an arrow on each end.

C. Write line or line segment.

9.   **10.**   **11.**   **12.**

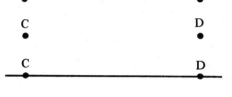

Practice

Write line or line segment.

1.   **2.**   **3.**   **4.**

5.   **6.**   **7.**   **8.**

Rectangles, Squares, and Triangles

This figure is a rectangle.

A rectangle has 4 sides and 4 square corners. Square corners are called **right angles.**

A. Get an index card.

   1. Use a centimeter ruler. Measure the sides.

      AB __?__   BD __?__   CD __?__   AC __?__

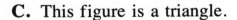

   2. Are any sides the same length?

▶ The opposite sides of a rectangle are the same length.

B. This figure is a square.

   3. Are the corners right angles?

   4. Measure the sides.

   5. Are any sides the same length?

   6. Is a square a rectangle?

     ▶ A square has all sides the same length.

C. This figure is a triangle.

   7. How many sides?

   8. How many corners?

     ▶ A triangle has 3 sides and 3 corners.

D. Write triangle, rectangle, or square.

9. 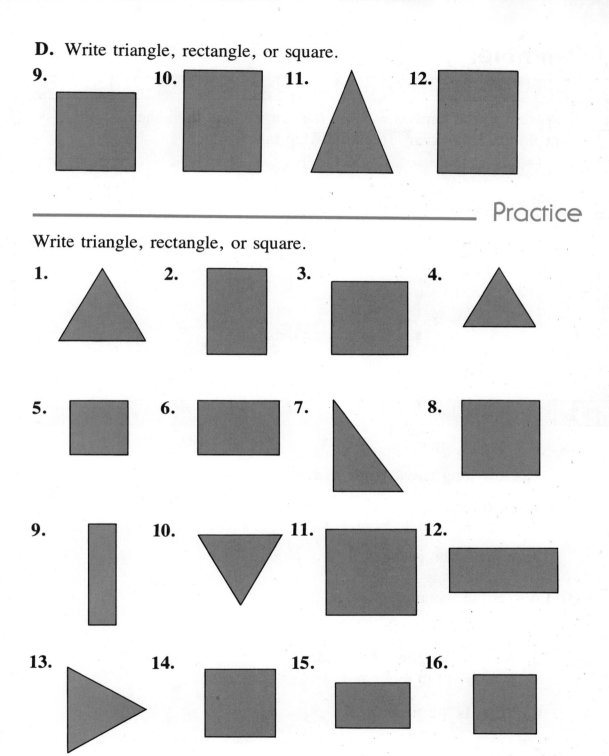   10.   11.   12.

Write triangle, rectangle, or square.

1.   2.   3.   4.

5.   6.   7.   8.

9.   10.   11.   12.

13.   14.   15.   16.

Perimeter

Meg went to the hardware store, the library, and then she went home. How many steps did Meg take?

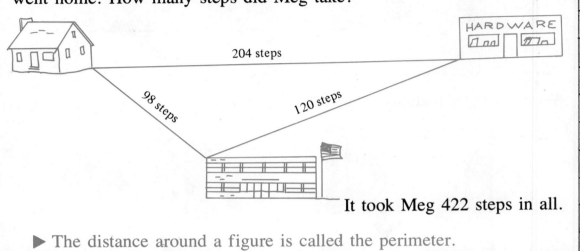

204 steps

98 steps

120 steps

HARDWARE

It took Meg 422 steps in all.

▶ The distance around a figure is called the perimeter.

A. Look at the square.

    1. How long is each side of the square?

    2. Add the lengths.
      3 cm + 3 cm + 3 cm + 3 cm = ___?___ cm

    3. What is the perimeter?

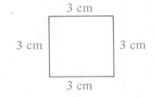

3 cm

3 cm   3 cm

3 cm

B. Look at the rectangle.

    4. How long is each side?

    5. Add the lengths of the sides.
      3 cm + 4 cm + 3 cm + 4 cm = ___?___ cm

    6. What is the perimeter?

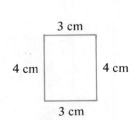

3 cm

4 cm   4 cm

3 cm

C. Find the perimeters.

7.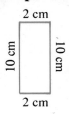
2 cm
10 cm
10 cm
2 cm

8.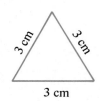
3 cm
3 cm
3 cm

9.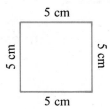
5 cm
5 cm
5 cm
5 cm

──────────────────────────────────── Practice

Find the perimeters.

1.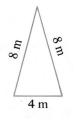
8 m
8 m
4 m

2.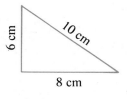
6 cm
10 cm
8 cm

3.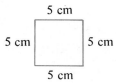
5 cm
5 cm
5 cm
5 cm

4.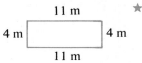
24 cm
12 cm
12 cm
24 cm

5.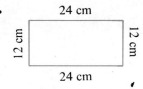
5 cm
10 cm
7 cm

6.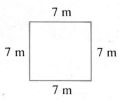
7 m
7 m
7 m
7 m

7.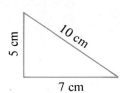
11 m
4 m
4 m
11 m

★ **8.**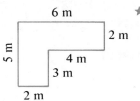
6 m
2 m
5 m
4 m
3 m
2 m

★ **9.**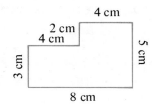
4 cm
2 cm
4 cm
5 cm
3 cm
8 cm

- - - - - - - - - - - - - - - - - - - **Find Out!**
Brainteasers

1. The perimeter of a square is 16 cm. Draw the square.

2. The perimeter of a rectangle is 16 cm. Draw the rectangle.

Circles

These are circles.

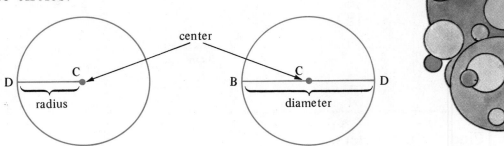

center

▶ A radius is a line segment
from the center to a point on
the circle.
Radii means more than one radius.

▶ A diameter is a line segment
that connects two points on
the circle and goes through
the center.

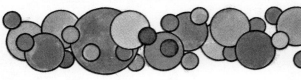

A. Look at the circle.

1. Point __?__ is the center.

2. One radius is between points
C and __?__ .

3. The diameter is between
points A and __?__ .

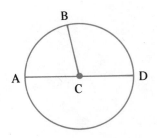

How many radii are shown?

4.   5.

How many diameters are shown?

6.   7.

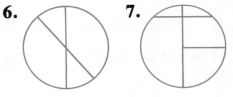

Other Shapes

Globe

Garbage Can

Building

Road Marker

A. Look at the picture above. Which objects have these shapes?

1.

cylinder

2.

cone

3.

sphere

4.

cube

B. Name one other object for each shape.

Practice

Write the shape of each figure.

1.

2.

3.

4.

5.

6.

7.

8.

Write the name of each figure.

1.
(282)

2.
(282)

3.
(284)

4.
(284)

5.
(284)

6.
(289)

7.
(289)

8.
(289)

9. How many radii are shown?
(288)

10. How many diameters are shown?
(288)

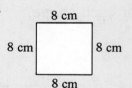

Find the perimeters. (286)

11. 4 cm

6 cm

4 cm

12. 8 cm

8 cm · 8 cm

8 cm

13. 9 cm

6 cm · 6 cm

9 cm

Find Out!
Brainteaser

Which figure completes the pattern?

     ____?____

Keeping Fit

Add.

1. 42 + 7	**2.** 82 + 16	**3.** 76 + 8
4. 36 + 24	**5.** 230 + 132	**6.** 265 + 9

7. 375 + 16	**8.** 268 + 135	**9.** 235 + 465	**10.** 359 + 196	**11.** 758 + 469

Subtract.

12. 39 − 6	**13.** 43 − 21	**14.** 62 − 4	**15.** 67 − 48	**16.** 90 − 25
17. 489 − 76	**18.** 637 − 124	**19.** 352 − 127	**20.** 893 − 685	**21.** 808 − 255
22. 624 − 86	**23.** 346 − 148	**24.** 504 − 327	**25.** 800 − 178	**26.** 600 − 587

Multiply.

27. 20 × 10	**28.** 40 × 3	**29.** 32 × 3	**30.** 42 × 2	**31.** 36 × 2
32. 48 × 3	**33.** 204 × 2	**34.** 323 × 3	**35.** 624 × 3	**36.** 317 × 3
37. 182 × 4	**38.** 360 × 3	**39.** 628 × 8	**40.** 352 × 5	**41.** 187 × 6

Divide.

42. $8\overline{)48}$	**43.** $9\overline{)72}$	**44.** $6\overline{)27}$	**45.** $6\overline{)39}$	**46.** $3\overline{)69}$
47. $4\overline{)84}$	**48.** $3\overline{)77}$	**49.** $4\overline{)47}$	**50.** $3\overline{)369}$	**51.** $2\overline{)840}$
52. $3\overline{)371}$	**53.** $5\overline{)674}$	**54.** $2\overline{)36}$	**55.** $7\overline{)85}$	**56.** $3\overline{)58}$

Problem Solving: Best Buy

One container of milk costs 76¢.
Two containers of milk cost $1.50.
Which is the better buy?

$$\begin{array}{r} 75 \\ 2\overline{)150} \\ 14 \\ \hline 10 \\ 10 \\ \hline 0 \end{array}$$ ⟵—— When you buy 2 containers
of milk each container
costs 75¢.

$76 - 75 = 1$¢
1¢ is saved on each container.
Buying 2 containers is the better buy.

Solve to find the better buy.

1. One package of flower seeds costs 35¢.
   3 packages cost 99¢.
   a. Find $3\overline{)99}$.
   b. $35 - 33 = \underline{\quad ? \quad}$
   c. How much is saved on each package?
   d. Which is the better buy?

Practice

Solve to find the better buy.

1. One pencil cost 5¢.
   Five pencils cost 20¢.
   a. Find $5\overline{)20}$
   b. $5 - 4 = \underline{\quad?\quad}$
   c. How much is saved on each pencil?
   d. Which is the better buy?

2. One can of soup costs 45¢.
   Two cans of soup cost 80¢.
   a. Find $2\overline{)80}$
   b. $45 - 40 = \underline{\quad?\quad}$
   c. How much is saved on each can?
   d. Which is the better buy?

3. One toothbrush costs 65¢.
   Three toothbrushes cost $1.50.
   a. Find $3\overline{)150}$
   b. $65 - 50 = \underline{\quad?\quad}$
   c. How much is saved on each toothbrush?
   d. Which is the better buy?

Symmetry

Some figures can be folded along a line so the two parts match.
If you folded each figure on the line, the two parts would match.

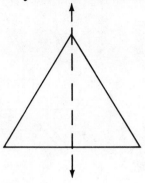 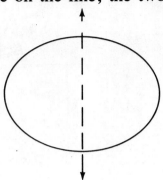 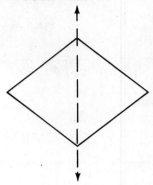

▶ If the two parts match, the figures are **symmetric.** The line is
called a **line of symmetry.**

A. Take a sheet of paper.

   1. Draw lines as shown.

   2. Fold on the black line.

   3. Do the parts match?

   4. Is the line a line of symmetry?

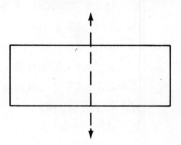

B. Trace each figure. Draw a line of symmetry.

  5.   **6.**   **7.**

 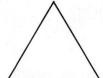 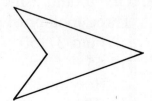

Which are symmetric? Write yes or no.

1.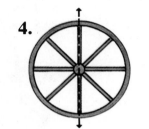

2.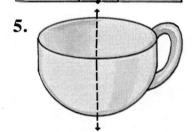

3.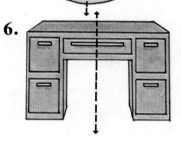

4.

5.

6.

Trace each figure. Draw a line of symmetry.

7.

8.

9.

10.

11.

12.

Find Out!
Activity

A square has 4 lines of symmetry.
Get a piece of square paper.
Fold it to see if you can find the lines of symmetry.

Area

Area is measured in square units.

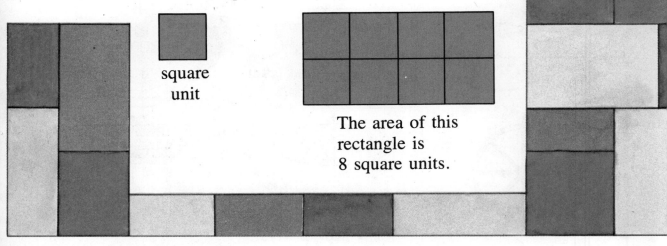

square unit

The area of this rectangle is 8 square units.

A. Look at this figure.

1. How many square units are in the figure?

2. The area of the figure is ___?___ square units.

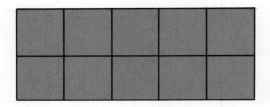

B. Find the areas.

3.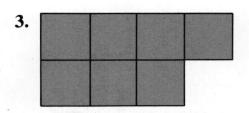

4.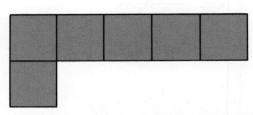

5.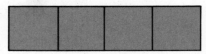

6.

Find the areas.

1.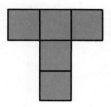

2.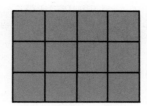

3.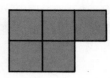

4.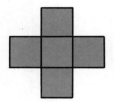

5.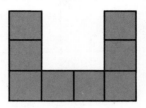

6.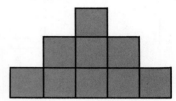

7.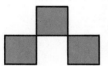

8.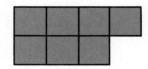

9.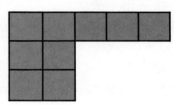

10.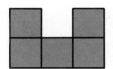

11.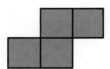

12.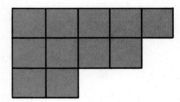

Find the areas of the shaded parts.

★ 13.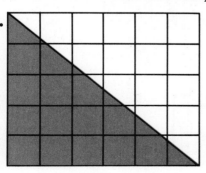

★ 14.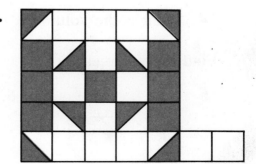

Volume

A cubic unit is used to measure volume.

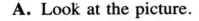

1 cubic unit   The volume is 8 cubic units.

A. Look at the picture.

   1. How many cubic units are there?

   2. What is the volume?

B. Look at the picture.

   3. Count the cubic units.

   4. What is the volume?

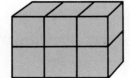

C. Find the volumes.

   5.

   6.

   7.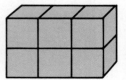

Find the volumes.

1.

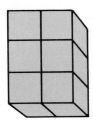

2.

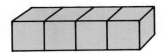

3.

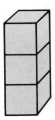

4.

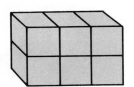

5.

6.

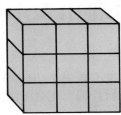

7.

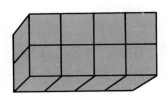

8.

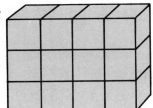

9.

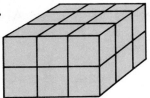

10.

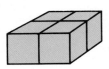

★11.

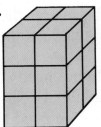

★12.

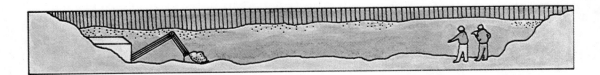

Problem Solving

1. In one week Ron spent $1.98 for clay and $1.15 for paint. About how much did he spend?
[HINT: Estimate $2.00 + $1.00 = __?__]

2. Pat's model plane has 716 pieces. She has put together 360 of the pieces. About how many pieces are left?

3. Leah has 216 large stamps and 167 small stamps. About how many stamps does she have?

4. Dick's jigsaw puzzle has 75 blue pieces for the sky. The rest of the puzzle has 88 pieces. About how many pieces does the puzzle have?

5. Miguel needs 67 pieces of paper to make a large mobile. He has cut 32 pieces. About how many pieces does he need to cut?

6. Emily had $7.23 to spend on art supplies. She spent $4.80 on paint. About how much money did she have left?

Write the name of each.

1.
(282)

2.
(284)

3.
(284)

4.
(289)

5.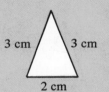
(289)

6.
(289)

Find the perimeters. (286)

7.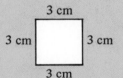
3 cm
3 cm   3 cm
3 cm

8.
3 cm   3 cm
2 cm

9.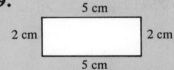
5 cm
2 cm   2 cm
5 cm

10. How many diameters? (288)

11. How many radii? (288)

12. Find the area. (296)

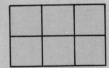

13. Find the volume. (298)

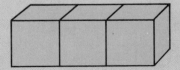

Which is the better buy? (292)

14. One pen for 45¢
Two for 80¢

Solve. (300)

15. There are 32 dogs and 26 cats. About how many animals?

Write the name of each.

1. (282)

2. (284)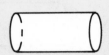

3. (284)

4. (289)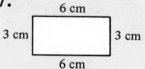

5. (289)

6. (289)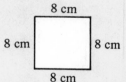

Find the perimeters. (286)

7.

6 cm
3 cm ___ 3 cm
6 cm

8.

5 cm / 5 cm
3 cm

9.

8 cm
8 cm ___ 8 cm
8 cm

10. How many diameters? (288)

11. How many radii? (288)

12. Find the area. (296)

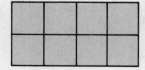

13. Find the volume. (298)

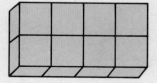

Which is the better buy? (292)

14. One tomato for 25¢
Three for 69¢

Solve. (300)

15. There are 18 adults and 23 children. About how many people?

Basic Skills Check

1. Who has the most crayons?

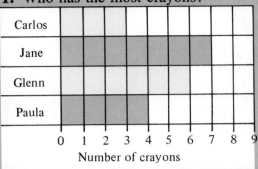

A Carlos   B Jane

C Glenn   D Paula

---

2. How many sunny days were there last week?

E 2   F 3

G 4   H 5

---

3. Which unit would be used to measure the height of the doorway in your class?

A meter   B gram

C liter   D kilogram

---

4. How many pounds does the bag of potatoes weigh?

E 2   F 4

G 9   H 10

---

5. Leonard is making a cake. He puts the ingredients in the bowl. He mixes it. Now he pours the batter into the pan. What is the next thing he will do?

A cut it   B frost it

C put it in the oven   D cool it

---

6. Michael bought a loaf of bread. He gave the clerk 3 dimes, 4 nickels, and 3 pennies. How much did he pay?

E 33¢   F 48¢

G 49¢   H 53¢

On The Wing

Alexis, Don, Gail, and Joy have started collecting butterflies. They are keeping a record of how many each has caught.

Alexis	🦋	🦋	🦋						
Don	🦋	🦋	🦋	🦋	🦋	🦋			
Gail	🦋	🦋	🦋	🦋					
Joy	🦋	🦋	🦋	🦋	🦋	🦋	🦋	🦋	

Each 🦋 means one butterfly.

A. Look at the chart above.

    1. How many butterflies did Gail catch?

    2. Who caught more, Don or Alexis?

    3. Who caught the most?

CHAPTER 12
GRAPHS

This chart shows how many days each child spent collecting butterflies.

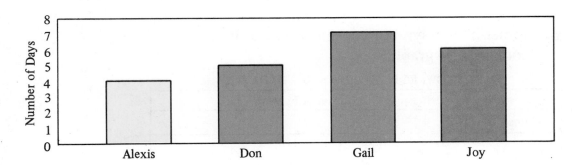

Look at the chart above.

1. Who spent the most days collecting butterflies?

2. Who spent the fewest?

3. How many days did Joy spend collecting?

Pictographs

Graphs show facts. This is a pictograph.

TREES PLANTED ON EARTH DAY

Trees	Number of Trees
Maple	🌳 🌳 🌳 🌳 🌳
Oak	🌳 🌳
Birch	🌳 🌳 🌳 🌳 🌳 🌳

Each 🌳 means 1 tree.

A. Look at the graph above.

    1. How many maple trees were planted?

    2. What kind of tree was planted the most?

    3. How would the graph show 12 oak trees?

B. Sometimes a symbol can mean more than one. Look at this graph.

FLOWERS PLANTED ON EARTH DAY

Flowers	Number of Flowers
Rose	🌼 🌼 🌼
Daisy	🌼 🌼 🌼 🌼 🌼
Violet	🌼 🌼 🌼 🌼

Each 🌼 means 2 flowers.

    4. How many flowers does each 🌼 mean?

    5. How many violets were planted?

    6. How many roses were planted?

Use these pictographs to find the answers.

PEOPLE WHO HELPED ON EARTH DAY

People	Number of People
Girls	👤 👤 👤 👤
Boys	👤 👤
Women	👤 👤 👤 👤 👤 👤
Men	👤 👤 👤 👤 👤 👤 👤 👤

Each 👤 means 1 person.

1. How many girls helped?

2. How many boys helped?

3. How many women helped?

TASKS ON EARTH DAY

Tasks	Number of People
Planting trees	👤 👤 👤 👤 👤 👤
Planting flowers	👤 👤 👤 👤
Serving refreshments	👤 👤
Clean up	👤 👤 👤 👤 👤 👤 👤 👤 👤 👤

Each 👤 means 2 people.

4. How many people planted trees?

5. How many people served refreshments?

6. How many people helped clean up?

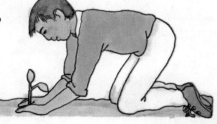

Bar Graphs

A **bar graph** shows information.
Patricia and her friends are cleaning a small park.

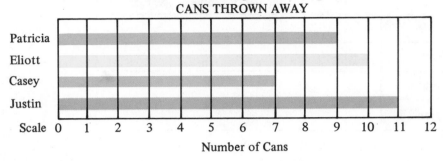

CANS THROWN AWAY

Patricia												
Eliott												
Casey												
Justin												

Scale 0 1 2 3 4 5 6 7 8 9 10 11 12

Number of Cans

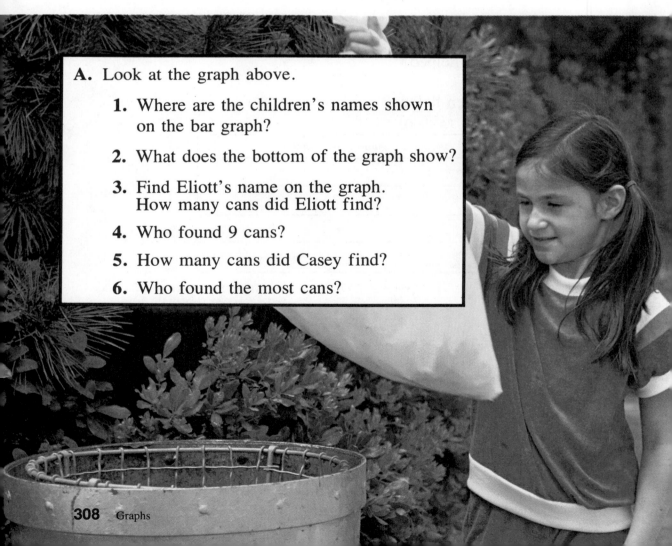

A. Look at the graph above.

1. Where are the children's names shown on the bar graph?

2. What does the bottom of the graph show?

3. Find Eliott's name on the graph. How many cans did Eliott find?

4. Who found 9 cans?

5. How many cans did Casey find?

6. Who found the most cans?

Use these bar graphs to find the answers.

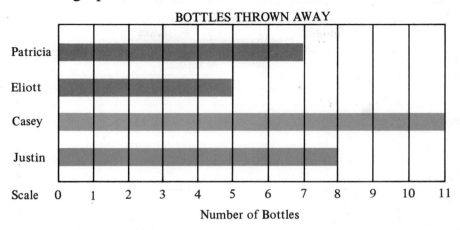

BOTTLES THROWN AWAY

1. How many bottles did Casey find?

2. Who found 8 bottles?

3. Who found the fewest bottles?

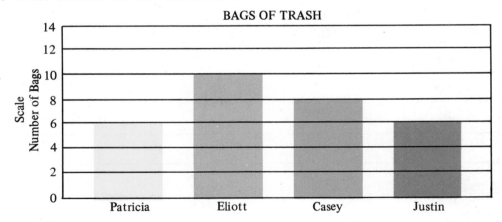

BAGS OF TRASH

4. Who collected the most bags of trash?

5. Who had the same number of bags as Patricia?

6. What scale is used?

★ **7.** How many bags of trash were collected in all?

Making a Pictograph

Mrs. Williamson's class studied the seasons in science class. The children graphed their birthdays by seasons.

BIRTHDAYS BY SEASONS

Seasons	Number of Birthdays
Spring	
Summer	
Autumn	
Winter	

Each 🎂 means 1 birthday.

Make your own pictograph.

BIRTHDAYS BY SEASONS

Season	Number of Birthdays
Spring	
Summer	
Autumn	
Winter	

Each 🎂 means 1 birthday.

1. Find out all the birthdays in your class.

2. Find out in what season each birthday is.

3. Draw a graph like the one above.

4. Put the information on the graph.

Making a Bar Graph

Corrine made a graph of how she spent her day.

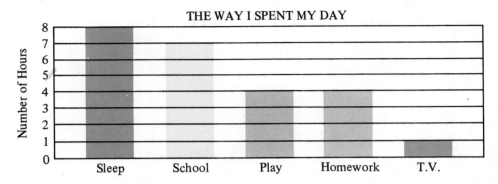

THE WAY I SPENT MY DAY

Make your own bar graph. Copy this chart.

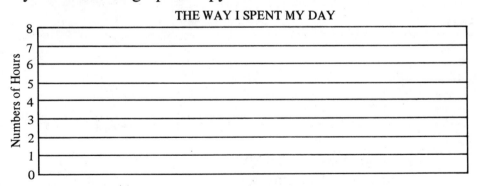

THE WAY I SPENT MY DAY

1. Keep a record of the things you do today.

2. Draw a graph like the one above.

3. Draw in the bars to show the information.
Remember to label each of the bars.

Circle Graphs

A **circle graph** shows parts of a whole. This graph shows what children did on their first day of summer camp.

Saturday

swimming | horseback riding
hiking | canoeing

A. Look at the graph above.

1. $\frac{1}{4}$ of the group went swimming. What part of the group went horseback riding?

2. What part went hiking?

3. What part went canoeing?

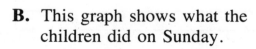

B. This graph shows what the children did on Sunday.

4. What part of the group played baseball?

5. What part did crafts?

6. What part played volleyball?

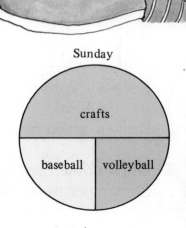

Sunday

crafts

baseball | volleyball

Use these circle graphs to find the answers.

1. What part of the group was in the relay races?

2. What part did archery?

3. What part played kickball?

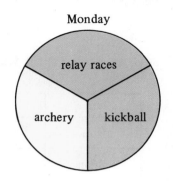

Monday

relay races

archery   kickball

4. What part of the group went hiking?

5. What part played volleyball?

★ 6. What part did crafts?

★ 7. What part went horseback riding?

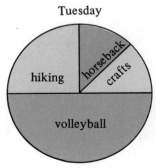

Tuesday

hiking   horseback   crafts

volleyball

Use this pictograph to find the answers. *(306, 308)*

GLASSES OF LEMONADE SOLD

Name	Number of Glasses
Maurice	
Brian	
Erica	

Each ⬜ means 2 glasses.

1. How many glasses did Maurice sell?

2. Who sold 6 glasses?

3. Who sold the most?

4. Who sold the least?

Use this bar graph to find the answers.

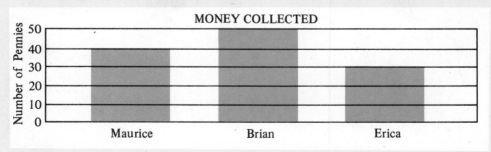

5. How many pennies did Maurice collect?

6. Who collected 50 pennies?

7. How many pennies did Erica collect?

Add.

1.	33 + 6	**2.**	58 + 4	**3.**	43 + 17
4.	139 + 4	**5.**	295 + 18	**6.**	425 + 175

Subtract.

7.	48 − 5	**8.**	74 − 6	**9.**	92 − 27	**10.**	80 − 14	**11.**	265 − 13
12.	461 − 135	**13.**	482 − 279	**14.**	508 − 243	**15.**	513 − 265	**16.**	900 − 135

Multiply.

17.	21 × 4	**18.**	15 × 3	**19.**	42 × 3	**20.**	70 × 6	**21.**	123 × 3
22.	104 × 5	**23.**	124 × 4	**24.**	253 × 5	**25.**	317 × 6	**26.**	346 × 8

Divide.

27. 6)54 **28.** 8)51 **29.** 4)88 **30.** 4)90 **31.** 7)105

32. 6)325 **33.** 3)609 **34.** 5)653 **35.** 8)925 **36.** 6)800

Match the name with the figure.

37. triangle

38. cube

39. cylinder

40. line segment

41. line

42. cone

a.   d.

b.   e.

c.    f.

Problem Solving

The Save With Us Bank has 3 branch banks in Flower
City. It has 4 branch banks in Garden City.
Ms. Outler works 4 days a week. How many branch
banks in all?

$3 + 4 = 7$ There are 7 branch banks in all.

You do not need to know Ms. Outler works 4 days a week.
This is extra information.

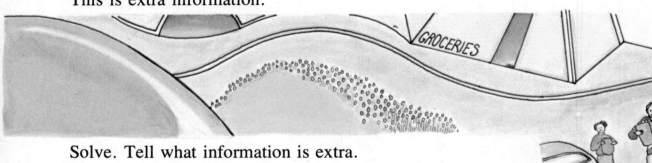

Solve. Tell what information is extra.

1. Shelley saves money at the Save With Us Bank. She
   saved $4.25 in January, $5.00 in March, and $8.00
   in April. How much did Shelley save in March and
   April?

2. Lou had $28.75 in the bank. He took out $5.00 last
   week. He took out $8.00 this week. How much did
   he take out?

3. Willie wants a watch. The watch costs $20. He has
   $18 in the bank now. He took out $9 last week. How
   much more money does Willie need to buy the watch?

4. Marie works at the bank. She works 4 hours at a
   time. She worked 12 hours last week and 16 hours
   this week. How many more hours did Marie work
   this week?

Solve. Tell what information is extra.

1. The bank gardener bought flowers to plant. He bought 23 tulips, 14 crocuses, and 42 daffodils. How many more tulips than crocuses are there?

2. Sarah has worked at the bank for 3 years. She works 7 hours a day. She works 5 days a week. How many hours does she work each week?

3. Mr. Costa works 6 hours a day. He spends $3 each day for lunch. How much does he spend for lunch for 5 days?

4. Samuel had $345 in the bank. Yesterday he put $155 more in the bank. He also made a car payment of $68.20. How much does Samuel have in the bank now?

5. The Save With Us Bank has 2 parking lots. The large parking lot holds 80 cars. There are 62 cars in the large parking lot. How many more cars can park in the large lot?

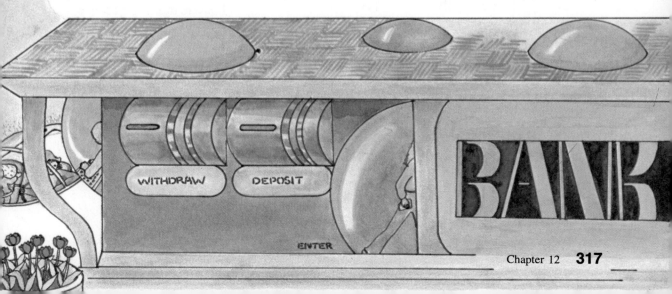

Probability

A. Look at the box.

    1. How many blocks are there?

    2. How many are blue?

    3. How many are red?

    4. If you pick a block it will be either
   __?__ or __?__ .

        ▶ The chances of picking the red
   block are 1 out of 2.

    5. What are the chances of picking the
   blue block?

B. Try this probability.

    6. How many sides does a dime have?

    7. What are the sides called?

    8. Flip your dime. Which side came up?

    9. Flip the dime again. Which side
   came up now?

    10. This chart shows a record of
   flips.
   Did heads come up about the same as
   tails?

Heads	Tails
卌 卌 卌 l	卌 卌 卌

C. Make a chart like the one above.

    11. Flip your dime 30 times. Record the results.

    12. Is the number of heads about the same as the
   number of tails?

You will need 2 blocks. One block should
be red and the other blue.

1. How many colors are there?

2. What are the chances that you will pick
the red block?

3. What are the chances that you will pick
the blue block?

Red	Blue

4. Make a chart like the one above. Shake
the box of blocks. Pick a block from
the box. Record your results.

5. Place the block back in the box. Shake,
then pick a block again. Record your results.

6. Do this 38 more times.

7. Count your marks. Is the number of red draws
about the same as the number of blue draws?

More Probability

A. Look at this spinner.

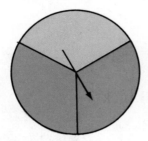

    1. How many parts are on this spinner?

    2. What color does the arrow point to?

▶ The chances of the arrow pointing to red are 1 out of 3.

    3. What are the chances of the arrow pointing to purple?

    4. What are the chances of the arrow pointing to blue?

B. Look at this spinner.

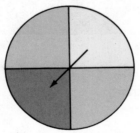

    5. How many parts are on this spinner?

    6. What color does the arrow point to?

▶ The chances of the arrow pointing to green are 1 out of 4.

    7. What are the chances of the arrow pointing to pink?

    8. What are the chances of the arrow pointing to yellow?

    9. What are the chances of the arrow pointing to blue?

1. Copy this chart. You will use it to play a game.

Blue	Red	Yellow	Green

You will also need 4 crayons and a box. One crayon should be blue; one red; one yellow; and one green.

2. Place the crayons in the box. Shake it.

3. Without looking, pick a crayon.

4. Record a mark in the correct place on the chart.

5. Put the crayon back into the box.

6. Shake the box again. Pick another crayon.

7. Record a mark in the correct place on the chart.

8. Pick a crayon 20 times.

9. How many times did you pick a blue crayon?

10. How many times did you pick a red crayon?

11. How many times did you pick a yellow crayon?

12. How many times did you pick a green crayon?

Problem Solving

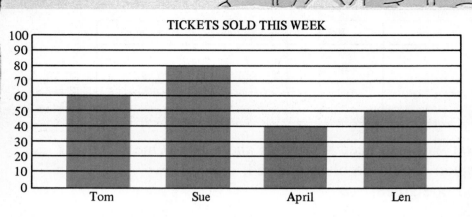

TICKETS SOLD THIS WEEK

Solve by using the graph.

1. How many tickets did Tom and April sell together?

2. How many more tickets did Sue sell than Len?

3. Who sold twice as many tickets as April?

4. Who sold 20 less tickets than Sue?

5. Last week April sold three times as many tickets as she sold this week. How many tickets did she sell last week?

6. Last week Len sold 24 more tickets than he did this week. How many tickets did Len sell last week?

7. How many tickets did the four children sell this week?

★ **8.** Each ticket costs 50¢. How much money did April collect?

★ **9.** How much money was earned by the four children this week?

Use this pictograph to find the answers. *(306, 307)*

MARBLES COLLECTED

Name	Number of Marbles
Sonya	Ⓞ Ⓞ Ⓞ Ⓞ
Louis	Ⓞ Ⓞ Ⓞ Ⓞ Ⓞ Ⓞ
Alvin	Ⓞ Ⓞ Ⓞ Ⓞ Ⓞ Ⓞ Ⓞ Ⓞ
Trudy	Ⓞ Ⓞ Ⓞ Ⓞ

Each Ⓞ means 1 marble.

1. How many marbles does each Ⓞ mean?

2. How many marbles did Louis collect?

3. Who collected the most?

4. Who collected the least?

5. How many marbles did Trudy collect?

Use this bar graph to find the answers. *(308, 309)*

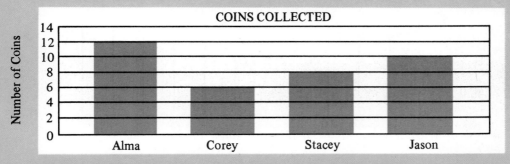

6. How many coins has Corey collected?

7. Who collected the most coins?

8. How many coins did Jason collect?

9. What scale is used?

Use this pictograph to find the answers. *(306,307)*

KINDS OF FISH CAUGHT

Name	Number of Fish
Catfish	⊳○ ⊳○ ⊳○ ⊳○
Trout	⊳○ ⊳○
Bass	⊳○ ⊳○ ⊳○

Each ⊳○ means 3 fish

1. How many fish does each ⊳○ mean?

2. How many trout were caught?

3. What kind of fish was caught the most?

4. How many catfish were caught?

5. How many bass were caught?

Use this bar graph to find the answers. *(308,309)*

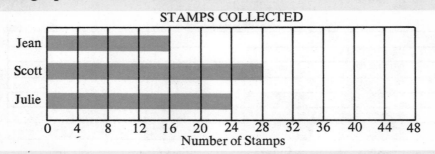

6. Who collected the fewest stamps?

7. How many did Julie collect?

8. Who collected the most stamps?

9. What scale is used?

Basic Skills Check

1.

$16 \div 4 = $ ___?___

A	B	C	D
2	4	6	8

2.

$4 \times 3 = $ ___?___

E	F	G	H
7	12	13	14

3.

$12 \div 2 = $ ___?___

A	B	C	D
3	4	6	10

4.

$2 \times 4 = $ ___?___

E	F	G	H
6	7	8	10

5.

$5 \times 3 = $ ___?___

A	B	C	D
12	14	15	18

6.

$25 \div 5 = $ ___?___

E	F	G	H
4	5	6	7

7.

$$\begin{array}{r} 3 \\ \times\, 4 \\ \hline \end{array}$$

A	B	C	D
12	15	18	20

8.

$20 \div 4 = $ ___?___

E	F	G	H
2	3	4	5

9.

$9 \div 3 = $ ___?___

A	B	C	D
0	1	3	5

10.

$15 \div 3 = $ ___?___

E	F	G	H
5	6	7	8

11.

$$\begin{array}{r} 2 \\ \times\, 5 \\ \hline \end{array}$$

A	B	C	D
2	4	6	10

12.

$$\begin{array}{r} 6 \\ \times\, 2 \\ \hline \end{array}$$

E	F	G	H
12	15	19	20

The Addition Table

+	0	1	2	3	4	5	6	7	8	9
0	0	1	2	3	4	5	6	7	8	9
1	1	2	3	4	5	6	7	8	9	10
2	2	3	4	5	6	7	8	9	10	11
3	3	4	5	6	7	8	9	10	11	12
4	4	5	6	7	8	9	10	11	12	13
5	5	6	7	8	9	10	11	12	13	14
6	6	7	8	9	10	11	12	13	14	15
7	7	8	9	10	11	12	13	14	15	16
8	8	9	10	11	12	13	14	15	16	17
9	9	10	11	12	13	14	15	16	17	18

The Multiplication Table

X	0	1	2	3	4	5	6	7	8	9
0	0	0	0	0	0	0	0	0	0	0
1	0	1	2	3	4	5	6	7	8	9
2	0	2	4	6	8	10	12	14	16	18
3	0	3	6	9	12	15	18	21	24	27
4	0	4	8	12	16	20	24	28	32	36
5	0	5	10	15	20	25	30	35	40	45
6	0	6	12	18	24	30	36	42	48	54
7	0	7	14	21	28	35	42	49	56	63
8	0	8	16	24	32	40	48	56	64	72
9	0	9	18	27	36	45	54	63	72	81

EXTRA PRACTICE

Add. *(Use with page 2.)*

1. 3 + 4	**2.** 2 + 1	**3.** 0 + 3	**4.** 5 + 4	**5.** 7 + 0	**6.** 9 + 1	**7.** 7 + 2
8. 4 + 4	**9.** 8 + 2	**10.** 5 + 3	**11.** 6 + 2	**12.** 7 + 3	**13.** 5 + 2	**14.** 6 + 4
15. 6 + 1	**16.** 5 + 5	**17.** 4 + 1	**18.** 6 + 3	**19.** 2 + 7	**20.** 4 + 6	**21.** 2 + 5
22. 3 + 7	**23.** 2 + 6	**24.** 4 + 5	**25.** 2 + 8	**26.** 3 + 5	**27.** 4 + 3	**28.** 1 + 9

★ How many ways can you write each of these as the sum of two numbers?

Example   8   2 + 6 = 8

29. 8   **30.** 5   **31.** 9

Add. *(Use with page 4.)*

1. 7 + 7	**2.** 9 + 5	**3.** 8 + 7	**4.** 9 + 4	**5.** 8 + 5	**6.** 9 + 6	**7.** 8 + 8
8. 6 + 7	**9.** 8 + 4	**10.** 9 + 7	**11.** 6 + 6	**12.** 7 + 5	**13.** 5 + 6	**14.** 9 + 8
15. 9 + 3	**16.** 6 + 8	**17.** 9 + 9	**18.** 7 + 4	**19.** 8 + 6	**20.** 7 + 9	**21.** 8 + 3
22. 4 + 9	**23.** 7 + 6	**24.** 6 + 9	**25.** 5 + 7	**26.** 8 + 9	**27.** 5 + 8	**28.** 3 + 9

★ How many ways can you write each of these as the sum of two numbers under 10?

29. 17   **30.** 11   **31.** 14

Subtract. *(Use with page 8.)*

1. 9 − 4	**2.** 10 − 5	**3.** 8 − 6	**4.** 9 − 2	**5.** 10 − 4	**6.** 9 − 5	**7.** 10 − 6
8. 8 − 2	**9.** 9 − 6	**10.** 10 − 7	**11.** 9 − 3	**12.** 8 − 5	**13.** 9 − 7	**14.** 10 − 3
15. 8 − 4	**16.** 10 − 8	**17.** 7 − 3	**18.** 10 − 2	**19.** 8 − 3	**20.** 6 − 2	**21.** 7 − 4
22. 6 − 4	**23.** 5 − 2	**24.** 7 − 5	**25.** 10 − 1	**26.** 6 − 3	**27.** 7 − 2	**28.** 5 − 3
29. 10 − 9	**30.** 8 − 8	**31.** 6 − 0	**32.** 4 − 3	**33.** 7 − 1	**34.** 9 − 0	**35.** 6 − 1

★ How many ways can you write each of these as the difference of two numbers. The numbers must be less than 11.

Example 3 $10 - 7 = 3$

36. 3   **37.** 8   **38.** 5

Subtract. *(Use with page 10.)*

1. 16 − 7	**2.** 15 − 6	**3.** 18 − 9	**4.** 14 − 6	**5.** 15 − 7	**6.** 14 − 9	**7.** 17 − 9
8. 14 − 7	**9.** 16 − 8	**10.** 13 − 6	**11.** 17 − 8	**12.** 11 − 3	**13.** 16 − 9	**14.** 14 − 8
15. 12 − 8	**16.** 13 − 7	**17.** 13 − 5	**18.** 15 − 9	**19.** 13 − 8	**20.** 12 − 6	**21.** 15 − 8
22. 12 − 5	**23.** 11 − 4	**24.** 12 − 7	**25.** 13 − 9	**26.** 12 − 4	**27.** 13 − 4	**28.** 12 − 9
29. 11 − 9	**30.** 15 − 9	**31.** 13 − 7	**32.** 12 − 3	**33.** 11 − 3	**34.** 14 − 5	**35.** 11 − 8

★ Complete.

36. $17 - \square = 8$ **37.** $15 - \square = 9$ **38.** $12 - \square = 7$ **39.** $11 - \square = 6$

Which operation would you use? Write + or −. *(Use with page 16.)*

1. 5 apples
6 oranges
How many in all?

2. 15 balls
6 lost
How many are left?

3. 11 bees
4 dead
How many alive?

4. 9 dresses
5 skirts
How many in all?

5. 7 pens
Bought 3 more
How many in all?

6. 18 roses
9 tulips
How many more roses?

7. 8 rings
7 watches
How many in all?

8. 14 children
8 boys
How many girls?

9. 13 blue lamps
9 yellow lamps
How many more blue lamps?

10. 8 large boxes
4 small boxes
How many in all?

★ Make up stories to go with these facts.

11. $10 - 3$

12. $7 + 6$

Add. *(Use with page 25.)*

1.	**2.**	**3.**	**4.**	**5.**	**6.**	**7.**
4 + 3	7 + 8	6 + 1	8 + 0	9 + 9	3 + 2	2 + 8

8.	**9.**	**10.**	**11.**	**12.**	**13.**	**14.**
6 + 7	5 + 5	8 + 5	4 + 9	6 + 9	5 + 4	7 + 3

Subtract.

15.	**16.**	**17.**	**18.**	**19.**	**20.**	**21.**
14 − 5	10 − 7	12 − 8	6 − 3	15 − 9	8 − 6	11 − 6

22.	**23.**	**24.**	**25.**	**26.**	**27.**	**28.**
9 − 2	17 − 8	13 − 7	8 − 3	12 − 6	5 − 0	16 − 9

Write the number. *(Use with page 36.)*

1. Seventy-six

2. Sixty-eight

3. Thirty-one

4. Fifty

5. Eight hundred

6. Seven hundred ninety

7. Three hundred four

8. Six hundred forty-one

Write the number. *(Use with page 38.)*

1. Two thousand

2. Two thousand, one hundred

3. Three thousand, nine

4. Four thousand, thirty

5. Nine thousand, fifty-two

6. Eight thousand, ten

7. One thousand, six hundred seventy

8. Five thousand, nine hundred forty-six

★ **9.** Fifteen hundred

★ **10.** Thirty-six hundred

What is the value of each underlined digit? *(Use with page 40.)*

1. 4<u>7</u>

2. 8<u>6</u>

3. 9<u>8</u>

4. <u>7</u>3

5. 6<u>4</u>

6. 9<u>5</u>3

7. <u>6</u>59

8. 7<u>6</u>0

9. 80<u>5</u>

10. <u>4</u>32

11. <u>3</u>,486

12. 1,08<u>9</u>

13. 6,4<u>5</u>7

14. <u>9</u>,372

15. 3,<u>4</u>56

Write the number.

16. 5 tens and 6 ones

17. 70 + 4

18. 4 hundreds, 8 tens, and 7 ones

19. 300 + 0 + 5

20. 3 thousands, 5 hundreds, 9 tens, and 1 one

21. 2,000 + 600 + 90 + 4

Which number sentence fits the story? *(Use with page 46.)*

1. 12 cakes
4 pies
How many more cakes?
12 + 4 = __?__
12 − 4 = __?__
16 − 4 = __?__

2. 7 glasses
8 cups
How many in all?
8 − 7 = __?__
8 − 1 = __?__
7 + 8 = __?__

3. 11 books
9 read
How many more to read?
11 − 9 = __?__
11 + 9 = __?__
20 − 9 = __?__

4. 6 boxes
5 bags
How many in all?
6 + 5 = __?__
6 − 5 = __?__
11 − 6 = __?__

5. 4 large bows
9 small bows
How many in all?
9 − 4 = __?__
9 − 5 = __?__
4 + 9 = __?__

6. 15 cars
6 broken
How many work?
15 + 6 = __?__
15 − 6 = __?__
15 − 9 = __?__

★**7.** 9 boxes
15 wanted
How many more needed?
9 + □ = 15
9 + 15 = □
15 − 8 = □

★**8.** 12 boys
7 chairs
How many chairs needed?
12 + 7 = □
7 + □ = 12
7 + 12 = □

Compare. Use > or <. *(Use with page 48.)*

1. 35 ≡ 38

2. 46 ≡ 56

3. 81 ≡ 73

4. 15 ≡ 19

5. 645 ≡ 298

6. 776 ≡ 900

7. 824 ≡ 850

8. 743 ≡ 749

9. 2,719 ≡ 3,732

10. 1,400 ≡ 1,500

11. 4,892 ≡ 4,829

12. 7,304 ≡ 8,149

13. 9,496 ≡ 9,486

14. 7,352 ≡ 8,471

★**15.** 48,639 ≡ 52,113

★**16.** 34,428 ≡ 32,128

Round each to the nearest ten. *(Use with page 50.)*

1. 42	**2.** 71	**3.** 39	**4.** 25	**5.** 72
6. 55	**7.** 84	**8.** 78	**9.** 15	**10.** 53
11. 67	**12.** 94	★ **13.** 234	★ **14.** 585	★ **15.** 718

Round each to the nearest hundred.

16. 175	**17.** 284	**18.** 341	**19.** 750	**20.** 813
21. 555	**22.** 545	**23.** 678	**24.** 421	**25.** 251
26. 883	**27.** 634	★ **28.** 3,492	★ **29.** 7,218	★ **30.** 4,553

Round each to the nearest dollar.

31. $1.65	**32.** $3.48	**33.** $7.50	**34.** $1.38	**35.** $5.21
36. $1.89	**37.** $5.65	**38.** $3.98	**39.** $5.45	**40.** $5.55
41. $2.17	**42.** $6.73	★ **43.** $23.98	★ **44.** $38.52	★ **45.** $849.49

Add. *(Use with page 58.)*

1. $\begin{array}{r} 4 \\ 3 \\ +8 \\ \hline \end{array}$	**2.** $\begin{array}{r} 7 \\ 1 \\ +6 \\ \hline \end{array}$	**3.** $\begin{array}{r} 4 \\ 4 \\ +5 \\ \hline \end{array}$	**4.** $\begin{array}{r} 1 \\ 8 \\ +7 \\ \hline \end{array}$	**5.** $\begin{array}{r} 3 \\ 4 \\ +5 \\ \hline \end{array}$	**6.** $\begin{array}{r} 2 \\ 6 \\ +7 \\ \hline \end{array}$
7. $\begin{array}{r} 5 \\ 4 \\ 6 \\ +2 \\ \hline \end{array}$	**8.** $\begin{array}{r} 4 \\ 4 \\ 4 \\ +3 \\ \hline \end{array}$	**9.** $\begin{array}{r} 6 \\ 4 \\ 7 \\ +2 \\ \hline \end{array}$	**10.** $\begin{array}{r} 5 \\ 7 \\ 3 \\ +4 \\ \hline \end{array}$	**11.** $\begin{array}{r} 3 \\ 4 \\ 1 \\ +5 \\ \hline \end{array}$	**12.** $\begin{array}{r} 2 \\ 3 \\ 4 \\ +5 \\ \hline \end{array}$
13. $\begin{array}{r} 2 \\ 4 \\ 1 \\ +6 \\ \hline \end{array}$	**14.** $\begin{array}{r} 5 \\ 7 \\ 3 \\ +2 \\ \hline \end{array}$	**15.** $\begin{array}{r} 8 \\ 5 \\ 2 \\ +4 \\ \hline \end{array}$	**16.** $\begin{array}{r} 7 \\ 1 \\ 2 \\ +5 \\ \hline \end{array}$	**17.** $\begin{array}{r} 3 \\ 7 \\ 4 \\ +5 \\ \hline \end{array}$	**18.** $\begin{array}{r} 1 \\ 6 \\ 8 \\ +3 \\ \hline \end{array}$

★ **19.** 6 + 9 + 5 + 4 + 3   ★ **20.** 1 + 3 + 5 + 6 + 7

Add. *(Use with page 62.)*

1.	12 + 6	**2.**	35 + 4	**3.**	60 + 7	**4.**	14 + 3	**5.**	71 + 8
6.	33 + 25	**7.**	20 + 70	**8.**	45 + 42	**9.**	36 + 41	**10.**	30 + 60
11.	243 + 5	**12.**	350 + 6	**13.**	702 + 7	**14.**	600 + 300	**15.**	254 + 23
16.	316 + 52	**17.**	821 + 148	★ **18.**	930 + 147	★ **19.**	508 + 961	★ **20.**	812 + 476

Add. *(Use with page 64.)*

1.	35 + 8	**2.**	47 + 6	**3.**	53 + 9	**4.**	18 + 8	**5.**	46 + 4	**6.**	35 + 5
7.	38 + 48	**8.**	57 + 23	**9.**	26 + 46	**10.**	75 + 5	**11.**	54 + 38	**12.**	57 + 17
13.	25 + 8	**14.**	75 + 15	**15.**	38 + 26	**16.**	29 + 43	**17.**	54 + 9	**18.**	42 + 29

★ Complete.

19. $39 + \square = 84$ **20.** $63 + \square = 91$ **21.** $47 + \square = 86$

Add. *(Use with page 66.)*

1.	468 + 7	**2.**	524 + 6	**3.**	843 + 9	**4.**	107 + 5	**5.**	372 + 8
6.	705 + 28	**7.**	809 + 67	**8.**	327 + 46	**9.**	633 + 57	**10.**	256 + 35
11.	408 + 409	**12.**	524 + 138	**13.**	609 + 135	**14.**	256 + 434	**15.**	729 + 148
16.	724 + 238	**17.**	456 + 436	★ **18.**	451 + 739	★ **19.**	537 + 625	★ **20.**	724 + 336

Add. *(Use with page 68.)*

1. 263 + 74	2. 842 + 90	3. 650 + 73	4. 785 + 83	5. 371 + 65
6. 474 + 175	7. 657 + 280	8. 183 + 572	9. 392 + 174	10. 446 + 172
11. 584 + 235	12. 358 + 591	13. 146 + 483	14. 587 + 362	15. 717 + 192
16. 134 + 393	17. 641 + 198	★ 18. 379 + 860	★ 19. 153 + 854	★ 20. 592 + 743

Write the number sentence that fits the story. *(Use with page 72.)*

1. 8 red balloons
5 green balloons
How many in all?

2. 14 birds
6 flew away.
How many are left?

3. 27 boys
31 girls
How many in all?

4. 125 red pencils
48 green pencils
How many in all?

5. 11 scouts
2 leaders
How many more scouts?

6. 17 monkeys
9 hats
How many more monkeys?

7. 178 trucks
21 cars
35 buses
How many in all?

8. 23 apples
45 oranges
14 pears
How many in all?

9. 65 boxes
29 filled
How many empty?

10. 286 ants
141 bees
How many in all?

★**11.** 3 dozen eggs
2 eggs broken
How many not broken?

★ **12.** 7 pairs of shoes
4 socks
How many more shoes?

Add. *(Use with page 74.)*

1. 95 + 9	**2.** 47 + 78	**3.** 65 + 85	**4.** 298 + 7	**5.** 475 + 75
6. 649 + 73	**7.** 493 + 58	**8.** 536 + 288	**9.** 354 + 167	**10.** 497 + 306
11. 368 + 242	**12.** 276 + 428	**13.** 637 + 165	**14.** 581 + 199	**15.** 537 + 385
16. 286 + 476	**17.** 143 + 779	**18.** 147 + 753	**19.** 194 + 788	**20.** 174 + 179
★ **21.** 284 + 929	★**22.** 174 + 892	★ **23.** 329 + 875	★ **24.** 648 + 563	★ **25.** 285 + 949

Add. *(Use with page 76.)*

1. 34 21 + 43	**2.** 53 8 + 14	**3.** 47 29 + 63	**4.** 26 75 + 38	**5.** 41 54 + 5
6. 63 25 + 47	**7.** 93 87 + 61	**8.** 45 234 + 351	**9.** 382 47 + 174	**10.** 371 55 + 236
11. 215 132 + 452	**12.** 321 416 + 133	**13.** 546 172 + 231	★ **14.** 829 512 + 351	★ **15.** 733 156 + 234

Add. *(Use with page 78.)*

1. $ 4.26 + 0.43	**2.** $ 5.65 + 1.70	**3.** $ 3.82 + 1.45	**4.** $ 6.78 + 2.05	**5.** $ 3.55 + 2.75
6. $ 1.91 + 0.87	**7.** $ 3.75 + 0.79	**8.** $ 4.28 + 3.45	**9.** $ 2.84 + 3.16	**10.** $ 4.08 + 3.79
11. $ 4.95 2.87 + 1.52	**12.** $ 1.86 0.94 + 2.47	**13.** $ 2.53 1.98 + 4.72	★ **14.** $ 6.48 7.29 + 0.37	★ **15.** $ 1.56 3.98 + 6.74

Estimate the sums. Round to the nearest ten. *(Use with page 80.)*

1. 53 + 29	**2.** 67 + 23	**3.** 42 + 37	**4.** 29 + 55	**5.** 71 + 18

1. 53
    + 29

2. 67
    + 23

3. 42
    + 37

4. 29
    + 55

5. 71
    + 18

6. 84
    + 12

7. 36
    + 49

8. 44
    + 33

9. 25
    + 51

10. 59
    + 28

11. 35
    + 47

12. 15
    + 64

★ **13.** 371
    + 212

★ **14.** 245
    + 132

★ **15.** 183
    + 349

Estimate the sums. Round to the nearest hundred or dollar.

16. 473
    + 327

17. 259
    + 481

18. 519
    + 350

19. 782
    + 149

20. 379
    + 451

21. 284
    + 249

22. 408
    + 371

23. 179
    + 513

24. 333
    + 527

25. 125
    + 156

26. $ 1.57
    + 4.83

27. $ 3.49
    + 2.87

28. $ 7.15
    + 1.52

29. $ 6.23
    + 1.48

30. $ 4.54
    + 4.35

31. $ 6.19
    + 2.65

32. $ 8.41
    + 1.20

★ **33.** $ 21.67
    + 15.98

★ **34.** $ 14.13
    + 43.56

★ **35.** $ 26.21
    + 12.74

Add. *(Use with page 85.)*

1. 7
    3
    + 2

2. 3
    2
    + 6

3. 8
    4
    + 5

4. 3
    6
    4
    + 2

5. 7
    1
    4
    + 5

6. 86
    + 13

7. 234
    + 561

8. 458
    + 24

9. 547
    + 349

10. 683
    + 294

11. 583
    + 274

12. 347
    + 84

13. 465
    + 398

14. 275
    + 485

15. 749
    + 154

16. 37
    25
    + 41

17. 146
    285
    + 394

18. $ 3.47
    + 2.98

19. $ 1.54
    + 3.86

20. $ 4.98
    2.56
    + 1.83

Subtract. *(Use with page 90.)*

1.	87	2.	49	3.	76	4.	97	5.	88
	− 5		− 28		− 4		− 40		− 58

6.	29	7.	68	8.	90	9.	300	10.	463
	− 6		− 53		− 60		− 100		− 41

11.	987	12.	734	13.	79	14.	854	15.	796
	− 5		− 124		− 38		− 623		− 245

16.	456	17.	387	★ 18.	3,478	★ 19.	2,436	★ 20.	5,432
	− 41		− 247		− 155		− 325		− 1,210

Subtract. *(Use with page 94.)*

1.	34	2.	53	3.	94	4.	52	5.	370
	− 9		− 7		− 36		− 35		− 8

6.	157	7.	943	8.	687	9.	483	10.	726
	− 28		− 38		− 339		− 434		− 318

11.	247	12.	531	13.	173	14.	536	15.	840
	− 29		− 529		− 57		− 229		− 527

★ Complete.

16. $738 - \square = 529$ **17.** $586 - \square = 239$

Subtract. *(Use with page 98.)*

1.	849	2.	638	3.	789	4.	644	5.	348
	− 73		− 45		− 293		− 352		− 73

6.	327	7.	989	8.	453	9.	226	10.	546
	− 295		− 396		− 291		− 194		− 482

11.	647	12.	833	13.	346	14.	524	15.	769
	− 395		− 93		− 184		− 73		− 186

★ Complete.

16. $734 - \square = 493$ **17.** $625 - \square = 594$

Subtract. *(Use with page 104.)*

1. 562 − 84	**2.** 923 − 38	**3.** 921 − 75	**4.** 715 − 378	**5.** 437 − 189
6. 938 − 839	**7.** 745 − 397	**8.** 415 − 298	**9.** 650 − 179	**10.** 337 − 58
11. 647 − 258	**12.** 340 − 287	**13.** 485 − 96	**14.** 752 − 383	**15.** 712 − 55
16. 840 − 294	**17.** 635 − 298	**18.** 946 − 847	★ **19.** 1,532 − 486	★ **20.** 6,784 − 589

★ Complete.

21. $656 - \square = 398$ **22.** $483 - \square = 394$

Subtract. *(Use with page 106.)*

1. 500 − 6	**2.** 703 − 9	**3.** 809 − 79	**4.** 600 − 7	**5.** 700 − 85
6. 900 − 45	**7.** 402 − 149	**8.** 307 − 298	**9.** 200 − 158	**10.** 605 − 409
11. 400 − 286	**12.** 505 − 249	**13.** 608 − 599	**14.** 350 − 86	**15.** 200 − 45
16. 803 − 495	**17.** 904 − 838	★ **18.** 6,000 − 473	★ **19.** 8,000 − 684	★ **20.** 1,000 − 475

Subtract. *(Use with page 108.)*

1. $ 4.25 − 0.75	**2.** $ 5.00 − 1.79	**3.** $ 3.07 − 1.98	**4.** $ 7.50 − 6.46	**5.** $ 3.85 − 1.19
6. $ 3.00 − 2.19	**7.** $ 7.00 − 5.39	**8.** $ 8.50 − 7.34	**9.** $ 2.00 − 1.59	**10.** $ 9.00 − 5.63
11. $ 6.05 − 3.87	**12.** $ 4.53 − 2.98	**13.** $ 9.47 − 8.69	★ **14.** $ 24.07 − 19.44	★ **15.** $ 30.05 − 25.98

Estimate the differences. Round to the nearest ten. *(Use with page 110.)*

1. 47 − 32	**2.** 89 − 29	**3.** 61 − 49	**4.** 78 − 27	**5.** 65 − 19
6. 34 − 15	**7.** 52 − 37	**8.** 94 − 27	**9.** 67 − 43	**10.** 29 − 13
11. 82 − 74	**12.** 43 − 25	★ **13.** 485 − 253	★ **14.** 861 − 437	★ **15.** 683 − 456

Estimate the differences. Round to the nearest hundred or dollar.

16. 923 − 481	**17.** 654 − 347	**18.** 784 − 199	**19.** 415 − 322	**20.** 850 − 585
21. 347 − 198	**22.** 727 − 384	**23.** 609 − 425	**24.** 583 − 256	**25.** 943 − 215
26. $4.51 − 3.35	**27.** $8.15 − 3.49	**28.** $7.74 − 3.83	**29.** $2.59 − 1.87	**30.** $6.43 − 4.86
31. $4.67 − 2.64	**32.** $9.15 − 7.84	★ **33.** $9.57 − 3.84	★ **34.** $26.89 − 5.74	★ **35.** $53.18 − 1.47

Subtract. *(Use with page 115.)*

1. 75 − 23	**2.** 83 − 52	**3.** 689 − 245	**4.** 734 − 523	**5.** 186 − 9
6. 93 − 27	**7.** 347 − 138	**8.** 473 − 245	**9.** 857 − 39	**10.** 453 − 62
11. 356 − 194	**12.** 877 − 793	**13.** 948 − 53	**14.** 783 − 95	**15.** 367 − 298
16. 534 − 376	**17.** 247 − 189	**18.** 851 − 363	**19.** 600 − 375	**20.** 406 − 289
21. 800 − 349	**22.** 608 − 599	**23.** $6.25 − 4.89	**24.** $5.39 − 3.84	**25.** $7.00 − 3.87

Multiply. *(Use with page 122.)*

1.	2 × 2	2.	3 × 4	3.	2 × 3	4.	3 × 2	5.	2 × 4	6.	3 × 3
7.	3 × 5	8.	2 × 5	9.	4 × 2	10.	5 × 2	11.	5 × 4	12.	5 × 5

★ Name the missing factors.

13. __?__ × __?__ = 8 **14.** __?__ × __?__ = 12 **15.** __?__ × __?__ = 10

Use the four steps to solve. *(Use with page 126.)*

1. There are 23 children in the class.
   Peg made 27 cookies for them.
   How many extra cookies are there?

2. Maria bought a shirt for $5.75.
   She also bought a pair of slippers for $2.99.
   How much did she spend in all?

3. Bob found 136 shells at the beach.
   John found 264 shells.
   How many more shells did John find?

4. Juan bought 8 balloons at the circus.
   He gave 5 to his friends.
   How many did he have left?

5. Jeff has 36 papers to sell.
   Marty has 53 papers to sell.
   How many papers do they have to sell in all?

6. There are 64 cars in the lot.
   Mrs. Graff has to sell 39 of them.
   How many will be left?

7. Fran has 135 baseball cards.
   She bought 9 more.
   How many does she have in all?

Multiply. *(Use with page 130.)*

1. 2 ×1	**2.** 3 ×0	**3.** 1 ×4	**4.** 0 ×0	**5.** 5 ×1	**6.** 0 ×4
7. 1 ×1	**8.** 0 ×5	**9.** 2 ×2	**10.** 2 ×7	**11.** 5 ×0	**12.** 2 ×3
13. 2 ×4	**14.** 3 ×1	**15.** 4 ×1	★**16.** 45 ×0	★**17.** 54 ×1	★**18.** 80 ×1

Multiply. *(Use with page 132.)*

1. 3 ×3	**2.** 4 ×9	**3.** 3 ×4	**4.** 4 ×7	**5.** 3 ×6	**6.** 4 ×6
7. 5 ×3	**8.** 3 ×8	**9.** 4 ×8	**10.** 7 ×3	**11.** 5 ×4	**12.** 9 ×3
13. 7 ×4	**14.** 3 ×7	**15.** 8 ×4	**16.** 4 ×5	**17.** 1 ×4	**18.** 6 ×4

★ Complete.

19. $4 \times 9 \times 1 = $ __?__   **20.** $1 \times 3 \times 8 = $ __?__   **21.** $2 \times 3 \times 3 = $ __?__

Multiply. *(Use with page 136.)*

1. 5 ×5	**2.** 6 ×4	**3.** 5 ×8	**4.** 6 ×7	**5.** 8 ×5	**6.** 9 ×6
7. 5 ×6	**8.** 6 ×3	**9.** 5 ×9	**10.** 6 ×8	**11.** 7 ×5	**12.** 8 ×6
13. 5 ×7	**14.** 6 ×6	**15.** 9 ×5	**16.** 6 ×9	**17.** 6 ×5	**18.** 7 ×6
19. 4 ×6	**20.** 5 ×4	**21.** 3 ×6	**22.** 2 ×5	**23.** 6 ×1	**24.** 6 ×2

★ Complete.

25. $4 \times 2 \times 5 = $ __?__   **26.** $3 \times 3 \times 4 = $ __?__   **27.** $1 \times 4 \times 7 = $ __?__

Multiply. *(Use with page 140.)*

1.	6 × 7	2.	8 × 8	3.	9 × 5	4.	7 × 9	5.	7 × 8	6.	5 × 8
7.	8 × 7	8.	9 × 8	9.	5 × 6	10.	7 × 5	11.	9 × 9	12.	6 × 9
13.	8 × 5	14.	8 × 9	15.	6 × 5	16.	9 × 6	17.	5 × 9	18.	7 × 6
19.	5 × 7	20.	6 × 6	21.	9 × 7	22.	7 × 8	23.	6 × 8	24.	7 × 7

★ Complete.

25. $3 \times 2 \times 8 = \underline{\quad ? \quad}$ **26.** $4 \times 2 \times 9 = \underline{\quad ? \quad}$

27. $3 \times 3 \times 9 = \underline{\quad ? \quad}$ **28.** $2 \times 2 \times 8 = \underline{\quad ? \quad}$

Multiply. *(Use with page 143.)*

1.	2 × 3	2.	4 × 2	3.	5 × 4	4.	3 × 3	5.	2 × 2	6.	3 × 4
7.	2 × 8	8.	7 × 2	9.	2 × 5	10.	9 × 2	11.	6 × 2	12.	2 × 1
13.	4 × 0	14.	9 × 1	15.	0 × 7	16.	1 × 6	17.	3 × 6	18.	4 × 9
19.	3 × 8	20.	4 × 4	21.	0 × 3	22.	6 × 4	23.	6 × 6	24.	7 × 5
25.	6 × 9	26.	5 × 5	27.	6 × 7	28.	6 × 5	29.	8 × 6	30.	8 × 8
31.	7 × 9	32.	9 × 8	33.	3 × 7	34.	7 × 8	35.	8 × 1	36.	7 × 7
37.	8 × 5	38.	4 × 7	39.	8 × 4	40.	5 × 9	41.	9 × 9	42.	3 × 9

Which operation would you use? Write × or ÷. *(Use with page 158.)*

1. Bake 6 cakes a day
8 days
How many cakes in all?

2. 16 cupcakes
4 in a box
How many boxes?

3. Run 5 miles an hour
6 hours
How many miles in all?

4. 5 notebooks
Cost 5 cents each
How much in all?

5. 35 flowers
7 in a row
How many rows?

6. 72 stamps
9 on a page
How many pages?

7. 9 shirts
5 buttons on each
How many buttons in all?

8. 42 books
7 on each shelf
How many shelves?

Divide. *(Use with page 160.)*

1. $10 \div 2$ **2.** $5 \div 1$ **3.** $16 \div 2$ **4.** $24 \div 3$

5. $3 \div 3$ **6.** $8 \div 2$ **7.** $9 \div 1$ **8.** $18 \div 3$

9. $6 \div 1$ **10.** $9 \div 3$ **11.** $14 \div 2$ **12.** $6 \div 3$

★ Complete.

13. $18 \div \square = 2$ **14.** $27 \div \square = 3$ **15.** $12 \div \square = 3$

Divide. *(Use with page 162.)*

1. $4\overline{)20}$ **2.** $6\overline{)48}$ **3.** $5\overline{)5}$ **4.** $4\overline{)16}$ **5.** $6\overline{)42}$

6. $3\overline{)15}$ **7.** $4\overline{)28}$ **8.** $6\overline{)24}$ **9.** $5\overline{)25}$ **10.** $3\overline{)27}$

11. $5\overline{)45}$ **12.** $6\overline{)18}$ **13.** $5\overline{)40}$ **14.** $4\overline{)36}$ **15.** $4\overline{)4}$

★ Complete.

16. $30 \div \square = 6$ **17.** $15 \div \square = 5$ **18.** $32 \div \square = 4$

Divide. *(Use with page 164.)*

1. $7\overline{)42}$ **2.** $8\overline{)72}$ **3.** $4\overline{)36}$ **4.** $8\overline{)64}$ **5.** $2\overline{)18}$

6. $8\overline{)56}$ **7.** $3\overline{)24}$ **8.** $7\overline{)14}$ **9.** $6\overline{)54}$ **10.** $8\overline{)40}$

11. $5\overline{)35}$ **12.** $8\overline{)8}$ **13.** $9\overline{)81}$ **14.** $6\overline{)48}$ **15.** $1\overline{)9}$

16. $7\overline{)49}$ **17.** $4\overline{)32}$ **18.** $7\overline{)63}$ **19.** $5\overline{)45}$ **20.** $8\overline{)16}$

21. $9\overline{)72}$ **22.** $7\overline{)7}$ **23.** $3\overline{)27}$ **24.** $7\overline{)28}$ **25.** $7\overline{)56}$

26. $9\overline{)63}$ **27.** $3\overline{)21}$ **28.** $9\overline{)54}$ **29.** $8\overline{)48}$ **30.** $6\overline{)42}$

★ Complete.

31. $40 \div \square = 5$ **32.** $28 \div \square = 4$ **33.** $45 \div \square = 9$

34. $36 \div \square = 9$ **35.** $21 \div \square = 7$ **36.** $24 \div \square = 8$

Divide. *(Use with page 169.)*

1. $2\overline{)8}$ **2.** $4\overline{)4}$ **3.** $4\overline{)12}$ **4.** $3\overline{)3}$ **5.** $1\overline{)4}$

6. $2\overline{)10}$ **7.** $3\overline{)6}$ **8.** $2\overline{)6}$ **9.** $1\overline{)5}$ **10.** $4\overline{)8}$

11. $5\overline{)30}$ **12.** $4\overline{)28}$ **13.** $6\overline{)48}$ **14.** $3\overline{)12}$ **15.** $2\overline{)2}$

16. $6\overline{)42}$ **17.** $5\overline{)25}$ **18.** $6\overline{)12}$ **19.** $4\overline{)36}$ **20.** $6\overline{)54}$

21. $5\overline{)15}$ **22.** $3\overline{)21}$ **23.** $5\overline{)40}$ **24.** $6\overline{)36}$ **25.** $7\overline{)49}$

26. $5\overline{)25}$ **27.** $8\overline{)72}$ **28.** $7\overline{)35}$ **29.** $9\overline{)81}$ **30.** $7\overline{)7}$

31. $6\overline{)24}$ **32.** $8\overline{)56}$ **33.** $4\overline{)20}$ **34.** $9\overline{)63}$ **35.** $8\overline{)32}$

36. $8\overline{)8}$ **37.** $4\overline{)16}$ **38.** $5\overline{)45}$ **39.** $9\overline{)27}$ **40.** $2\overline{)18}$

41. $8\overline{)64}$ **42.** $3\overline{)24}$ **43.** $7\overline{)63}$ **44.** $1\overline{)7}$ **45.** $9\overline{)72}$

46. $7\overline{)56}$ **47.** $2\overline{)4}$ **48.** $8\overline{)16}$ **49.** $8\overline{)48}$ **50.** $9\overline{)54}$

Estimate. Is the answer reasonable? *(Use with page 186.)*

1. 39 green boxes
47 blue boxes
How many in all?
Answer: 86 boxes

2. 325 pictures
174 torn
How many not torn?
Answer: 251 pictures

3. Ball: $1.98
Bat: $5.25
How much in all?
Answer: $6.23

4. 59 large hats
22 small hats
How many in all?
Answer: 81 hats

5. 823 cartons
284 empty
How many are not empty?
Answer: 539 cartons

6. 75 birds
28 flew away.
How many left?
Answer: 57 birds

Multiply. *(Use with page 208.)*

1. 34 $\times 2$	**2.** 13 $\times 2$	**3.** 42 $\times 4$	**4.** 51 $\times 6$	**5.** 82 $\times 3$	**6.** 33 $\times 2$
7. 71 $\times 9$	**8.** 92 $\times 4$	**9.** 63 $\times 3$	**10.** 52 $\times 3$	**11.** 44 $\times 2$	**12.** 61 $\times 9$

★ Complete.

13. $24 \times \square = 48$ **14.** $32 \times \square = 96$ **15.** $12 \times \square = 36$

Multiply. *(Use with page 210.)*

1. 47 $\times 2$	**2.** 18 $\times 6$	**3.** 24 $\times 4$	**4.** 43 $\times 5$	**5.** 45 $\times 6$	**6.** 24 $\times 6$
7. 78 $\times 5$	**8.** 67 $\times 4$	**9.** 46 $\times 8$	**10.** 79 $\times 6$	**11.** 86 $\times 9$	**12.** 35 $\times 5$
13. 93 $\times 8$	**14.** 79 $\times 7$	**15.** 53 $\times 8$	**16.** 47 $\times 9$	**17.** 36 $\times 6$	**18.** 68 $\times 4$

★ Complete.

19. $63 \times \square = 252$ **20.** $18 \times \square = 108$ **21.** $45 \times \square = 225$

Which number sentence fits the story? *(Use with page 214.)*

1. Cut 8 logs an hour
7 hours
How many logs?
$56 \div 7 = \underline{\quad?\quad}$
$8 \times 7 = \underline{\quad?\quad}$
$8 \div 7 = \underline{\quad?\quad}$

2. 36 monkeys
4 in a cage
How many cages?
$36 \div 4 = \underline{\quad?\quad}$
$36 \times 4 = \underline{\quad?\quad}$
$4 \times 9 = \underline{\quad?\quad}$

3. 18 ribbons
2 for each girl
How many girls?
$18 \times 2 = \underline{\quad?\quad}$
$18 \div 9 = \underline{\quad?\quad}$
$18 \div 2 = \underline{\quad?\quad}$

4. 9 boxes
6 pens in each box
How many pens in all?
$9 \times 6 = \underline{\quad?\quad}$
$9 \div 6 = \underline{\quad?\quad}$
$54 \div 9 = \underline{\quad?\quad}$

5. 8 children
2 cookies each
How many cookies in all?
$8 \div 2 = \underline{\quad?\quad}$
$16 \div 2 = \underline{\quad?\quad}$
$8 \times 2 = \underline{\quad?\quad}$

6. 35 houses
5 on a street
How many streets?
$35 \times 5 = \underline{\quad?\quad}$
$35 \div 5 = \underline{\quad?\quad}$
$35 \div 7 = \underline{\quad?\quad}$

Multiply. *(Use with page 216.)*

1. 400 $\times 3$	**2.** 900 $\times 4$	**3.** 700 $\times 6$	**4.** 800 $\times 5$	**5.** 600 $\times 3$	**6.** 100 $\times 6$
7. 300 $\times 9$	**8.** 200 $\times 9$	**9.** 900 $\times 7$	**10.** 700 $\times 8$	★ **11.** 3,000 $\times 3$	★ **12.** 1,200 $\times 4$

Multiply. *(Use with page 218.)*

1. 324 $\times 2$	**2.** 402 $\times 3$	**3.** 143 $\times 2$	**4.** 304 $\times 2$	**5.** 221 $\times 4$	**6.** 111 $\times 5$
7. 332 $\times 3$	**8.** 112 $\times 4$	**9.** 434 $\times 2$	**10.** 101 $\times 7$	**11.** 243 $\times 2$	**12.** 303 $\times 3$
13. 312 $\times 3$	**14.** 221 $\times 3$	**15.** 444 $\times 2$	★ **16.** 1,323 $\times 3$	★ **17.** 1,012 $\times 4$	★ **18.** 3,213 $\times 3$

Multiply. *(Use with page 220.)*

1. 128 $\times 2$	**2.** 314 $\times 3$	**3.** 208 $\times 4$	**4.** 307 $\times 6$	**5.** 224 $\times 3$
6. 214 $\times 6$	**7.** 105 $\times 9$	**8.** 218 $\times 4$	**9.** 316 $\times 5$	**10.** 518 $\times 5$
11. 802 $\times 4$	**12.** 705 $\times 8$	**13.** 624 $\times 4$	**14.** 417 $\times 5$	**15.** 309 $\times 9$
16. 503 $\times 8$	**17.** 413 $\times 7$	★**18.** 1,114 $\times 5$	★**19.** 2,123 $\times 4$	★**20.** 3,225 $\times 3$

Multiply. *(Use with page 222.)*

1. 182 $\times 2$	**2.** 341 $\times 3$	**3.** 281 $\times 4$	**4.** 370 $\times 6$	**5.** 242 $\times 3$
6. 832 $\times 4$	**7.** 751 $\times 8$	**8.** 361 $\times 5$	**9.** 151 $\times 9$	**10.** 241 $\times 3$
11. 363 $\times 3$	**12.** 461 $\times 6$	**13.** 372 $\times 4$	**14.** 251 $\times 8$	**15.** 352 $\times 4$
16. 282 $\times 4$	**17.** 573 $\times 3$	★**18.** 2,153 $\times 3$	★**19.** 5,273 $\times 3$	★**20.** 7,384 $\times 2$

Multiply. *(Use with page 224.)*

1. 436 $\times 4$	**2.** 857 $\times 3$	**3.** 644 $\times 5$	**4.** 783 $\times 9$	**5.** 238 $\times 6$
6. 385 $\times 7$	**7.** 764 $\times 8$	**8.** 958 $\times 7$	**9.** 869 $\times 8$	**10.** 435 $\times 7$
11. 647 $\times 5$	**12.** 876 $\times 8$	**13.** 493 $\times 6$	**14.** 987 $\times 6$	**15.** 786 $\times 3$
16. 853 $\times 9$	**17.** 964 $\times 5$	★**18.** 2,345 $\times 6$	★**19.** 5,634 $\times 5$	★**20.** 6,783 $\times 4$

Multiply. *(Use with page 227.)*

1. 40 $\times$ 2	**2.** 30 $\times$ 3	**3.** 24 $\times$ 2	**4.** 32 $\times$ 3	**5.** 21 $\times$ 4
6. 35 $\times$ 8	**7.** 49 $\times$ 9	**8.** 73 $\times$ 4	**9.** 200 $\times$ 6	**10.** 800 $\times$ 9
11. 314 $\times$ 2	**12.** 433 $\times$ 3	**13.** 403 $\times$ 3	**14.** 515 $\times$ 3	**15.** 409 $\times$ 8
16. 437 $\times$ 2	**17.** 648 $\times$ 2	**18.** 451 $\times$ 5	**19.** 364 $\times$ 2	**20.** 872 $\times$ 3
21. 753 $\times$ 3	**22.** 456 $\times$ 7	**23.** 875 $\times$ 9	**24.** 634 $\times$ 4	**25.** 752 $\times$ 9
26. 341 $\times$ 8	**27.** 436 $\times$ 2	**28.** 643 $\times$ 5	**29.** 735 $\times$ 3	**30.** 562 $\times$ 3

Divide. *(Use with page 233.)*

1. $2\overline{)60}$	**2.** $3\overline{)90}$	**3.** $6\overline{)60}$	**4.** $2\overline{)80}$	**5.** $9\overline{)90}$
6. $4\overline{)400}$	**7.** $6\overline{)600}$	**8.** $3\overline{)300}$	**9.** $4\overline{)800}$	**10.** $2\overline{)400}$
11. $7\overline{)490}$	**12.** $5\overline{)400}$	**13.** $8\overline{)640}$	**14.** $3\overline{)270}$	**15.** $9\overline{)720}$
★**16.** $3\overline{)1,200}$	★**17.** $7\overline{)2,100}$	★**18.** $8\overline{)6,400}$	★**19.** $9\overline{)2,700}$	★**20.** $4\overline{)2,400}$

Divide. *(Use with page 236.)*

1. $9\overline{)75}$	**2.** $7\overline{)43}$	**3.** $3\overline{)19}$	**4.** $5\overline{)47}$	**5.** $4\overline{)27}$
6. $7\overline{)45}$	**7.** $8\overline{)63}$	**8.** $9\overline{)86}$	**9.** $4\overline{)39}$	**10.** $6\overline{)49}$
11. $9\overline{)57}$	**12.** $3\overline{)16}$	**13.** $7\overline{)52}$	**14.** $6\overline{)53}$	**15.** $5\overline{)48}$

★ Complete.

16. $74 \div \square = 8\,r\,2$ **17.** $59 \div \square = 7\,r\,3$ **18.** $47 \div \square = 5\,r\,2$

Divide. *(Use with page 238.)*

1. $4\overline{)52}$ **2.** $3\overline{)84}$ **3.** $8\overline{)96}$ **4.** $3\overline{)96}$ **5.** $4\overline{)88}$ **6.** $5\overline{)75}$

7. $4\overline{)76}$ **8.** $3\overline{)87}$ **9.** $7\overline{)84}$ **10.** $2\overline{)56}$ **11.** $3\overline{)81}$ **12.** $6\overline{)72}$

13. $5\overline{)95}$ **14.** $4\overline{)92}$ **15.** $2\overline{)98}$ **16.** $3\overline{)45}$ **17.** $3\overline{)99}$ **18.** $3\overline{)57}$

★ **Solve.**

19. $\square \div 4 = 16$ **20.** $\square \div 6 = 15$ **21.** $\square \div 7 = 14$

Divide. *(Use with page 240.)*

1. $4\overline{)87}$ **2.** $4\overline{)67}$ **3.** $2\overline{)75}$ **4.** $3\overline{)98}$ **5.** $3\overline{)80}$ **6.** $3\overline{)76}$

7. $5\overline{)83}$ **8.** $2\overline{)87}$ **9.** $7\overline{)85}$ **10.** $4\overline{)75}$ **11.** $5\overline{)99}$ **12.** $4\overline{)97}$

13. $8\overline{)92}$ **14.** $3\overline{)88}$ **15.** $7\overline{)89}$ **16.** $6\overline{)93}$ **17.** $3\overline{)95}$ **18.** $6\overline{)91}$

★ **Solve. Use a calculator if you need to.**

19. $67 \div \square = 11\,r\,1$ **20.** $87 \div \square = 12\,r\,3$

Which number sentence fits the story? *(Use with page 244.)*

1. A race car went 168 miles an hour for 4 hours. How many miles did it go in all?

$168 \div 4 =$ ___?___ $168 \times 4 =$ ___?___ $168 + 4 =$ ___?___

2. Tim has a coin book with 56 coins in it. Each page has 8 coins. How many pages does he have?

$56 \times 8 =$ ___?___ $56 + 8 =$ ___?___ $56 \div 8 =$ ___?___

3. Toni has 78 comic books. She bought 64 more. How many does she have now?

$78 + 64 =$ ___?___ $78 - 64 =$ ___?___ $78 \times 64 =$ ___?___

4. Mr. Lander has 24 hats. He keeps 4 hats in each box. How many boxes does he have?

$24 \times 4 =$ ___?___ $24 \div 4 =$ ___?___ $24 + 4 =$ ___?___

Divide. *(Use with page 248.)*

1. 2)846 **2.** 7)875 **3.** 6)882 **4.** 3)366 **5.** 4)484

6. 3)936 **7.** 4)488 **8.** 2)486 **9.** 3)543 **10.** 3)936

11. 3)693 **12.** 2)654 **13.** 3)654 **14.** 5)585 **15.** 4)468

★ **16.** 5)5,965 ★ **17.** 3)9,546 ★ **18.** 4)8,604 ★ **19.** 2)4,342

Divide. *(Use with page 250.)*

1. 4)485 **2.** 2)625 **3.** 3)647 **4.** 4)406 **5.** 3)947

6. 3)683 **7.** 5)814 **8.** 7)962 **9.** 5)947 **10.** 8)999

11. 4)569 **12.** 2)689 **13.** 7)800 **14.** 5)706 **15.** 8)874

16. 6)937 **17.** 4)807 **18.** 3)998 **19.** 5)732 **20.** 6)735

★ **21.** 3)8,425 ★ **22.** 6)7,315 ★ **23.** 8)9,369 ★ **24.** 5)6,713

Divide. *(Use with page 252.)*

1. 5)395 **2.** 3)261 **3.** 9)855 **4.** 4)324 **5.** 6)354

6. 9)729 **7.** 4)384 **8.** 7)518 **9.** 6)384 **10.** 8)568

11. 8)656 **12.** 5)405 **13.** 4)312 **14.** 3)279 **15.** 7)546

★ **16.** 7)3,682 ★ **17.** 8)6,352 ★ **18.** 3)1,962 ★ **19.** 6)1,572

Divide. *(Use with page 254.)*

1. 3)196 **2.** 5)183 **3.** 7)647 **4.** 9)462 **5.** 7)583

6. 9)806 **7.** 6)547 **8.** 5)426 **9.** 8)473 **10.** 4)313

11. 7)431 **12.** 9)641 **13.** 5)307 **14.** 8)234 **15.** 7)176

★ **16.** 5)2,863 ★ **17.** 7)3,498 ★ **18.** 6)4,315 ★ **19.** 3)2,642

Divide. *(Use with page 257.)*

1. 4)80   **2.** 3)90   **3.** 8)800   **4.** 2)400   **5.** 6)36

6. 9)54   **7.** 8)36   **8.** 7)45   **9.** 4)84   **10.** 3)93

11. 5)55   **12.** 6)77   **13.** 4)85   **14.** 7)97   **15.** 2)486

16. 5)615   **17.** 8)912   **18.** 7)875   **19.** 4)783   **20.** 3)644

21. 4)268   **22.** 7)427   **23.** 9)846   **24.** 5)375   **25.** 6)436

26. 8)427   **27.** 5)363   **28.** 4)143   **29.** 9)864   **30.** 5)437

Solve. *(Use with page 272.)*

1. Sam bought meat for $2.70 and fruit for $1.55. How much
change did he get from $5.00?
Step 1: $2.70 + $1.55 = ___?___
Step 2: $5.00 − $4.25 = ___?___
Sam got ___?___ in change.

2. Ann had 4 boxes of crayons. Each box had 12 crayons. Jim
gave her 14 more crayons. How many did she have then?
Step 1:   4 × 12 = ___?___
Step 2:   48 + 14 = ___?___
She had ___?___ crayons.

3. Jamie had 24 brownies. She divided them evenly with her 3
friends. Then she ate 2. How many did she have left?
Step 1:   24 ÷ 4 = ___?___
Step 2:   6 − 2 = ___?___
She had ___?___ brownies.

4. Mrs. Lenz had 36 flowers. She bought 12 more. Then she
divided them evenly into 4 vases. How many flowers were
in each vase?
Step 1:   36 + 12 = ___?___
Step 2:   48 ÷ 4 = ___?___
There were ___?___ flowers in each vase.

Table of Measures

Metric   Customary

Length

1 centimeter (cm) = 10 millimeters (mm)   1 foot (ft) = 12 inches (in.)
1 meter (m) = 100 centimeters   1 yard (yd) = 3 feet
1 kilometer (km) = 1,000 meters   1 yard = 36 inches
                                             1 mile (mi) = 5,280 feet
                                             1 mile = 1,760 yards

Mass/Weight

1 kilogram (kg) = 1,000 grams (g)   1 pound (lb) = 16 ounces (oz)
1 metric ton (t) = 1,000 kilograms   1 ton = 2,000 pounds

Liquid

1 liter (L) = 1,000 milliliters (mL)   1 pint (pt) = 2 cups
                                             1 quart (qt) = 2 pints
                                             1 gallon (gal) = 4 quarts

Time

1 minute (min) = 60 seconds (s)
1 hour (h) = 60 minutes
1 day = 24 hours
1 week = 7 days
12 months = 1 year
1 decade = 10 years
1 century = 100 years

GLOSSARY

This glossary contains an example, an illustration, or a brief description of important terms used in this book.

Addends The numbers that are added. (page 2)
Example $3 + 5 = 8$
3 and 5 are addends.

Area The number of square units it takes to cover the inside of a flat figure. The area of this figure is 8 square units. (page 296)

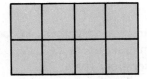

Bar graph A graph that shows number information with bars of different lengths. (page 308)

Circle A path that begins and ends at the same point. All the points of the circle are the same distance from a point inside, called the center. (page 288)

Decimal A number named by a numeral such as 0.3 or 0.8. (page 274)

Degree The unit used to measure temperature with a thermometer. (page 182)

Denominator The bottom number of a fraction. (page 262)
Example $\frac{1}{6}$ ← denominator

Diameter A line segment that goes through the center of a <u>circle</u> with its two endpoints on the circle. $\overline{AB}$ is a diameter. (page 288)

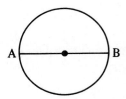

Difference The answer in subtraction. (page 8)
Example $9 - 5 = 4$
4 is the difference.

Digit Any one of the numbers. (page 40)

0, 1, 2, 3, 4, 5, 6, 7, 8, 9

Equation A number sentence in which the equals sign (=) is used. (page 2)
Examples $2 + 5 = 7$ $9 - 1 = 8$

Estimate An answer that is found by using rounded numbers. (page 80)
Example $22 + 39 = \underline{\quad?\quad}$
$20 + 40 = 60$
60 is the estimate.

Glossary

Even number   A number that ends in 0, 2, 4, 6, or 8. (page 42)
Examples   16; 48; 134

Expanded numeral   A name for a number that shows the value of the digits. (page 40)
Example   35 = 30 + 5

Factors   Numbers to be multiplied. (page 120)
Example   2 × 4 = 8
2 and 4 are factors.

Flow chart   A list of steps. (page 246)

Fraction   A number named by a numeral such as $\frac{1}{2}$. (page 262)

Graph   Two sets of related information shown by use of pictures or bars. (page 304)

Grouping property of addition   Changing the grouping of the addends does not change the sum. (page 5)
Example   (3 + 4) + 2 = 3 + (4 + 2)

Grouping property of multiplication   Changing the grouping of factors does not change the product. (page 207)
Example   (5 × 2) × 3 = 5 × (2 × 3)

Line   A straight path that goes in two directions without end. (page 282)

Line of symmetry   A line that separates a figure so that the two halves match when folded. (page 294)

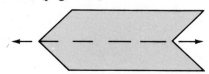

Line segment   A straight path that has two endpoints. (page 282)

Measure   To compare a unit of measure with the thing to be measured. (page 172)

Multiple   The product of a number and a given number. (page 204)
Example   15 is a multiple of 5 because 3 × 5 = 15. (3 is also a multiple of 15.)

Multiplication-addition property   A property that relates addition and multiplication. (page 141)
Example   2 × (4 + 3) = (2 × 4) + (2 × 3)

Number families   Number sentences that use the same numbers and the same or opposite operation. (page 12)
Example   4 + 3 = 7
3 + 4 = 7
7 − 4 = 3
7 − 3 = 4

Number sentence   A number sentence tells about numbers. (page 12)
Examples   2 + 6 = 8
8 − 6 = 2
8 > 6
6 < 8

Numeral   A symbol used to name a number. A name for the number three is 3. (page 1)

Numerator   The top number of a fraction. (page 262)
Example $\frac{1}{6}$ ← numerator

Odd number   A number that ends in 1, 3, 5, 7, or 9. (page 42)
Examples   19; 37; 153

Glossary

Order property of addition Changing the order of the addends does not change the sum. (page 6)
Example $7 + 5 = 5 + 7$

Order property of multiplication Changing the order of the factors does not change the product. (page 128)
Example $4 \times 9 = 9 \times 4$

Parentheses These marks ( ) are parentheses. They are used to show grouping. In $(4 + 3) + 2$, 4 and 3 are grouped and are added first. Then 2 is added to their sum. (page 5)

Perimeter The distance around a figure. The perimeter of this figure is 10 inches. (page 286)

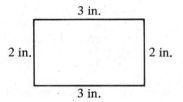

3 in.

2 in.   2 in.

3 in.

Periods in numerals The groups of three digits set off by commas in a numeral. (page 52)
Example In 142,257, the digits 1, 4, and 2 are in the thousands period, and the digits 2, 5, and 7 are in the ones period.

Pictograph A graph that uses picture symbols to show number information. (page 306)

Point An exact location in space. (page 288)

Probability The chance of something happening. (page 318)

Product The answer in multiplication. (page 120)
Example $2 \times 3 = 6$
6 is the product.

Quotient The answer in division. (page 146)
Example $8 \div 2 = 4$
4 is the quotient.

Radius A line segment from the center of a circle to a point on the circle. (Radii is the plural of radius.) The radius goes from point A to point B. (page 288)

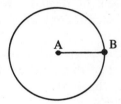

Rectangle A figure formed by four line segments. It has four right angles. (page 284)

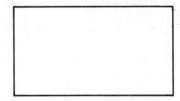

Related sentences Related sentences use the same numbers and the same or opposite operation. (page 154)
Example $2 \times 5 = 10$
$5 \times 2 = 10$
$10 \div 5 = 2$
$10 \div 2 = 5$

Glossary

Remainder In the division $17 \div 5$, the quotient is 3 and the remainder is 2. (page 236)

Right angle An angle that looks like a square corner, such as a page of a book. (page 284)

Square A figure that has all four sides the same length and four right angles. (page 284)

Standard numeral The usual name for a number. The standard numeral for eight is 8. (page 36)

Sum The answer in addition. (page 2)
Example $3 + 2 = 5$
5 is the sum.

Symmetric If the parts match when a figure is folded on a line, the figure is symmetric. (page 294)

Temperature Tells how hot or cold something is. (page 182)

Thermometer Measures the temperature. (page 182)

Triangle A figure formed by three line segments. (page 284)

Volume The number of cubic units that it takes to fill a space. The volume of this box is 24 cubic units. (page 298)

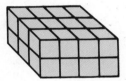

Glossary

SYMBOL LIST

Glossary

INDEX

G means the word is listed in the Glossary.

Index

G

Gallon, 197
Geometry, 212, 282–303
  area, 296–297
  circles, 288
  cone, 289, 301, 302, 315
  cube, 289, 301, 315
  cylinder, 289, 301, 302,
    315
  diameter, 288
  Keeping Fit, 315
  line segments, 282–283,
    301, 315
  lines, 282–283, 302, 315
  perimeter, 286–287
  radius, 288
  rectangles, 284–285, 302
  shapes, 289
  sphere, 289, 302
  squares, 284–285, 301
  symmetry, 294–295
  triangles, 284–285, 301,
    302, 315
  volume, 298–299
Grams (g), 179, 180, 181
Graphs, 304–314, 322–
    324, **G**
  bar, 308–309, 311, 322
  circle, 312–313
  pictographs, 306–307,
    310
Greater than, 48–49, 276–
    277
**Grouping property of
    addition,** 5, **G**
**Grouping property of
    multiplication,** 207, **G**

H

Half dollars, 32–33, 35
Half inch, 194–195
Hour and half hour, 18–
    19
Hour hand, 18; *see also*
    Time
Hours, later and earlier,
    190–191

Hundreds, 36–37, 40–41

Hundreds, 36–37, 40–41
  comparing, 48–49
  multiples of, 216–217
  rounding to nearest, 50–
    51, 80–81

I

Inch (in.), 194–196, 199
  half, 194–195
  quarter, 194–195

K

Keeping Fit
  addition, 15, 44, 101,
    167, 291, 315
  diagnostic review, 101,
    125, 243, 271
  division, 185, 271, 291,
    315
  geometry, 315
  measurement, 213
  multiplication, 152, 243,
    291, 315
  numeration, 63
  subtraction, 15, 44, 65,
    125, 167, 315
  time, 131, 185, 243, 271
Kilograms (kg), 179, 180,
    181

L

Less than, 48–49, 276–
    277
Line of symmetry, 294–
    295, **G**
Line segments, 282–283,
    301, 315, **G**
Linear measurement, 174–
    177, 194–196
Lines, 282–283, 302, 315,
    G
Liquid measurement, 178,
    180, 181, 197
Liters (L), 178, 180, 181

M

Maintenance, *see* Basic
    Skills Check; Keeping
    Fit
Making
  a bar graph, 311
  a pictograph, 310
Mass measurement, 179
Measurement, 172–203, **G**
  customary, 194–199
  Keeping Fit, 213
  linear, 174–177, 194–196
  liquid, 178, 180, 181, 197
  mass, 179
  metric, 174–181
  using arbitrary units, 172–
    173
  weight, 198, 199
Meters (m), 176–177, 180
Metric measurement
  Celsius, 182–183
  centimeters (cm), 174–
    177, 180
  choosing a unit of, 180
  grams (g), 179, 180, 181
  kilograms (kg), 179, 180,
    181
  liters (L), 178, 180, 181
  meters (m), 176–177, 180
  milliliters (mL), 178,
    180, 181
Mid-Chapter Review, 14,
    43, 70, 100, 124, 156,
    184, 212, 242, 270,
    290, 314
Milliliters (mL), 178, 180,
    181
Minute(s)
  after the hour, 20–21
  before the hour, 22–23
  Keeping Fit, 101, 131,
    185, 243, 271
  later and earlier, 192–
    193
  time to five, 20–23
  time to the, 188–189
Minute hand, 18; *see also*
    Time
Missing factors, 153

Index

Index

Index

ANSWERS

This section contains answers to learning stage items only.

CHAPTER 1

PAGE 1
 A. **1.** 10   **2.** 10

PAGE 2
 A. **1.** 4   **2.** 3   **3.** 7   **4.** 7
 B. **5.** 5, 3   **6.** 8
 C. **7.** 9   **8.** 10   **9.** 5   **10.** 1   **11.** 10
 12. 6   **13.** 4   **14.** 10   **15.** 4   **16.** 9

PAGE 4
 1. 8   **2.** 5   **3.** 13
 4. 13   **5.** 11   **6.** 11   **7.** 12   **8.** 11   **9.** 14   **10.** 12
 11. 16   **12.** 15   **13.** 16   **14.** 14   **15.** 14   **16.** 12
 17. 12   **18.** 11   **19.** 17   **20.** 15   **21.** 18   **22.** 13

PAGE 8
 A. **1.** 4   **2.** 2   **3.** 2   **4.** 2
 B. **5.** 2   **6.** 0   **7.** 8   **8.** 8   **9.** 4
 10. 7   **11.** 1   **12.** 1   **13.** 3   **14.** 3
 15. 7   **16.** 4   **17.** 9   **18.** 1   **19.** 3

PAGE 10
 A. **1.** 14   **2.** 8   **3.** 6   **4.** 6
 B. **5.** 7   **6.** 7   **7.** 9   **8.** 9   **9.** 5   **10.** 4
 11. 8   **12.** 5   **13.** 4   **14.** 8   **15.** 6   **16.** 5
 17. 7   **18.** 6   **19.** 9   **20.** 4   **21.** 8   **22.** 8

PAGE 13
 A. **1.** 6   **2.** 2   **3.** 2

PAGE 16
 A. **1.** How many more frogs?   **2.** subtract
 B. **3.** +   **4.** −

PAGE 18
 A. **1.** on 1   **2.** on 12   **3.** 1:00
 B. **4.** a little past the 2   **5.** on 6   **6.** 2:30
 C. **7.** 3, 3:00   **8.** 12, 12:00   **9.** 7, 7:30

PAGE 20
 A. **1.** between the 9 and 10   **2.** on 7   **3.** 35 minutes
 4. 35 minutes after 9; 9:35
 B. **5.** 20 minutes after 7   **6.** 5 minutes after 10
        7:20   10:05
 7. 45 minutes after 11; 11:45

A. 1. 20   **2.** 40   **3.** 20 minutes to 3; 2:40
B. 4. 10 minutes to 5   **5.** 20 minutes to 7
        4:50   6:40
6. 25 minutes to 1; 12:35

CHAPTER 2
PAGES 30–31
A. 1. 12
   2. January, February, March, April, May, June, July, August, September, October, November, December
   3. January, March, May, July, August, October, December
   4. July
B. 5. 2/14/83   **6.** 5/2/81   **7.** 8/9/80
C. 8. April 3, 1982   **9.** September 2, 1970   **10.** December 25, 1985

PAGES 32–33
A. 1. 20, 25, 30, 35, 40   **2.** 55, 60, 65, 70, 75
B. 3. 40, 50, 60, 70, 80   **4.** 60, 70, 80, 90, 100
C. 5. 75¢   **6.** 46¢
D. 7. 35¢   **8.** 80¢   **9.** 35¢   **10.** 61¢
E. 11. 3 dimes   **12.** 5 nickels   **13.** 1 quarter   **14.** 4 dimes

PAGES 34–35
A. 1. 2 dollars and 45 cents   **2.** 9 dollars and 5 cents
   3. 3 dollars and 23 cents   **4.** 4 dollars and 60 cents
   5. 1 dollar and 39 cents
B. 6. $2.15   **7.** $2.30   **8.** $3.12   **9.** $1.16
C. 10. $1.30   **11.** $5.61
D. 12. $4.20   **13.** $1.50   **14.** $2.35

PAGE 36
A. 1. thirty   **2.** sixty   **3.** forty-seven
   4. ninety-eight   **5.** thirty-six   **6.** four hundred
   7. five hundred six   **8.** eight hundred nintey-one
   9. six hundred fifty   **10.** seven hundred twenty-eight
B. 11. 94   **12.** 56   **13.** 210   **14.** 600   **15.** 480   **16.** 392

PAGE 38
A. 1. one thousand   **2.** three thousand
   3. five thousand   **4.** eight thousand
   5. two thousand
continued on next page

Answers

B. 6. 7,000   **7.** 3,000   **8.** 6,000

C. 9. five thousand, four

    10. seven thousand, thirty-nine

    11. six thousand, seven hundred twenty

    12. two thousand, eight hundred fifteen

    13. three thousand, five hundred twenty-six

D.14. 3,007   **15.** 2,023   **16.** 9,466

PAGES 40–41

A. 1. hundreds, 500   **2.** tens, 0

    3. ones, 6   **4.** thousands, 3,000

B. 5. 7   **6.** 30   **7.** 40   **8.** 300   **9.** 3

    10. 200   **11.** 6,000   **12.** 0   **13.** 40   **14.** 9,000

C.15. 99   **16.** 60   **17.** 43   **18.** 68

    19. 238   **20.** 121   **21.** 4,062

PAGES 46–47

A. 1. How many in all?

    2. 9 big pumpkins and 7 small pumpkins

    3. add

    4. $9 + 7 = \underline{?}$

    5. $13 - 7 = \underline{?}$ **6.** $9 + 8 = \underline{?}$

PAGES 48–49

A. 1. yes   **2.** yes   **3.** no

B. 4. >   **5.** <   **6.** >   **7.** <   **8.** >   **9.** >

C.10. yes   **11.** no   **12.** >   **13.** >

D.14. <   **15.** >   **16.** >   **17.** <

PAGES 50–51

A. 1. 80   **2.** 90   **3.** 60   **4.** 90   **5.** 40

    6. 70   **7.** 90   **8.** 70   **9.** 20   **10.** 60

B.11. 200   **12.** 200   **13.** 400   **14.** 700   **15.** 100

    16. 300   **17.** 500   **18.** 800   **19.** 300   **20.** 300

C.21. $2.00   **22.** $3.00   **23.** $3.00   **24.** $1.00   **25.** $5.00

    26. $2.00   **27.** $7.00   **28.** $2.00   **29.** $5.00   **30.** $6.00

PAGE 52

B. 4. fifty-seven thousand, one hundred twenty-two

    5. thirty-six thousand, four hundred eighty

    6. eighty-six thousand, three hundred two

    7. four hundrd thirty-six thousand, nine hundred eighty-one

    8. six hundred thirty thousand, four hundred sixty-four

    9. nine hundred four thousand, seven hundred forty-six

C.10. 6,000   **11.** 10,000   **12.** 100

    13. 80,000   **14.** 90,000   **15.** 800,000

Answers

CHAPTER 3
PAGE 58
A. 1. 9 **2.** 14 **3.** 15 **4.** 15 **5.** yes
B. 6. 13 **7.** 16 **8.** 14 **9.** 15 **10.** 18 **11.** 13

PAGE 61
1. G, 7, 8 **2.** D, 40, E, 50
3. G, H, 45 **4.** V, U, 22, 21

PAGE 62
A. 1. 76 **2.** 43 **3.** 97 **4.** 79 **5.** 86
B. 6. 7 **7.** 6 **8.** 5 **9.** 567
C.10. 585 **11.** 467 **12.** 594 **13.** 788 **14.** 956
15. 349 **16.** 847 **17.** 662 **18.** 579 **19.** 979

PAGE 64
A. 1. 14
2. 4 in the ones place and 1 over the tens place
3. 6
4. 64
B. 5. 67 **6.** 41 **7.** 92 **8.** 40 **9.** 93
10. 32 **11.** 82 **12.** 72 **13.** 83 **14.** 63

PAGE 66
A. 1. 12
2. 2 in the ones place and 1 over the tens place
3. 8
4. 2
5. 281
B. 6. 727 **7.** 960 **8.** 987 **9.** 483 **10.** 995
C.11. 740 **12.** 461 **13.** 594 **14.** 481 **15.** 642

PAGE 68
A. 1. 9 **2.** 12
3. 2 in the tens place and 1 over the hundreds place
4. 6 **5.** 629
B. 6. 467 **7.** 902 **8.** 975 **9.** 749 **10.** 626
C.11. 908 **12.** 253 **13.** 817 **14.** 684 **15.** 748

PAGE 71
A. 3. 50, 50
4. 35, 34, 34
5. 97, 96, 96
B. 6. 47 **7.** 77 **8.** 28 **9.** 51 **10.** 75

PAGE 72
A. 1. How many are not stores?
2. There are 135 buildings and 14 stores.
3. subtract
4. $135 - 14 = $ __?__
B. 5. $252 + 108 = $ __?__ **6.** $13 - 5 = $ __?__

PAGE 74

   A. 1. 12   **2.** 2 in the ones place and 1 over the tens place
       3. 13
       4. 3 in the tens place and 1 over the hundreds place   **5.** 232
   B. 6. 701   **7.** 532   **8.** 615   **9.** 560   **10.** 435
   C.11. 503   **12.** 350   **13.** 906   **14.** 881   **15.** 922

PAGE 76

   A. 1. 11   **2.** 1 in the ones place and 1 over the tens place
       3. 20
       4. 901
   B. 5. 76   **6.** 202   **7.** 838   **8.** 974   **9.** 949
   C.10. 138   **11.** 220   **12.** 905   **13.** 921   **14.** 801

PAGE 78

   A. 1. 17   **2.** 7 in the ones place and 1 over the tens place
       3. 22
       4. $8.27
   B. 5. $1.86   **6.** $9.80   **7.** $6.67   **8.** $9.08   **9.** $6.63
   C.10. $7.63   **11.** $5.39   **12.** $6.18   **13.** $9.01   **14.** $8.54

PAGE 80

   A. 1. 60   **2.** 60   **3.** 80   **4.** 70   **5.** 80
   B. 6. 200   **7.** 100   **8.** 300   **9.** 300
   C.10. $2.00   **11.** $2.00   **12.** $4.00   **13.** $4.00
   D.14. 800   **15.** 500   **16.** 900   **17.** $4.00   **18.** $8.00

PAGE 82

   A. 1. 12   **2.** 2 in the ones place and 1 over the tens place
       3. 13
       4. 3 in the tens place and 1 over the hundreds place
       5. 8,032
   B. 6. 8,180   **7.** 5,676   **8.** 6,585   **9.** 7,854
   C.10. 7,570   **11.** 3,561   **12.** 9,478   **13.** 7,203

CHAPTER 4
PAGE 88

   A. 1. 6   **2.** 2   **3.** 4
   B. 4. 5   **5.** 3   **6.** 2   **7.** 2

PAGE 90

   A. 1. 1   **2.** 4   **3.** 3   **4.** 341
   B. 5. 63   **6.** 38   **7.** 901   **8.** 75   **9.** 230

Answers

A. 1. 3   **2.** 18

       ³¹⁷   ⁵¹¹   ⁶¹⁷   ³¹⁰   ⁷¹⁶

3. 4̷7̷   **4.** 6̷1̷   **5.** 7̷7̷   **6.** 4̷0̷   **7.** 2 8̷6̷

A. 1. 78   **2.** 34   **3.** 36   **4.** 45   **5.** 12

B. 6. 7   **7.** 5   **8.** 2   **9.** 257

C. 10. 528   **11.** 103   **12.** 518   **13.** 269   **14.** 124

A. 1. 326   **2.** 113   **3.** 439   **4.** yes

B. 5. 87   **6.** 32   **7.** 334   **8.** 343   **9.** 426

A. 1. 3   **2.** 15   **3.** 8

       ⁷¹⁶   ¹¹⁴   ⁶¹⁸   ⁵¹¹   ³¹⁷

B. 4. 8̷6̷3   **5.** 2̷4̷4   **6.** 7̷8̷2   **7.** 6̷1̷1   **8.** 4̷7̷8

A. 1. 6   **2.** 9   **3.** 2   **4.** 296

B. 5. 672   **6.** 536   **7.** 775   **8.** 278   **9.** 242

C. 10. 373   **11.** 826   **12.** 484   **13.** 81   **14.** 246

Step 2. add   **Step 3.** 10

A. 1. 7   **2.** 5   **3.** 6   **4.** 657

B. 5. 171   **6.** 488   **7.** 736   **8.** 264   **9.** 198

C. 10. 275   **11.** 889   **12.** 491   **13.** 555   **14.** 335

A. 1. 2   **2.** 9   **3.** 10

B. 4. 4 hundreds and 10 tens

     5. 9 tens and 10 ones

     7. 374

C. 8. 393   **9.** 448   **10.** 535   **11.** 172   **12.** 284

A. 1. 9   **2.** 2   **3.** $1.29

B. 4. $1.74   **5.** $.29   **6.** $2.41   **7.** $1.94   **8.** $.71

A. 1. no   **2.** 40¢

A. 1. 70   **2.** 40   **3.** 30   **4.** 10   **5.** 10

B. 6. 600   **7.** 200   **8.** 400

C. 9. $4.00   **10.** $1.00   **11.** $3.00

D. 12. 300   **13.** 400   **14.** 200   **15.** $2.00   **16.** $3.00

A. 1. 9   **2.** 6   **3.** 5   **4.** 2,569

B. 5. 1,676   **6.** 1,879   **7.** 3,737   **8.** 678   **9.** 2,487

C. 10. 2,159   **11.** 5,466   **12.** 1,775   **13.** 1,996   **14.** 776

Answers

CHAPTER 5

PAGE 118

A. 1. 2 **2.** 3 **3.** 6 **4.** 6
B. 5. 8; 8 **6.** 9; 9 **7.** 10; 10
C. 8. $3 \times 2 = 6$; 6 **9.** $2 \times 3 = 6$; 6 **10.** $4 \times 3 = 12$; 12

PAGES 120–121

A. 1. 2 **2.** 5 **3.** 10 **4.** 5, 2 **5.** 10
B. 6. 8 **7.** 4
C. 8. 9 **9.** 12 **10.** 6 **11.** 8 **12.** 4 **13.** 15

PAGE 122

A. 1. 12 **2.** 16 **3.** 10 **4.** 15
B. 5. 12 **6.** 20 **7.** 15 **8.** 20 **9.** 25 **10.** 16

PAGE 126

A. 1. How many did not find gold? **2.** $6 - 4 = $?
3. 2 divers **4.** yes
B. 5. How many starfish seen in all? **6.** $2 + 3 = $?
7. 5 starfish **8.** yes

PAGE 128

A. 1. 4, 6, 8, 10, 12, 14, 16, 18
B. 2. 6 **3.** 6
C. 4. 8 **5.** 8 **6.** 10 **7.** 10 **8.** 12 **9.** 12
10. 14 **11.** 14 **12.** 16 **13.** 16 **14.** 18 **15.** 18

PAGES 130–131

A. 1. 0 **2.** 0 **3.** 0 **4.** 0 **5.** 0 **6.** 0
7. 0 **8.** 0 **9.** 0 **10.** 0 **11.** 0 **12.** 0
B. 13. 1 **14.** 2 **15.** 3 **16.** 4 **17.** 5
18. 1 **19.** 2 **20.** 3 **21.** 4 **22.** 5
C. 23. 0 **24.** 4 **25.** 5 **26.** 0 **27.** 2 **28.** 0

PAGES 132–133

A. 18, 21, 24, 27
B. 1. 3, 6, 9, 12, 15, 18, 21, 24, 27
2. 3, 6, 9, 12, 15, 18, 21, 24, 27 **3.** increase by 3
C. 24, 28, 32, 36
D. 4. 4, 8, 12, 16, 20, 24, 28, 32, 36
5. 4, 8, 12, 16, 20, 24, 28, 32, 36 **6.** increase by 4
E. 7. 21 **8.** 28 **9.** 32 **10.** 24 **11.** 27 **12.** 0

PAGES 136–137

A. 25, 30, 35, 40
B. 1. 5, 10, 15, 20, 25, 30, 35, 40, 45
2. 5, 10, 15, 20, 25, 30, 35, 40, 45 **3.** increase by 5
C. 4. 6, 12, 18, 24, 30, 36, 42, 48, 54
5. 6, 12, 18, 24, 30, 36, 42, 48, 54 **6.** increase by 6
D. 7. 45 **8.** 42 **9.** 40 **10.** 35 **11.** 0 **12.** 36
E. See table on page 327.

Answers

PAGE 138

   A. **1.** 7, 14, 21, 28, 35, 42, 49, 56, 63
        2. 7, 14, 21, 28, 35, 42, 49, 56, 63
        3. increase by 7
   B. **4.** 8, 16, 24, 32, 40, 48, 56, 64, 72
        5. 8, 16, 24, 32, 40, 48, 56, 64, 72
        6. increase by 8
   C. **7.** 56   **8.** 72   **9.** 49   **10.** 64   **11.** 48   **12.** 0
   D. See table on page 327.

PAGE 140

   A. **1.** 9, 18, 27, 36, 45, 54, 63, 72, 81
        2. 9, 18, 27, 36, 45, 54, 63, 72, 81
        3. increase by 9
   B. **4.** 63   **5.** 54   **6.** 0   **7.** 81   **8.** 72   **9.** 36
   C. See table on page 327.

CHAPTER 6
PAGE 146

   A. **1.** 6   **2.** 3   **3.** 3   **4.** 3
   B. **5.** 4   **6.** 2   **7.** $4 \div 2 = 2$ **8.** 2

PAGE 148

   A. **1.** 5   **2.** 5   **3.** 5   **4.** 5
   B. **5.** 5   **6.** 4   **7.** 3   **8.** 4
   C. **9.** 3   **10.** 2   **11.** 2   **12.** 2

PAGE 150

   A. **1.** 2   **2.** 4   **3.** 5   **4.** 3
   B. **5.** 3   **6.** 1   **7.** 1   **8.** 5

PAGE 153

   A. **1.** 5
   B. **2.** 3   **3.** 4   **4.** 2
        5. 7   **6.** 3   **7.** 4

PAGE 154

   A. **1.** $8 \div 4 = 2$ **2.** $10 \div 5 = 2$ **3.** $6 \div 3 = 2$
        or $8 \div 2 = 4$ or $10 \div 2 = 5$ or $6 \div 2 = 3$
   B. **4.** $3 \times 3 = 9$ **5.** $3 \times 1 = 3$ **6.** $3 \times 4 = 12$
   C. **7.** 5, 5   **8.** 4, 4   **9.** 4, 4

PAGE 157

   A. **1.** 6   **2.** 6

PAGE 158

   A. **1.** How many children in each class?   **2.** divide
   B. **3.** $\div$

A. 1. 7, 7   **2.** 7

B. 3. 6, 6   **4.** 6, 6   **5.** 9, 9   **6.** 9, 9

   7. 8, 8   **8.** 7, 7

C. 9. 8   **10.** 7   **11.** 6   **12.** 5

   13. 8   **14.** 5   **15.** 9   **16.** 4

PAGE 162

A. 1. 9   **2.** 9

B. 3. 4   **4.** 7   **5.** 6

      4   7   6

   6. 9   **7.** 8   **8.** 9

      9   8   9

C. 9. 7   **10.** 6   **11.** 5   **12.** 3   **13.** 5

   14. 7   **15.** 4   **16.** 8   **17.** 6   **18.** 5

PAGE 164

A. 1. 8   **2.** 8   **3.** 7

      8   8   7

   4. 9   **5.** 9   **6.** 6

      9   9   6

B. 7. 8   **8.** 8   **9.** 7   **10.** 6   **11.** 5

   12. 9   **13.** 7   **14.** 7   **15.** 9   **16.** 8

CHAPTER 7

PAGE 172

   2. no   **3.** no   **4.** Answers may vary. Example: hand

PAGES 174–175

A. 4 cm

B. 10 cm

C. 1. 7 cm   **2.** 4 cm   **3.** 6 cm   **4.** 5 cm

PAGE 176

A. 6. 100 cm

B. 7. 300   **8.** 600

C. 9. 4   **10.** 5

PAGE 178

A. 1. 2,000   **2.** 4,000

B. 3. 3   **4.** 5

PAGE 179

A. 1. 3,000   **2.** 4,000

B. 3. 2   **4.** 6

PAGE 183

A. 1. 32°C   **2.** 8°C   **3.** 10°C below zero

Answers

A. 1. 90   **2.** yes   **3.** yes

B. 4. no   **5.** yes

PAGE 188

A. 1. a little past 1   **2.** at 16   **3.** 1:16

B. 4. 47   **5.** 5:47

C. 6. 7:27   **7.** 1:52   **8.** 12:04

PAGE 190

A. 1. 9:32   **2.** 10:32

B. 3. 7:07   **4.** 6:07

PAGE 192

A. 1. 6:20   **2.** 6:40   **3.** 6:00

B. 4. 4:50   **5.** 2:42   **6.** 1:37

C. 7. 11:00   **8.** 4:20   **9.** 6:35

PAGE 196

A. 1. 24   **2.** 6   **3.** 72

PAGE 197

A. 1. 4   **2.** 4   **3.** 8

PAGE 198

A. 1. 16   **2.** 16

B. 3. 32

PAGE 199

A. 1. 92° F   **2.** 4° F below zero

CHAPTER 8
PAGE 204

A. 1. yes   **2.** yes   **3.** yes   **4.** no   **5.** yes   **6.** no

B. 7. 4, 40   **8.** 8, 80   **9.** 10, 100

C. 10. 90   **11.** 60   **12.** 70   **13.** 80   **14.** 90

PAGE 207

A. 1. 16, 16   **2.** 20, 20

PAGE 208

A. 1. 3   **2.** 9   **3.** 93

B. 4. 44   **5.** 26   **6.** 55   **7.** 122   **8.** 96   **9.** 168

C. 10. 68   **11.** 69   **12.** 70   **13.** 84   **14.** 45   **15.** 105

16. 63   **17.** 88   **18.** 47   **19.** 88   **20.** 46   **21.** 60

PAGE 210

A. 1. 16

2. 6 in the ones place and 1 over the tens place

3. 12, 13   **4.** 136

B. 5. 75   **6.** 92   **7.** 91   **8.** 78   **9.** 144   **10.** 90

11. 96   **12.** 42   **13.** 170   **14.** 258   **15.** 96   **16.** 54

Answers

   A. 1. How many sets of dancers?
     2. 72 people, 8 in each set
     3. Divide
     4. $72 \div 8 = \underline{\quad ? \quad}$
   B. 5. $16 \times 2 = \underline{\quad ? \quad}$

PAGE 216
   A. 1. yes   **2.** no   **3.** yes   **4.** yes   **5.** no
   B. 6. 4, 40, 400   **7.** 6, 60, 600   **8.** 18, 180, 1,800
     9. 28, 280, 2,800   **10.** 27, 270, 2,700
   C. 11. 600   **12.** 900   **13.** 1,400   **14.** 6,300   **15.** 800
     16. 1,200   **17.** 4,800   **18.** 700   **19.** 1,500   **20.** 1,600

PAGE 218
   A. 1. 6   **2.** 0   **3.** 24   **4.** 2,406
   B. 5. 840   **6.** 1,064   **7.** 969   **8.** 408   **9.** 693
   C. 10. 550   **11.** 936   **12.** 1,288   **13.** 824   **14.** 1,608

PAGE 220
   A. 1. 18
     2. 8 in the ones place and 1 over the tens place
     3. 6, 7   **4.** 1,278
   B. 5. 654   **6.** 515   **7.** 1,092   **8.** 1,260   **9.** 694
   C. 10. 1,548   **11.** 878   **12.** 3,035   **13.** 896   **14.** 1,692

PAGE 222
   A. 1. 21
     2. 1 in the tens place and 2 over the hundreds place
     3. 6, 8   **4.** 819
   B. 5. 968   **6.** 1,755   **7.** 1,346   **8.** 780   **9.** 1,687
   C. 10. 750   **11.** 906   **12.** 1,476   **13.** 1,708   **14.** 788

PAGE 224
   A. 1. 32
     2. 2 in the ones place and 3 over the tens place
     3. 36, 39   **4.** 1,592
   B. 5. 702   **6.** 1,156   **7.** 860   **8.** 1,344   **9.** 952
   C. 10. 1,270   **11.** 1,716   **12.** 734   **13.** 1,308   **14.** 468

CHAPTER 9
PAGE 233
   A. 1. 8, 4, 4   **2.** 80, 40, 40   **3.** 800, 400, 400
   B. 4. 30   **5.** 10   **6.** 100   **7.** 80   **8.** 90
PAGES 236–237
   A. 1. 6   **2.** 30   **3.** 2   **4.** 6   **5.** 2
   B. 6. 3 r 1   **7.** 2 r 2   **8.** 5 r 2   **9.** 6 r 1   **10.** 7 r 1
   C. 11. 6 r 1   **12.** 9 r 2   **13.** 7 r 1   **14.** 7 r 3   **15.** 8 r 3

Answers

A. 1. 2   **2.** 28   **3.** $2 \times 28 = 56$

B. 4. 13   **5.** 11   **6.** 19   **7.** 23   **8.** 12

A. 1. 32 r 1   **2.** 19 r 1   **3.** 14 r 3   **4.** 11 r 1   **5.** 11 r 1

B. 6. 12 r 1   **7.** 32 r 2   **8.** 14 r 2   **9.** 30 r 1   **10.** 18 r 3

A. 1. How many ribbons given?

    2. 16 kinds entered; 3 ribbons given for each kind.

    3. Multiplication   **4.** $16 \times 3 = \underline{\quad ? \quad}$

B. 5. $156 \div 2 = \underline{\quad ? \quad}$

A. 1. Multiply by the number you divided by.

    2. Divide again.

B. 3. 4 r 1   **4.** 1 r 3   **5.** 6 r 1   **6.** 9 r 1   **7.** 9 r 1

    8. 32 r 2   **9.** 13 r 4   **10.** 27   **11.** 24 r 1   **12.** 32 r 1

A. 1. 243   **2.** 169   **3.** 131   **4.** 121

B. 5. 431   **6.** 123   **7.** 152   **8.** 247

A. 1. 322 r 1   **2.** 176 r 1   **3.** 142 r 2   **4.** 231 r 2

B. 5. 122 r 1   **6.** 344 r 1   **7.** 322 r 1   **8.** 234 r 1

A. 1. 0, 7   **2.** 7   **3.** 74

B. 4. 72   **5.** 81   **6.** 66   **7.** 68

A. 1. 0, 3   **2.** 12   **3.** 32 r 1

B. 4. 91 r 2   **5.** 92 r 1   **6.** 68 r 3   **7.** 66 r 5

CHAPTER 10
A. 1. 4   **2.** 2   **3.** $\frac{2}{4}$

B. 4. $\frac{1}{2}$ **5.** $\frac{2}{3}$ **6.** $\frac{1}{4}$

A. 1. 5   **2.** 2   **3.** $\frac{2}{5}$

B. 4. 6   **5.** 6   **6.** $\frac{6}{6}$

C. 7. $\frac{3}{7}$ **8.** $\frac{2}{5}$ **9.** $\frac{3}{3}$

A. 1. 8   **2.** 2, 2

B. 3. 4   **4.** 2

A. **1.** $\frac{1}{3}$ **2.** $\frac{2}{6}$ **3.** 2

B. **4.** 2   **5.** 4

PAGE 272

   1. 7   **2.** 13   **3.** 13

PAGE 274

A. **1.** 2   **2.** 2   **3.** 0.2

B. **4.** 0.7   **5.** 0.3

PAGES 276–277

A. **1.** $\frac{1}{3}$ **2.** $\frac{1}{5}$ **3.** $\frac{1}{3}$ **4.** >, <

B. **5.** $\frac{2}{3}$ **6.** $\frac{4}{9}$ **7.** $\frac{2}{3}$ **8.** >, <

C. **9.** >   **10.** <

CHAPTER 11

PAGES 282–283

C. **9.** line segment   **10.** line

   11. line segment   **12.** line

PAGE 284

A. **1.** $AB = 8$ cm, $BC = 13$ cm, $CD = 8$ cm, $DA = 13$ cm

   2. yes, the opposite sides

B. **3.** yes   **4.** 3 cm   **5.** yes   **6.** yes

C. **7.** 3   **8.** 3

D. **9.** square   **10.** rectangle   **11.** triangle   **12.** rectangle

PAGES 286–287

A. **1.** 3 cm   **2.** 12   **3.** 12 cm

B. **4.** 3 cm, 3 cm, 4 cm, 4 cm   **5.** 14   **6.** 14 cm

C. **7.** 24 cm   **8.** 9 cm   **9.** 20 cm

PAGE 288

A. **1.** C   **2.** A, B, or D   **3.** D

PAGE 289

A. **1.** garbage can   **2.** road marker

   3. globe   **4.** building

PAGE 292

   1.a. 33   **b.** 2   **c.** 2¢   **d.** 3 for 99¢

PAGE 294

A. **3.** yes   **4.** yes

PAGE 296

A. **1.** 10   **2.** 10

B. **3.** 7 square units   **4.** 6 square units

   5. 4 square units   **6.** 7 square units

Answers

PAGE 298

A. 1. 3   **2.** 3 cubic units

B. 3. 6   **4.** 6 cubic units

C. 5. 2 cubic units   **6.** 4 cubic units   **7.** 6 cubic units

CHAPTER 12

PAGE 304

A. 1. 4   **2.** Don   **3.** Joy

PAGE 306

A. 1. 5   **2.** Birch   **3.** 12 tree symbols

B. 4. 2   **5.** 8   **6.** 6

PAGE 308

A. 1. on the left   **2.** the number of cans thrown away   **3.** 10

    4. Patricia   **5.** 7   **6.** Justin

PAGE 312

A. 1. $\frac{1}{4}$ **2.** $\frac{1}{4}$ **3.** $\frac{1}{4}$ **B. 4.** $\frac{1}{4}$ **5.** $\frac{1}{2}$ **6.** $\frac{1}{4}$

PAGE 316

    1. $13.00; $4.25 saved in January   **2.** $13.00; $28.75 in the bank

    3. $2; He took out $9 last week.   **4.** 4 hours; She works 4 hours at a time.

PAGE 318

A. 1. 2 blocks   **2.** 1   **3.** 1   **4.** red or blue   **6.** 1 out of 2

B. 7. 2 sides   **8.** heads and tails   **11.** yes   **12.** yes

PAGE 320

A. 1. 3 parts   **2.** red   **3.** 1 out of 3   **4.** 1 out of 3

B. 5. 4 parts   **6.** green   **7.** 1 out of 4   **8.** 1 out of 4   **9.** 1 out of 4

PHOTO CREDITS

All HRW Photos by Jim Kiernan except the following:

    Chapter 1: pp. 16–17—HRW Photo by Ken Lax; p. 24—HRW Photo by Russell Dian.

    Chapter 2: All HRW Photos by Ken Lax.

    Chapter 3: pp. 58–59—HRW photos by Ken Lax; p. 64—HRW Photo by Russell Dian Courtesy of West Side YMCA; p. 66—Focus on Sports; p. 76—HRW Photo by Russell Dian.

    Chapter 4: p. 90—HRW Photo by Ken Lax Courtesy of Gimbels; p. 114—HRW Photo by Ken Lax.

    Chapter 5: p. 129—HRW Photo by Ken Lax; p. 139—HRW Photo by Russell Dian.

    Chapter 6: p. 155—HRW Photo by Ken Lax; p. 163—HRW Photo by Russell Dian; p. 168—HRW Photo by Ken Lax.

    Chapter 7: p. 177—HRW Photo by Russell Dian; p. 180—*left* Focus on Sports; *center* HRW Photo by Ken Lax; *right* HRW Photo by Ken Lax; *top left* HRW Photo by Ken Lax; *bottom left* Alpha; *upper right* HRW Photo by Russell Dian; p. 181—*bottom left* HRW Photo by Ken Lax; *top left* Alton Anderson; p. 197—HRW Photos by Bill Hubbell.

    Chapter 8: p. 212—HRW Photo by Russell Dian; p. 220—Louis Goldman/Rapho Guillumette/Photo Researchers; p. 224—Dennis Hallinan/Alpha; p. 226—HRW Photo by Ken Lax.

    Chapter 9: p. 241—HRW Photo by Ken Lax; p. 250—HRW Photo by Russell Dian; p. 253—HRW Photo by Ken Lax; p. 256—HRW Photo by Ken Lax.

    Chapter 10: pp. 260–261—HRW Photo by Ken Lax; pp. 268–277—HRW Photo by Ken Karp; p. 278—HRW Photo by Ken Lax.

    Chapter 11: p. 300—HRW Photo by Russell Dian.

    Chapter 12: p. 308—HRW Photo by Ken Lax.

ART CREDITS

Illustrated by Leigh Grant, represented by Publishers' Graphics.

Answers